HOUSE GUESTS

HOUSE
PESTS

A Note on the Author

Richard Jones is a fellow of the Royal Entomological Society and past president of the British Entomological Society. Richard writes about insects, nature and the environment for *BBC Wildlife*, *the Guardian*, *Gardeners' World* and *Countryfile*. His previous book for Bloomsbury, *Little Book of Nits* (with Justine Crow), also addressed invaders, but of an even more personal kind.

RICHARD JONES

HOUSE
GUESTS

*A Natural History
of Animals in the Home*

HOUSE
PESTS

BLOOMSBURY
LONDON • NEW DELHI • NEW YORK • SYDNEY

Dedication

For more than 30 years Catrina Ure has had to suffer my unending and unwavering zeal for all things insect. Perhaps this was all very well with me spotting an unusual fly visiting flowers in the picnic meadow. However, her patience has sometimes been sorely tried by my enthusiasm at finding biscuit beetles invading every foodstuff in the larder, or my insistence for a detailed examination of thousands of bacon beetle larvae wriggling about under the kitchen carpet of our new home. So, for her tolerance of my life-long obsession with insects, outside and inside the home, I dedicate this book to her.

Bloomsbury Natural History
An imprint of Bloomsbury Publishing Plc

50 Bedford Square
London
WC1B 3DP
UK

1385 Broadway
New York
NY 10018
USA

www.bloomsbury.com

First published 2015

British Library Cataloguing-in-Publication Data
A catalogue record for this book is available from the British Library.

ISBN: HB: 978-1-4729-0623-6
PB: 978-1-4729-2185-7
ePDF: 978-1-4729-2212-0
ePub: 978-1-4729-0624-3

2 4 6 8 10 9 7 5 3 1

Typeset in UK by Susan McIntyre
Printed and bound in Great Britain by CPI Group (UK) Ltd, Croydon CR0 4YY

MIX
Paper from
responsible sources
FSC® C020471

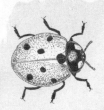

Contents

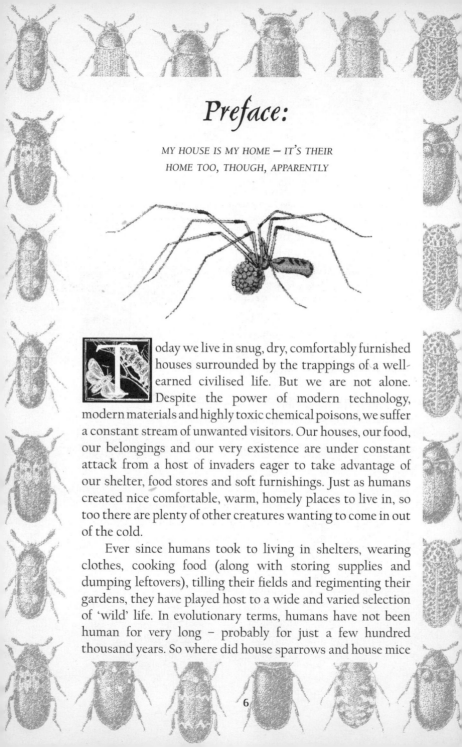

Preface:

*MY HOUSE IS MY HOME – IT'S THEIR
HOME TOO, THOUGH, APPARENTLY*

oday we live in snug, dry, comfortably furnished houses surrounded by the trappings of a well-earned civilised life. But we are not alone. Despite the power of modern technology, modern materials and highly toxic chemical poisons, we suffer a constant stream of unwanted visitors. Our houses, our food, our belongings and our very existence are under constant attack from a host of invaders eager to take advantage of our shelter, food stores and soft furnishings. Just as humans created nice comfortable, warm, homely places to live in, so too there are plenty of other creatures wanting to come in out of the cold.

Ever since humans took to living in shelters, wearing clothes, cooking food (along with storing supplies and dumping leftovers), tilling their fields and regimenting their gardens, they have played host to a wide and varied selection of 'wild' life. In evolutionary terms, humans have not been human for very long – probably for just a few hundred thousand years. So where did house sparrows and house mice live before there were houses? What did biscuit beetles eat before there were custard creams, Oreo cookies and fig rolls? What did clothes moths eat before there were designer jeans and hand-knitted cardies? Did the cigarette beetle breathe a little easier and live a healthier life before tobacco smoking took off? When the first carpets were laid, carpet beetles were waiting to take up residence in the deep pile, but where had they been living for the very many previous rug-free millennia? When the first caveman installed the first larder, it was soon infested with larder beetles; but which cupboards had they inhabited before the kitchen was invented? And long before the four-poster bed, where did bed bugs hide to sneak out for a night-time drink of blood?

These are just some of the strange, charming and sometimes annoying creatures that have taken up residence with us. From bats in the belfry to beetles in the cellar, moths in the wardrobe and mosquitoes in the bedroom, humans cannot escape the attentions of wild nature. So where have all these creatures come from? Can we live with them? Or can we get rid of them? Should we get rid of them? Taking a quizzical look at all manner of household 'visitors', we can get a taste of human history (and prehistory), and an understanding of how we fit into the wider world, how we are part of the environment at large, how we are influencing it and how it has influenced us.

One of the first discoveries is that, although a random hoverfly might take a wrong turn and fly in through the open back door to bump on the insides of the window panes for a bit trying to get out again, most of the truly domestic creatures (those carpet beetles and bed bugs, but also grain beetles, house crickets and flour moths) are not simply wild animals sneakily crossing the threshold of the back door to steal a bit of food. Throughout most of the world these household animals do not occur 'in the wild' – they are no longer wild animals and they only occur in buildings occupied by humans.

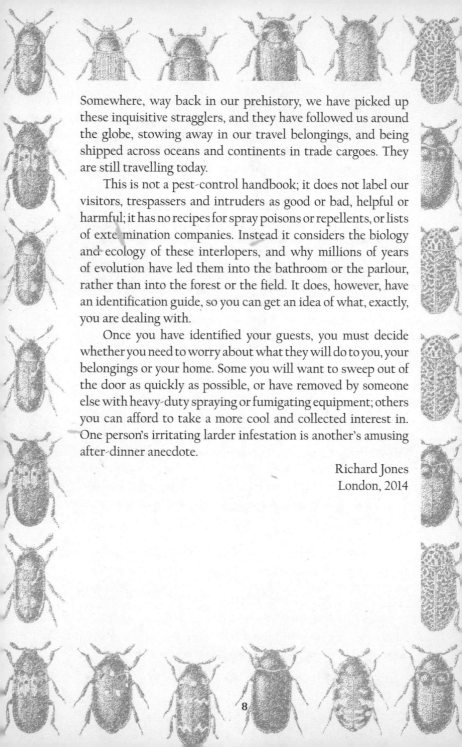

Somewhere, way back in our prehistory, we have picked up these inquisitive stragglers, and they have followed us around the globe, stowing away in our travel belongings, and being shipped across oceans and continents in trade cargoes. They are still travelling today.

This is not a pest-control handbook; it does not label our visitors, trespassers and intruders as good or bad, helpful or harmful; it has no recipes for spray poisons or repellents, or lists of extermination companies. Instead it considers the biology and ecology of these interlopers, and why millions of years of evolution have led them into the bathroom or the parlour, rather than into the forest or the field. It does, however, have an identification guide, so you can get an idea of what, exactly, you are dealing with.

Once you have identified your guests, you must decide whether you need to worry about what they will do to you, your belongings or your home. Some you will want to sweep out of the door as quickly as possible, or have removed by someone else with heavy-duty spraying or fumigating equipment; others you can afford to take a more cool and collected interest in. One person's irritating larder infestation is another's amusing after-dinner anecdote.

Richard Jones
London, 2014

I

Introduction:

*T*he British are a nation of nature lovers. That's not to say other nations are necessarily less caring of their wildlife. It's just that in the UK, there is a proud if slightly eccentric tradition of studying and celebrating nature. Wildlife documentaries are blockbuster productions here; their presenters are popular celebrities and national treasures. Birdwatching, rambling, horse riding, dog walking, sightseeing, rock pooling, pond dipping, or just strolling through the countryside delighting at butterflies and buntings, and picnicking in flowery meadows, are mainstream activities. Gardening is probably more popular, or it certainly comes a close second.

ccording to all the surveys, 'attracting wildlife' into our humdrum domestic lives is a major driver of horticultural interest, and a major commercial interest, what with all the merchants for birdfeeders, nest boxes, bat boxes, night-view trailcams, bug hotels, bumblebee boxes, mason-bee lodges and hedgehog houses. We love nature, and we want to see it close up.

Something odd, though, happens at the back door. It's fascinating to watch squirrel acrobatics along the fence and the birds squabbling at the seed ball; it is amazing to watch insects jostling on the flowers – bees, hoverflies, butterflies and plenty of smaller fry – and it may even be acceptable to suffer a few nibbles in the nasturtium leaves from the large, speckled caterpillar of a cabbage white butterfly, but our toleration seems to stop dead the moment any of these creatures has the temerity to step inside our homes.

A spider crawling up the wall off the recently cut flowers, a lone ant wandering over the kitchen table or a single fly buzzing in erratic zigzags under the light bulb is often enough to produce immediate feelings of disgust and revulsion. While a gentle waft of the hand may be enough to dissuade a curious wasp attracted to the cream tea on the patio, it will have the occupants of a living room reaching for the swat or the bug spray if it comes indoors. Sparrows are merely amusing figures of fun when landing perkily on the back of a garden chair and eyeing up the last of the sandwiches, but if they start roosting under the eaves, or dragging nest material into the loft, they become vermin. The mouldering, beetle-chewed fence post at the end of the lawn can be ignored, but a tiny, trickling pyramid of sawdust, just a milligram or two, beneath the exit hole of a woodworm under the stairs will elicit an immediate call to a pest-control agent. We do love nature, and we do want to see it up close, but not that close.

To understand this apparently contradictory human reaction, we simply have to understand the difference between a dwelling being a house and it being a home. The most important thing about a home is that it has become what anthropologists (and some entomologists, for example Robinson 1996) call a 'sacred space' – not a place of worship or superstition or New Age mumbo-jumbo, but a private living space, shared by a family and entered only by invitation.

The barrier to the living space is traditionally a door, but this need not be an impervious block of wood; it may be a symbolic barrier like a draped cloth, balanced sticks or hanging strings of beads. In almost every human culture a visitor must first ask permission to enter, before crossing the threshold into a family's sacred space. The unwelcome are not granted access, and in most societies violation of even a symbolic barrier is vigorously protected by law, so much so that 'reasonable force' (even armed force) can be used to eject intruders. It is no wonder that insects (and other animals) that invade human premises without permission are viewed at the very least with suspicion, and usually with outright opposition and extreme prejudice.

This protective feeling about our homes is so deep-seated and widespread in human societies around the globe that it is hard to imagine it to be anything other than a truly ancient and fundamental part of our very being. It is now not possible to know how and where the first door was put in place, but the temptation must be to suggest that wherever it was, it had to be defended against intruders, both human and non-human.

The house, as understood in our modern world, is on the verge of becoming a hermetically sealed brick box. Double glazing, plastic- or metal-framed windows and doors, draft excluders, and cavity and loft insulation all conspire to make entry virtually impossible, even to the smallest of insect explorers. Things were not always thus. So to get an idea of why we are invaded in our homes today, we need to take a look at how human homes have come about in the first place, and where and when in our history (and prehistory) we first came into contact with the myriad intruders that pester us and vex us today. So, by way of a slight digression, let's start way back in time and consider our long-gone ancestors, and where they lived.

IN A HOLE IN THE GROUND
THERE LIVED A ... CAVEMAN?

Contrary to popular belief, mostly influenced by children's cartoons and Hollywood B-movies, early humans did not all live in caves. Rocky overhangs and dark caverns no doubt offered some shelter, but they were also the lairs of bears, big cats, hyenas and a wealth of other dangerous and highly non-domesticated tenants. There are some cave connections, but there can be several explanations for this. Each new archaeological discovery puts another metaphorical brick into the housing puzzle of the past, but it's not immediately clear where most early hominids lived, because the fossil evidence is so sparse as to be sometimes almost non-existent, and what little there is can be difficult to interpret.

The latest in a series of typical caveman stories in the media was sparked by the discovery (by Brown *et al*. 2004) of tiny, human-like skeletons about 1m in length in a cave on the Indonesian island of Flores. Archaeologists are still debating the finds, which date from 'only' 95,000 to 13,000 years ago, and which may or may not represent a distinct and separate species, but even so the idea of humans and human-like creatures living in caves is firmly fixed in the minds of the general populace.

Before caves, though, trees would have been an obvious place for our ancestral primate relatives to live. A brief exploration of hominid development lays the foundation for understanding how, as humans, we came into being, how we took over the world, and started building, making and owning the stuff we now have to protect from pests.

About 4 million years ago Africa was home to various humanish apes, some of which walked about mostly on two legs. This upright stance is one of the most striking characteristics that make us human. The other is that we have only relatively light body hair; the two are possibly connected. At the time, those millions of years ago, this strange adaptation probably gave early hominids the edge over their hairy shuffling ape cousins; Harcourt-Smith (2007) gives a good overview. One explanation is that on the hot, dry, lightly wooded savannahs of southern and eastern Africa, standing upright took the head, with its rapidly evolving and energy-hungry brain, away from the radiated heat of the red, sun-baked African earth to catch the light breezes wafting gently at what would now, conveniently, be head height.

Other possible reasons for the evolution of walking upright include standing up to look out across the savannah for danger, reaching up to pick fruits from trees, and carrying things in our arms while we walked. Whatever the reason(s) for bipedalism, lack of body hair assisted those creatures on the hot, dry grasslands, and sweating became the paramount temperature-control mechanism for the body; any fur would immediately impede this cooling effect. As naked apes, early hominids were quite at home in the tropical and subtropical glare of the African sun. We remain one of the few mammals that can keep moderately active during the day in the hottest regions of the world, but lacking hair we have low cold tolerance. This adaptation would come back to haunt later humans when they finally ventured into the cooler north.

Pieced together from scattered bones and bits of bones, various pre-human species have been described, the earlier ones usually in the genus *Australopithecus*, from the words meaning southern (Latin *australis*) and ape (Greek *pithekos*), and echoing the old scientific name of the chimpanzee *Anthropithecus* (man-like ape). Some of the more dainty specimens have been called *Australopithecus afarensis* and *A. africanus*, while more heavily built skeletons have been assigned to *A. robustus*. Even at their most robust, though, australopiths were short – the males were around 1.2m tall, the females a head shorter.

There are suggestions (from fossils of slightly more curved finger bones and stronger arms than ours) that these early humanoids were more at home in trees than we are, but apart from a few other inferences based on pelvic-bone shape we can know little about these creatures. Although mostly walking upright (and probably being mostly naked of body hair), they had proportionally shorter legs than us, and a more shambling, less proudly striding gait. We do not know what they ate, where they sheltered (if at all) or how they interacted with the environment. The excellent *Masters of the Planet* by Tattershall (2012) gives a good review of early human development as far as body structure is concerned, as far as we know it, but he is candid about how little we know of the behaviour of our precursors.

The likelihood is that early humans were living wild on the savannah, without shelter, without homes, and at most making temporary roosts in which to sleep. Today, gorillas, chimps and orang-utans make rough nests, little more than platforms of twisted vegetation or branches on which to spend the night. Darkness is a dangerous time, what with big cats and other serious predators prowling about; diminutive australopiths would have done well to keep out of the way as best they could. The 'nests' of apes are used for only a few days at a time; they are by no means permanent, and this is why the higher primates do not have fleas. Let's just jump forward a few hundred thousand years to understand why we have them today.

FLEAS – WELCOME ABOARD

Modern humans are the only apes to have their own fleas. This is unfortunate, but is a direct consequence of our sedentary lifestyle. We do not, however, carry our fleas with us wherever we go (that's lice, see further on in this chapter). They jump aboard us to bite us and suck our blood, but really fleas are denizens of the nest. More particularly, only adult fleas jump on us to bite; the tiny (1–2mm), pale, worm-like larvae wriggle around in the deep nest detritus. This is where a permanent host nest (a home) becomes important.

Fleas living on an animal (bird or mammal) drop their tiny, smooth eggs willy-nilly, to fall down into the nest. The fleas also drop copious dark squiggles of hard, dry faeces. Since blood is on tap, as it were, the fleas feed freely, and their abundant excrement is little different from dried blood, still highly nutritious. A flea larva down below feeds on this secondhand blood, along with any other organic matter like host droppings and rotten nest material, until grown and matured enough to change into a pupa (chrysalis). It does not, however, automatically emerge as a new adult flea, but bides its time.

One of the features of birds and mammals is that they are active daily and seasonally, and there would be no point in a flea emerging from its pupa only to discover that its host had gone walkabout for a month. Instead it waits, dormant, sometimes for many months, until vibrations indicate that the host has returned to take up residence again. Within seconds the flea quickly shimmies out of its chrysalis and jumps aboard.

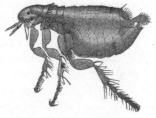

Anyone who has cats (more about them later) will recognise the phenomenon of returning from a few weeks' holiday, the pets having been shipped off to a cattery for the duration, and

Ctenocephalides felis

coming back into the empty home to be met with what seems a sudden plague of cat fleas *Ctenocephalides felis* jumping up and biting the ankles. They have not been multiplying wildly while the house occupants have been away, but have just been quietly reaching the end of their larval stage and waiting in their chrysalises. The vibrations of the returning humans trigger what has now become a synchronised mass emergence, where before the continual trickle turnover would have gone unnoticed. Except maybe by the cats.

Dogs are not immune to this either; they have their own very similar flea, *C. canis*. I'm a cat person myself, so I've had plenty of cat fleas jump upon my bare ankles as I pad around the kitchen making coffee first thing in the morning. There was a chicken flea *Ceratophyllus gallinae*, too, once, but that wasn't indoors. I encountered it when I was playing hide-and-seek in my grandfather's chicken coops, and I guess my childish stomping gave the flea in its chrysalis just the right signals to encourage it to emerge. That one hurt, if memory serves.

Cat/dog flea larva

The flea life cycle is only possible in conventionally nesting (rather than merely roosting) species, which is why all the nomad great apes live flea-free lives. It was only because humans returned, night after night, to sleep in the same shelter, and accumulated nest material in

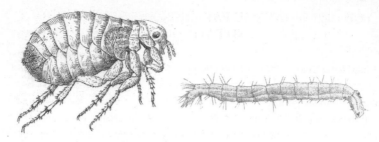

The human flea *Pulex irritans*, and larva

the form of bedding, that a human-based flea community could become established. Astonishingly, this was only a very recent occurrence.

The human flea *Pulex irritans* is a rather adaptable flea, and a fascinating insect – I thoroughly recommend *The Compleat Flea*, by Lehane (1969). It certainly did not start off sucking human or even *Australopithecus* blood.

There are about 2,600 flea species across the globe, most with varying degrees of host specificity. Fleas have been biting mammals and birds for over 200 million years, and had evolved their modern shape and form by 40–50 million years ago. Busvine (1976) goes into plenty of helpful detail on how the bloodsucking habit of fleas and other insects might have evolved. Usually a given flea species only occurs on one host species, although it might also occur on a small number of similar hosts. The mole flea *Hystrichopsylla talpae*, for example, only occurs on moles, but the chicken flea occurs on a wide range of other bird species apart from chickens, and on the occasional child playing in a chicken house. The human flea is one of six species in the genus *Pulex*, all of which originated in the Americas. Humans did not arrive in the New World to collect their fleas until about 14,000 years ago, when they crossed the land bridge between present day Chukotka and Alaska as the ice retreated after the last ice age. But when they did, they soon picked up some *Pulex* from their original hosts – prairie dogs, peccaries and guinea pigs (Buckland and Sadler 1989).

YOU ARE WHAT YOU EAT – HUMANS START HUNTING AND EATING MEAT

Meanwhile, from the Pleistocene epoch, many *Australopithecus* bones (and those from later humanoid species) have been recovered from caves and subterranean pits. They're still not cavemen bones, though. Various ideas are put forward. Streams and rivers that dried up long ago may have washed the scattered bones into the caves along with general debris during seasonal floods, or the unfortunate australopithecines could have been the victims of big-cat attacks, the bodies having been dragged down into the darkness to be devoured later. Caves, silted and in-filled with rubble, offer good preservation conditions over the aeons, and the bones remained moderately well preserved until excavated by excited archaeologists. But these were not homes.

By 2 million years ago more human-like primates had appeared. So like modern humans were they that they are generally included in our own genus – *Homo*. Various species names are bandied about, including *Homo habilis* and *H. erectus*. They were erect, but still some way off modern human height, with various estimates of around 1.5m.

At this point in time their diet, as suggested by their teeth, was very similar to that of the predominantly (but not all wholly) vegetarian large apes we still know today – gorillas, chimpanzees and orang-utans. A knowledge of pre-human diet is important for us because it gives clues to the beginnings of food preparation and storage, and a prehistoric technology that would eventually produce long-term shelters – homes. Two million years ago was roughly when human tool making began, with bashing one rock against another to make a sharp edge. At first, technological advance was very slow, and it took another million years before typical 'Stone Age' sharpened flint fragments appeared regularly. The presence of these blades begs the question of what the early humans were cutting. The usual suggestion is that they were butchering animals for food.

This immediately summons up, to the mind's eye, caricature images of unkempt, hairy (but not furry), brutish-looking people clutching wooden clubs, and casually dressed in draped animal skins knotted fashionably at the shoulder or cut to make loincloths of varying modesty. Too much of this is ill-informed myth. Meat eating (the obvious precursor to wearing fur) is so commonplace in modern societies that it is difficult to imagine how it began. It certainly did not start by some epiphany for a lone Stone Age forager wielding his club or launching his flint-tipped spear into the succulent and deliciously nutritious flank of a gazelle, thus suddenly elevating him from mere gatherer to the new-found iconic status of hunter. It seems much more likely that early humans stole kills (or at least bits of kills) from proper predators like lions and leopards.

Evidence for this comes from the unlikely study of tapeworms, the disturbing and distasteful gut parasites that feed the nightmares of many a squeamish new biology student. These huge intestinal worms are highly species specific, and at one time it was thought that humans acquired their several species with the domestication of cattle and pigs, only around 10,000 years ago, ingesting the egg-like larval cysts by eating the poorly cooked beef or pork meat in which they lodge. The flat, many-segmented worms developing in the human digestive tract can reach about 6m in length; segments full of eggs break off and are passed in the faeces. In the close human/animal confines of the shelter/barn or shelter/sty, the eggs soon get accidentally swallowed by the stock animals and hatch in their stomachs. The tiny worm embryos migrate out through the body to the muscle tissue, ready to be eaten by the next hungry person.

In fact, molecular analysis of these worms (Hopberg *et al*. 2001) across a range of mammal hosts shows that humans had tapeworms long before this, and that it was probably us who gave tapeworms to our stock animals. Humans picked up tapeworms from the same sources that lions, hyenas and wild dogs got theirs – from eating antelope or gazelle meat – and at a time well before stone (or indeed any) tools. The implication is that meat eating began as meat scavenging. Animal carcasses attract a huge variety of scavengers, including (after hyenas, vultures and humans) plenty of insects like flies and beetles. When early humans were using their small stone blades to slice morsels from freshly abandoned kills on the lightly wooded African savannah, it did not matter what came along to feed after them, but the moment they started to bring home the bacon (or venison, or beef or whatever), including any skins, horns, antlers, tendons, hooves and all the other useful bits, they were positively asking for trouble. We'll come back to this interesting larder-centric relationship later.

From about 600,000 years ago, the human fossil record becomes a little more enlightening. This is the era of the almost-modern humans – *Homo heidelbergensis* and *H. neanderthalensis*. *H. heidelbergensis*, although named after the illustrious city in south-west Germany where a fossil jaw was first found in 1908, was the first truly cosmopolitan human. Other modern-type human (*Homo*) fossils have been found scattered piecemeal across Africa, Europe and parts of Asia, but *H. heidelbergensis* was the first nearly worldwide human. This is notable because it coincides (roughly) with the apparently worldwide spread of a new stone-shaping technology (Acheulean, after the French town of St Acheul, where it was first excavated and identified) of large hand axes and chopping tools. What were they chopping? At a similar time humans may have started to understand, and maybe even 'use' fire. Were they chopping wood?

The current earliest known example of what is thought to be human use of fire comes from an apparent hearth at an 800,000-year-old site in Israel, but this is rather an archaeological outlier, and real evidence of regular controlled fire does not appear until about 400,000 years ago. Now, however, things start to get interesting, because this is also the time of the earliest documented human shelter.

THE FIRST HOMES AND THE FIRST HOME BUILDERS

The several ancient shelters, as they are fancifully reconstructed in the imaginative minds of palaeoanthropologists de Lumley and Boone (1976), were built about 350,000 years ago at the archaeological site of Terra Amata, in what is now Nice, in the south of France. A small group of hunters seems to have returned every so often to the site, but unfortunately left no traces of themselves. Each shelter is defined by a large, oval ring of heavy stones anchoring cut saplings that were embedded into what was at the time a sand and pebble beach. The presumption is that the saplings were drawn together overhead to create a hut that could shelter 20–40 people. There is conjecture as to whether the construction would have been covered with animal hides or turf, or thatched with leaves, but there are no remains to indicate any of this.

What is most interesting, however, is that a gap in the stones demarcates a doorway, and just inside this is a shallow, scooped-out hearth, multilayered with ash, surrounded by blackened cobbles and containing burned animal bones. Here are tantalising echoes of our sacred space, with its entry portal open to guests, but protected by flames against intrusion from ... what? Prowling animals? Prowling enemies? Howling wind? Biting flies? We still don't know quite enough, and there are plenty of arguments about the shelters' exact age, form and use, but this important excavation marks at least a theoretical start to the notion of home building. We're still not quite ready to leave the caves, though.

Around 150,000 years ago those most famous of 'cavemen' start to appear – the Neanderthals. *Homo neanderthalensis* is so well known to us because although it has been found as far afield as present-day Israel and Iraq (but not Africa), it is really Europe's endemic proto-human, and finds in the abundant caves of France, Germany, Switzerland, Italy and Spain have fixed it firmly in our consciousness.

The most striking thing about any reconstructed Neanderthal image in textbook or museum displays, apart from the prominent, stern-looking brow ridge, is that these people are usually portrayed (as per caveman stereotype) wearing animal-hide clothes and carrying flint-tipped weapons. There is at least some archaeological evidence for these.

Neanderthals made Europe their home at a time of world cold – during the series of regular ice ages that have characterised the northern hemisphere for the last 3 million years, since the tectonic plates of South and North America met to create the Panama isthmus, thus blocking out the warm circulating currents from the Pacific Ocean (Van Andel 1994). Incidentally, this same tectonic event earlier started the cooling and drying of Africa that transformed copious lush tropical rainforest into the savannahs where delicate (or robust) *Australopithecus* could evolve.

Several things seem to have allowed the Neanderthals to survive so far north. Their stout, stocky body form (they were seriously squatter, larger and heavier than modern humans) gave them some advantage in conserving body heat. However, they would have had to be sumo wrestlers in size and blubber content to feel comfortable in those skimpy loincloths. It is much more likely that they wore warm clothes – the discovery of stone scrapers and piercing awls certainly suggests that they were preparing and stitching animal hides. Coincidentally, rickets, a distorting disease of the bone joints from lack of vitamin D, also starts to appear, and since this vitamin is synthesised in the skin as a response to sunlight, covering the body with heavy, lightproof clothes appears to have been the cause.

Later humans, the Cro-Magnons, modern *Homo sapiens* to all appearances, colonised even further north and were well clothed, with tunics, leggings and cloaks decorated with beads, according to the archaeological records from their burials. The emergence of clothes would later usher in the era of clothes-destroying insects, but we're getting a bit ahead of ourselves here – first let's look at some clothes-infesting animals.

LICE – CLOSE UP AND VERY PERSONAL

The discovery of Neanderthal awls and Cro-Magnon needles dating to 100,000–40,000 years ago, and the suggestion that this is when humans first put on clothes, fits in very nicely with the evolution of perhaps our oldest personal guests – lice. Unlike fleas (see page 14), which hop on and off as the mood takes them, lice *never* leave the human body unless it is to move to another human brushing or lying against it. They never let go; only the death of the louse or the host will ever induce a louse to relinquish its hold (Maunder 1983). Consequently, we have had lice from a time before we were remotely human, and long before we ever settled down to make homes.

Head louse
Pediculus capitis

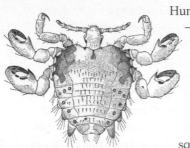

The crab louse *Pthirus pubis*

Humans are host to three louse species – the crab louse *Pthirus pubis*, the head louse *Pediculus capitis* and the body louse *P. humanus*.

The crab louse, sometimes also called the pubic louse due to its preferential occurrence around the nether regions, is a short (2mm), squat beast, and despite its name is really the generalist louse of coarse human body hair. It has stout, powerful claws for gripping the thick, fairly well-spaced hairs of the groin, but can also occur on men's hairy chests, and in beards, armpits, eyelashes and eyebrows. It's generally agreed that the crab louse is just about the most embarrassing insect in the world, so enough about it here.

The head louse is all too familiar to anyone with school-age children. It occurs on heads, and its claws are perfectly sized to grasp the much finer, more tightly packed hairs on the human scalp. It's an annoying nuisance, for sure, but completely harmless, and does not transmit any diseases. In *The Little Book of Nits*, Jones and Crow (2012) try to placate parents and dispel some of the many myths surrounding this irritating insect. There is an uneasy repugnance at the idea of tiny creatures living in your hair, but this is a modern phenomenon of a fastidious Western society that finds it unacceptable to scratch the head at the dinner table. I take a certain scholarly pride in claiming that I am alone, as far as I know, in being the only person who has ever exhibited a live head louse, plucked from their own head, at a meeting of a national entomological society (Jones 2001).

Thankfully the body louse is all but extinct in modern society. This is a nasty, unpleasant creature. It transmits typhus *Rickettsia prowazekii*, trench fever *Bartonella quintana* and relapsing fever *Borrelia recurrentis*, bacterial diseases that breed in the guts of the louse but infect human victims through cuts in the skin when the louse is squished during scratching, or by contamination with its copious bloody faeces. Busvine (1976) gives lots more gory details. Typhus epidemics throughout history have killed countless millions. Up until the middle of the 20th century it was the louse of the morbidly unclean, the homeless, the pitifully squalid and the unwashed poor, but also of the soldier in the trenches (hence trench fever), the famine victim and the refugee; this is the louse of natural and man-made disasters.

Although almost identical to the head louse, the body louse differed in one very important aspect – its behaviour, because instead of living on heads, it lived in the clothes. In fact 'clothing louse' would be a more accurate name for it, a conviction echoed in an old scientific name, *Pediculus vestimenti*. Ironically, it is the easiest louse to get rid of. All you need do is change your clothes, but people who suffered from body lice were the victims of situations where they could not take off their clothes for many weeks, and even months; the clothes they stood up in (or lay down in) were probably the only possessions they had. Louse infestation rates could reach appalling proportions in the occasional hapless person, and it was not uncommon for grim cleansing stations to report numbers of 30,000 body lice on a single individual.

There is still a certain squeamish shame attached to head lice, even though they actually do better on clean hair than on matted locks, and afflict middle-class children just as much as working-class kids. Part of this embarrassment is due to the close resemblance of the head louse to the body louse, and the fact that in the past the two have sometimes been regarded as one and the same species, just different subspecies or races. The differences between them are extremely slight: the adult body louse is usually slightly longer (2.3–4.1mm) than the adult head louse (2.1–3.3mm), but there is considerable overlap; in the laboratory head and body lice can be induced to interbreed, producing intermediate lice.

It is only through the advance of DNA studies that we can now see clearly how head and body lice are different. They have very similar DNAs, showing that they are indeed very closely related, but subtle differences in the double helix sequences have accumulated over evolutionary time. These changes

The head louse *Pediculus capitis*

23

(mutations) in the DNA strands of all organisms are well documented, and occur at a low but more or less constant rate over the aeons. By comparing DNA sequences, and counting the minor differences between head and body lice, it is possible to extrapolate backwards in time to estimate where the ancestral lineages of the two creatures meet – how long ago they shared a common ancestor. By these calculations (Kittler *et al.* 2003), body lice evolved from head lice about 70,000 years ago (give or take a few millennia). This, coincidentally, was just at the time when *Homo neanderthalensis* and slightly later *H. sapiens* were making themselves at home in the cool Eurasian wilderness, sitting around the fire, and cutting and stitching animal skins to make themselves something warm to wear – putting on the first clothes.

REAL CAVEMEN LIVED IN FRANCE

Back in the cave, despite fur coats it is dark and gloomy, and the cold, hard starkness of bare rock doesn't look very enticing to modern eyes. It's tempting to assume that the Neanderthals introduced at least some creature comforts to make life worth living. Animal fur bedding sounds about right.

The Neanderthals excelled in Mousterian stone technology, named after the French site at Le Moustier, in the Dordogne. This skilful working of hard stone produced razor-sharp cutting and slicing implements, and elegant long blades that look very like spearheads, to the point where it is generally accepted that the Neanderthals were successful hunters. Indeed, chemical analysis of their bones shows that they were probably top predators; it's all to do with different nitrogen isotopes accumulating in carnivores as opposed to herbivores. Neanderthals' arm and shoulder structure implies that they were spear thrusters rather than spear throwers; nevertheless they appear to have been capable of ambushing and bringing down mammoths and woolly rhinos, which were quite the most fearsome creatures of the day.

Evidence of healed and fatal bone fractures in the skeletons of the fearless Neanderthal hunters testifies, down the millennia, to the dangers of the large-mammal hunt using close-range stone weapons.

But when the big game was caught (and skinned), a veritable feast ensued, and judging from the increasing frequency of hearths, the feast was cooked on an open fire.

Cooking using fire is a clear indication that food, both animal and plant material, was being brought back to the home base for preparation. This may have also been the start of smoking and drying to preserve meat and fish for later consumption – unless the food storage pests got in there first. Even if the hunted and gathered food was consumed relatively quickly, it would still have offered plenty of opportunities for the unwelcome attentions of any local scavenger pests. As anyone who has lived in rural France will attest, leaving the supermarket shopping out on a work surface for a few minutes is a clear invitation for house flies to come and settle. Even in the dubious semi-darkness of the cave entrance, any food left unattended for a moment would have been abuzz.

All these clues to Neanderthal cuisine and loincloth fashions indicate, through the hazy window of patchy prehistoric archaeological remains, that although faced with an inhospitable or inclement climate these people were coping. Not only did they cope, but they also coped very well, enough to see them through 100,000 years, more than twice as long as 'modern' humans have been about in these latitudes. They coped by using the ingenuity of human (or pre-human?) inventiveness. They sought shelter in the cave openings and overhangs (French archaeologists have a special word for them – *abri*, from the Old French *abrier*, to shelter); they warmed themselves using animal pelts for clothing and probably for bedding too, and they warmed their 'homes' and prepared their food using fire.

Just as an aside, the common association, in the modern mind, of Stone Age peoples living in caves has much to do with European cave paintings. These actually came later, with the appearance of the Cro-Magnon people, a race of modern humans (*Homo sapiens*) that migrated out of Africa only about 40,000 years ago. The caves (occupied from about 33,000 to 11,000 years ago) were obviously special to the Cro-Magnons, but they were certainly not homes. The cave paintings are not domestic murals; they are seriously weird and symbolic images painted by the disciples of some lost and forgotten shamanic ritual. And the painted caverns are deep underground, so deep that they could take an hour of walking or crawling to get to, clutching feeble, guttering tallow torches. No one could live here. They were claustrophobic, cold, dark, dangerous places.

On a cheerier note, camping would have had all the advantages it still has today – you travel light; the tent or bivouac is quick and easy to establish; the materials are cheap, or at least readily available to hunt and forage; you have all the ease of healthy cooking over a barbecue or fire pit, and you can move with the seasons or with the hunting, or when you've got bored, or when the latrines and middens get too smelly.

Judging from 'recent' (that is, in the last 1,000 years or so) nomadic hunter-gatherer societies, seasonal migratory moves could follow the prey herds and the constantly changing forage crops. Easily dismantled, transported and reassembled shelters like tepees, wigwams, yurts and gers offer a fine balance of comfort with manoeuvrability. They still have their unwelcome visitors, though, climbing in through the flimsy animal-skin door or crawling through the air and smoke vents. It's not too much to imagine similar structures punctuating a Neolithic landscape 50,000 years ago. It's difficult, though, to imagine how any traces of them might be preserved for modern archaeologists to argue about.

There are precious few finds. We do, however, know that the 'modern' *Homo sapiens* (Cro-Magnon and other groups) moving out into Eurasia 40,000 years ago were skilled makers of all manner of artefact – a range of elegant yet practical tools made from stone, bone, antlers and wood, including hooks, harpoons and rope. It is only as we move towards the 'modern' era that a scattering of shelters is unearthed, some of which might be considered semi-permanent. Among the most unusual shelters we know of are the mammoth-bone huts of the Russian plains, built some 15,000 years ago. Excavations of massive bone piles at several sites show circular structures of 150–650 interlocking mammoth bones weighing up to 20 tonnes, using a heavy base of stacked jaws and skulls, and surmounted by a superstructure of arching tusks and timber, presumably covered with skins or turf.

The idea of these huge piles of mammoth bones might jar with modern readers wondering at the killing power of a few people armed with stone-tipped spears. There is a rather romantic idea that aboriginal peoples had little effect on the environment, and that their hunting schemes were somehow in balance with nature and ultimately sustainable. However, whenever humans arrived at a new 'empty' land, like they did in Australia (40,000 years ago), the Americas (15,000 years ago), New Zealand (3,500 years ago) and Madagascar (2,500 years ago), it did not take them long (just a few centuries) to wipe out many species of large, but slow, megafauna. The overhunting of mammoths and woolly rhinos (and all the other large animals) by Neolithic humans has been termed the Pleistocene overkill (Martin and Klein 1984), and although it may have provided meat, skins and building bones aplenty for many generations, it would later become one of the driving forces behind the change from hunting to farming considered in the next chapter.

Modern mammoth-bone shelter reconstructions (Fletcher 1993) indicate that it might have taken ten people about 15 days to build a settlement of half-a-dozen shelters, and that once completed they would have been weatherproof and snug enough. They don't, however, indicate more subtle attributes, like the smell.

Bones are not without a certain odour – this was, after all, a temperate region, and bones left out in the open did not become sun bleached and sterile as they do in a desert, say. Modern noses might be unaccustomed to it, but bone smell was familiar to all right up until well into the first half of the 20th century, when large industrial factories were rendering cow, pig and horse bones for glue. Textbooks of the time (for example Hinton 1945) list the many scavenger beetles that populated the bone-works. Although these beetles no longer feed on our stored bones, some of them are the same beetles we still find in our kitchens today, namely hide, bacon and larder beetles (more on them later). It is tempting to imagine that these same beetles were attracted to the mammoth-bone huts, and fascinating to consider what the occupants called them in their archaeo-Siberian tongue.

Smell is something that the already disjunct archaeological record cannot preserve. However, this primordial sense is what first brought so many domestic pest (and guest) species into the lives of humans. It is also the smell that might have first alerted humans to the idea that some of these visitors were less than healthy.

THE SMELLY EDGES OF SOCIETY

Back in the Stone Age camp, flimsy timber-framed shelters, roofed with hides, turf or thatch, continue not to leave archaeological remains; burial mounds have not been invented and traces of human day-to-day activity are very thin on the ground. Nevertheless, wherever humans go they do leave traces of themselves – in their litter. The best signs of a prehistoric human presence in the landscape often come from dumped rubbish. This may be in the form of huge coastal seashell middens (Waslkov 1987) accumulated over centuries (millennia even), or small piles of broken stone tools mixed with butchered animal bones. Eventually pottery shards would start turning up too. The discarded refuse of human enterprise still says much about us today; looking backwards it lets us surmise what our ancient ancestors were doing, and also how they were tested, early on, by the pests that still pester us.

Anthropologists and sociologists use a neat turn of phrase that is precisely apt here – the septic fringe (Robinson 1996). Today this may well mean the dishevelled, rambling, often lawless sprawl of the shanty town. In tropical conurbations it is still associated with squalid living quarters, lack of waste disposal and sewage facilities, contaminated water, poor hygiene, and diseases spread by rodent and insect pests. In prehistoric times it meant the edge of the settlement, the place where unwanted rubbish was dumped, and as well as broken tools it contained food waste, both cooked and uncooked.

Harking back for a moment to pre-humans scavenging their first tastes of animal flesh from lion kills on the African savannah, meat eating is not without its dangers. It does not take long for raw meat to become inedible, then toxic, and cooked meat also goes off pretty quickly. Humans, right the way back in their ancestral history, have never been adapted to eating the rancid meat that wolves and foxes down quite happily. Our herbivore forerunners had already evolved long, convoluted intestines to assist in vegetable digestion – intestines in which toxins easily build up to create food poisoning if we get our meal choices wrong. The smell of rotten meat (second only to the smell of dung perhaps) rightly repels us, an instinctive warning that it is not good to eat. Smells from the Palaeolithic midden would have been fairly strong too, enough to tell our ancestors that the dumped food scraps were beyond edibility, and probably enough to suggest that anything living in the refuse was not worth befriending. Here, then, would have been humans' first contacts with so many of the noisome nuisances we still have today – house flies, blow flies and cockroaches. This would be the metaphorical back door into human societies, before an actual entry into the real front door of the hut was tried later. The chances are that this is how dogs got inside our homes.

WHEN DID WE LET OUR BEST FRIENDS INDOORS?

Dogs are now part of every human society across the world. Irrespective of rules set down by the Kennel Club and other official dog-breeding groups, they occur in all shapes and sizes, and most colours and patterns, and have been used for everything from hunting to fashion accessory. But they are all dogs, all one, single interbreeding species, as demonstrated by unlikely crosses of the chihuahua with the bulldog, standard poodle with the St Bernard, and doberman with the basset hound. It is no surprise to discover that modern dogs are descended from wild grey wolves *Canis lupus*, and whatever their pedigree status all domestic dogs go by the scientific subspecies name *Canis lupus familiaris*, sometimes shortened to just *Canis familiaris*.

What is perhaps more surprising is the fact that although archaeologists have uncovered dog-like (but still also quite wolf-like) remains in close association with humans from about 35,000 years ago in Belgium, Ukraine and Russia, all modern dog lineages are actually descended from a single domestication event somewhere in Eurasia only 15,000 years ago. It would seem that for very many millennia, humans had almost-wolves for pets, but true dogs only became our best friends much later.

There are several ways in which wolves could have first come into contact

Canis familiaris

with humans, and become domesticated. They could have met at a carcass site, either group having made the kill, but the other hoping to scavenge or thieve. Wolves could have come into conflict with people during particular hunts, for example on the seasonal migrations of prey animals like reindeer. Wolves are curious animals, and although wolf attacks on humans are exceedingly scarce today, they have probably happened occasionally from time immemorial, with the possible consequences of humans seeking revenge or removal of the perceived threat. Cubs left after such an incident could have been taken alive for trophies, talismans or playthings. Humans and wolves are both pack animals, loosely based around family units, with a pecking hierarchy enforced by violence or threat; wolf cubs would have fitted in very well with a pack of hunter-gatherer humans.

An intriguing bit of genetic evidence, however, suggests that they may have first come face to face over the septic fringe, the midden rubbish heap at the edge of the camp. Dogs, as is well known, will eat anything; wolves, on the other hand, are carnivores. Dogs can easily digest starch in the form of bread, rice, potatoes and the like, but this is a recent physiological trait, one that has apparently been selected for by humans. Wild grey wolves do have two copies of the gene that codes for the starch-digesting enzyme amylase, but dogs have up to 30 copies. The implication from the researchers that carried out the DNA analysis is that any wolves that scavenged and could successfully process starchy food bits thrown out by humans would have the advantage over those that could not.

In good old natural-selection style they were more likely to thrive and pass on this ability to their similarly more successful offspring, who would continue to frequent the food-giving middens. At this point other selective pressures also came to bear on the increasingly human-acclimatised wolves. Flight distance decreased – this is the physical distance at which an animal feels threatened enough to run away from danger. It can be decreased by learning from a young age, but there is also a propensity in there, under genetic control, or at least under genetic influence. Connected to aggression (fight or flight being the two best responses to danger), flighty or aggressive wolves would not have been tolerated even at the encampment's rubbish dump.

By comparing the genomes of wild wolves and domestic dogs, the starch gene scientists (Axelsson *et al.* 2013) identified 36 regions in the DNA that probably represent real genetic changes caused by human selection (selective befriending and selective breeding). Nineteen regions contain genes important in brain function (eight controlling nervous-system pathways and potentially underling behaviour), and ten genes had key roles in starch digestion and fat metabolism.

Since the rendezvous at the rubbish dump, wolves have become dogs in various structural ways too. Today's breeds are the result of many centuries of increasingly selective breeding to produce animals for various purposes. In their (our) history dogs have been used for tracking, hunting, herding, guarding, companionship and warmth, as beasts of burden and occasionally for their flesh or skins (Millais 1911 recommends dog skin for the projectile pouch of a handy catapult). The huge variety in body shape, form and mass of modern dogs belies the fact that there are several key changes that have been orchestrated right across their range. They mostly became significantly smaller (as too did domesticated cattle, sheep, goats, horses and pigs a few millennia later), the jaws became shorter (initially leading to teeth crowding, but eventually to smaller teeth) and the skulls shrank, leading to smaller brain size. Maybe without the need to cope with the 'wild', domestic dogs don't need to be so wily. They do, however, need to be calm, friendly, loyal to the pack (now their human family) and able to digest processed, often starch-based pap delivered to their dinner bowl from the family leftovers or now from a tin. Even in a society where large, powerful dogs command respect as rather menacing status symbols, vicious uncontrollable wild animals are not tolerated, and will not be invited indoors.

THE FIRST HOUSES

Today 'house' usually means something built of brick, stone or concrete – something quite substantial and long-lasting. There are still plenty of timber-framed houses, and thatch is a perfectly acceptable roofing material; these are less obvious in the archaeological record, but where (and when) they occur, there are also signs of stone dwellings, or at the very least, stone foundations. The most important point about a house is that it is permanent (that is, it is not a seasonal camp), and that it is part of a settlement. By definition a settlement implies that the occupants are settled, no longer camping nomads; in prehistoric terms this means that they were no longer hunter-gatherers, but had become farmers.

This transition appears to occur very suddenly in the archaeological record, around 12,000–10,000 years ago (Henry 1989), and the Fertile Crescent, from Anatolia (present-day Turkey), Mesopotamia (the land in and around the Tigris and Euphrates rivers), and the Levantine coast of the Mediterranean to Upper Egypt, is usually portrayed as the hub of this great leap forward – the Neolithic Revolution.

Certainly this is the start of serious house building, and Jericho in Israel/Palestine, built in around 7500 BC, is usually cited as the first walled city, the stone remains of which are still being excavated today. Agriculture brought high returns in terms of food production; excesses could be stored against famine or even short-term seasonal hardship. It was able to support a much higher human population density, and although it gave rise to the disparity between rich landowner and poor serf labourer, or subsistence farmer, it also allowed for the appearance of commerce, trade and wealth, which in turn allowed for the flowering of art, literature, philosophy and science. It gave us, in effect, civilisation.

Domestic pests, however, were no respecters of human niceties, no matter how civilised, and merely took advantage of human beings' increased ability to create and own more things. The highest in the land were not beyond depredation. When the great pharaohs were laid to rest in their giant sarcophagi in or under their giant pyramids, the food stores set aside for their journey into the afterlife were tainted from the start with cockroaches, grain weevils and biscuit beetles, and their mummified bodies were polluted with carrion beetles (Pettrigrew 1834; Hope 1836).

Civilisation has brought mankind great advantages, but it has also brought with it plenty of hangers on.

II

The attractions of home:

*I*t's arguable, I suppose, whether human beings became so successful because they were able to make permanent homes, or that they were able to make permanent homes because they were so successful. This is something that archaeologists, anthropologists and historians are still debating. Whatever the answer to this conundrum, there can be little doubt that after modern humans made the first great cultural leap into symbolism and language, which paved the way for intercontinental migration, notably the colonisation of Australia 40,000 years ago, and widespread cooperation and trade (war too, probably), the second great advance was definitely settled agriculture.

arming the land had several effects. As well as giving humans a high-yielding, dependable food source (quietly brushing aside inconvenient famines caused by droughts, floods, locust swarms, disease blights, wars, internecine strife, pillage, plagues and the like), it also tied them to the land. They had to stay put in order to till soil and sow seeds, and tend, irrigate, weed, harvest and store crops. Humans finally put down firm roots. Ostensibly humans did well by this transition.

Received wisdom has it that agriculture began in the Near East around 10,000 years ago. This is where and when all the archaeology points. But it now seems unlikely that an irreversible agri-revolution occurred overnight, and the demise of hunter-gathering in favour of arable farming probably took many thousands of years. It also seems quite likely that farming did not just suddenly appear; it had probably been going on piecemeal for millennia.

From the point of view of household visitors, many of which are linked to the medium- or long-term storage of food after a harvest, this meant that there was a long period of people living in semi-settlements before moving on again, or regional overlap of settlers regularly interacting with passing hunter-vagrants. There was plenty of opportunity for animals of all shapes and sizes to come into contact with humans, either in their mobile camps, or in their progenitor hamlets and villages. This is something that is easy to forget when we try and work out where house pests and guests originated. If we try it by examining the archaeological record, we get disoriented, because the archaeological record appears to start, already in full flow, at that watershed 10,000 years ago.

Archaeoanthropologists still debate the finer details. Early settled farming was very tough – much harsher than previous itinerant foraging. The farmers were less robust than their hunting ancestors, suffered nutritional, traumatic and infectious diseases unknown to their forebears, and only had a diet limited to the plants they cultivated, rather than the rich and varied foods found in the seasonal wanderings of older hunting clans (Harris 1996). At first sight it would appear odd that our ancestors would choose to go down this seemingly harsh domestic route.

The suggestion is that even though they were wandering about and unsettled in the long term, the hunter-gatherers from, say, 40,000 years ago were nevertheless successfully managing their environment, encouraging some plants (fruit-bearing trees, for instance) and practising a sort of proto-farming in small, temporary plots for a few years before moving on. Those stone hand axes could be put to good use in clearing small plots of less useful scrub and coppicing trees, in favour of useful forage plants. Many archaeological sequences show a knowledge of agricultural and domestic plants long before the real shift from hunter-gathering to full arable farming. Tudge, in his book *Neanderthals, Bandits and Farmers* (1998), paints a convincing picture of this complex overlapping intermediate agriculture phase.

By a series of coincidental effects farming took over by insidious gain, rather than by any eureka moment. Game management became stock keeping; cultivation started from protecting various useful plants and taking cuttings (only later by planting seeds); land clearance by burning started the idea of arable fields, and the gradual decline of free-range large mammals to eat (due to the Pleistocene overkill by over-vigorous cavemen armed with sharp flint spears) reduced the impact and value of the grand hunt. Eventually there came a tipping point, at which time hunting and gathering was a loss maker not worth saving. The partially nomadic hunting could no longer compete with the attractions of a settled agricultural life. The farmers inherited the Earth; they actually inherited the very soil. And this event was best manifested in the Near East.

When it finally came, 10,000 years ago, the mass community change to settled farming did offer a few long-term advantages. Previously restricted by the limited food sources provided by prey animals and seasonal foraging, populations burgeoned. As mentioned earlier, farming on a small hobby scale had probably been going on for very many centuries, but what proper permanent settlement offered was the prospect of planned and cooperative food collection, organised transport, storage and preparation, and sharing. And by remaining still, the increasing numbers of people could now start to accumulate the well-earned luxuries of modern living – furniture, bedding, clothes, utensils, art, nick-nacks, storage units, heating and so on. Eventually, life was good.

Life was good for house visitors, too. It still is. They do well because humans have provided for them everything they will ever need – more even than that. They came and went, to and fro, during the many thousands of years of the nomad/settler interface. However, when humans finally stopped moving, the house pests and guests we have today were able to catch up completely, and bend all their attention to making themselves at home, too. Today roughly 3,000 animal species are recorded as living in, invading, or destroying or otherwise polluting human habitations (Bonnefoy *et al*. 2008).

FIRST, SOME TERMINOLOGY – WORDS AND MEANINGS

Human homes have now become an accredited biological habitat in their own right. We have been around long enough – as have our buildings – for the ecosystems they represent to have scientific names. Animals that 'live', wholly or significantly, with humans are called **synanthropes**; they exhibit **synanthropy**; they are, in character, **synanthropic**.

These animals may live with us intimately, or through gentle gradations across our cultivated land out into the wilderness whence they came. In their original haunts, they inhabited a **eubiocoenosis**. This is the natural habitat in which they lived before humans evolved, and depending on the individual species involved, it could have been caves, tropical rainforests, temperate woodland, savannah grassland, desert oases, riverbanks, marshes, sea cliffs or numerous other different ecological niches. As mankind started to have an effect on the environment, through farming, our lands attracted creatures out of their original homes and into the **agrobiocoenosis**, a farmed or managed zone that encompasses everything from hedgerows, ditches, paddocks and pastureland, to haystacks and arable fields. This is sometimes divided into types A (small-plot subsistence agriculture) and B (intensive industrial monoculture-production agriculture), although this is perhaps a technicality too far for this book. The agrobiocoenosis can also include managed woodland, whether this is intensive forestry or infrequently attended copses.

The human settlement of buildings arranged from a single small dwelling place, through hamlet and village, to larger urban agglomerations, now forms the **anthropobiocoenosis**, where organisms' relationships with mankind might be **domestic** (inside the house) or **peridomestic** (around, at the edge of or just outside the house). The garden might be considered an indistinct boundary zone, sometimes part of the agrobiococnosis (type A) and sometimes a peridomestic territory.

Getting even more personal, some invaders have become human parasites of varying degrees. **Obligate parasites** (lice, for example) are those that live entirely on their host, and cannot survive or reproduce without one. **Facultative parasites** sometimes take on a parasitic role (adult fleas, say, living on their victim and sucking its blood), but can survive away from the host and sometimes live a semi-autonomous existence elsewhere (as do flea larvae in the nest). Bloodsuckers like mosquitoes don't really count as parasites, but might be described as **facultative predators**, since they live almost all of their lives away from humans, but need to eat just a bit of us (or some other animal) to get the vital nutrition necessary for egg laying. More about these biting pests later.

Another group of organisms that deserves its own special category comprises those that come into the house, but don't really do any harm to us or our belongings; they simply take up lodgings there. These are usually referred to as **commensals** – from the Latin meaning 'eating at the same table'. Some people look upon all invaders with an equal disdain, but really things like window flies (which innocently feed on carpet beetle larvae) and assassin bugs (which mainly feed on bed bugs) could be considered here. Another subtle distinction is given to **inquilines**, a term usually applied to 'guest' organisms living in the nests of other animals, and feeding on any spilled detritus, or nest material, but not generally inflicting harm on the hosts. Humans have plenty of inquiline organisms, like silverfish, book lice (they don't feed on books, though) and spider beetles, which live hidden and discreet lives scavenging in secret corners.

Window flies
Scenopinus fenestralis

The exact status designated to an animal is very much a personal subjective assessment. I have my own definition, which I'd like to offer to distinguish pests from guests:

– it's only a pest if it reaches pest proportions.

WHY ARE HOMES SO ATTRACTIVE?

Attractiveness has nothing to do with tasteful decor, grandiose architectural flourishes or postcode snobbery. It doesn't even have anything to do with house size, floor-plan layout, age or style, although choice of building materials can have some minor effects. Homes are attractive to humans now for the same reasons that they were 50 millennia ago – they provide shelter from the elements (wet, cold, heat, wind), and a base for storing all our food and belongings.

The pests (and a few guests) that come indoors are also seeking the same things they have been seeking for many millions of years. Although humans have come on in leaps and bounds in the last 50,000 years, this is nothing to most animals, and many of them have remained unchanged for aeons – it's just that their needs now coincide with man's, and their life cycles now overlap with us. Good for them; bad for us, though, maybe.

Obviously, what turns up in a home depends on where in the world a home is. Tropical homes, by virtue of the higher animal diversity (especially of insects) in the tropics, have more species to contend with. A textbook of British household pests (Butler 1896) contains a completely different array from that presented in a tropical handbook (Stebbing 1909). When Francis X. Williams (1928) of the Hawaiian Sugar Planters Association went on a busman's holiday to the Philippines, he made a long list of over 100 different species inhabiting his nipa house, a rustic palm-thatched building 'of some antiquity'. He also described several species of wasp new to science, including the aptly named *Ancistrocerus domesticus* that was making its nest in a nail hole in a wall. Homes in higher latitudes, and at higher altitudes, have generally cooler climates, and the local faunas show lower diversity, as do homes on remote islands or deep in city centres. However, insects especially are highly adaptable and mind-numbingly numerous. Even the most remote and unattractive property will eventually be found out and in they will come.

There are four main reasons why our homes offer such good living space to animal invaders, or rather four factors that these invaders have been able to exploit to their obvious advantage. These are:

1. Dry shelter
2. Warmth
3. Food
4. Avoidance of natural predators and parasites

Future chapters will deal with some of the most familiar, important or revealing animals in more detail, but for now let's look briefly at the four basic principles of attraction behind the invasion of our homes.

SHELTER – MORE THAN JUST A ROOF OVER THEIR HEADS

Sitting writing this in London, in winter, I might be about to make a very common assumption – that my house is invaded because it is warm. But this misconception is merely the view from the centrally heated early 21st century. In temperate latitudes what a house really offers is dryness.

Despite the notion that rain is a natural phenomenon, this does not make it any less dangerous to animals. Venturing into the garden in the rain quickly shows that there is nothing about, and that all sensible creatures are seeking shelter, if only hiding in a hole or roosting under a curled leaf. Humans are not the only things to catch their deaths if caught out in the wet. There are plenty of diseases ready to strike the bedraggled; invertebrates, especially, are prone to attacks from fungus or mould. Cold they can cope with, but damp is a danger, so they need dry spaces in which to seek respite. Houses are dry, and as far as many animals are concerned they are simply suitable places in which to keep out of the rain.

Woodlice, the familiar domed, multi-segmented, multi-legged critters found beneath logs and stones, sometimes venture into houses when it rains. This is at an ironic end of the moisture-avoidance spectrum, because woodlice are really quite moisture-adapted animals, which don't really like the dry. Insects have a cuticle made of chitin, a complex amino-polysaccharide molecule laid down in alternating laminated layers to give a tough, flexible and waterproof (that is, water-retaining) coating. Woodlice, on the other hand, are among a very few land-dwelling crustaceans, and they have kept, from their marine ancestors, a relatively hard but porous shell derived from calcium carbonate, the brittle chalky chemical also found in seashells, cuttlefish 'bones', chalk and limestone. Marine crustacea do not have to worry about drying out, but woodlice rapidly lose water if it gets too hot. This is why they seek shelter most of the time, huddling together in damp crevices and dark corners in woodland, hedge and garden.

Woodlice come out to feed in the cool damp of the night, grazing on decaying plant material. During heavy rain they are liable to get flooded out, and the physiological adaptations they made to air breathing when they evolved out on land come back to haunt them. This is when they start to sneak in through the gap under the back door. The trouble is that modern human houses are not just dry; they are very dry indeed. As a consequence, most people who find woodlice usually find them days later, tucked into corners at the edges of carpets, where they have died from dehydration and shrivelled into dry, brittle, desiccated husks.

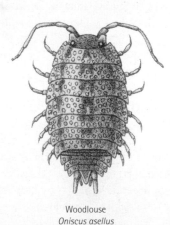

Woodlouse
Oniscus asellus

This process is hastened by modern central heating, air conditioning and climate control, but even way back when houses were first being constructed they were powder-dry places. Most of the animals that invade our sacred space today are not simply looking for brief shelter from the rain;

they are species that are, in essence, very well adapted to drought conditions. Household invaders are not just a random selection of animals already living outside in the garden, which have been tapping their noses on the windows and desperately trying to get indoors. They are a highly selected group of organisms which have discovered that the low-moisture habitat of the human household exactly matches the low-moisture habitat in which they had been evolving for millions of years beforehand. The dryness that allows our possessions to remain preserved and crisply rot free is a dryness that our household invaders have already had to contend with and overcome. Judging by their numbers, many have overcome it very well.

One of the supreme overcomers is the cellar beetle *Blaps mucronata* in the UK, and its various relatives around the world. This large, black, flightless beetle walks with the deliberate slowness of a clockwork model. It has a domed, hunched appearance, and long, gangling legs. It might look familiar to anyone who has seen video footage of its relatives, the *Onymacris* darkling beetles from the Namib Desert. These similarly hunched, long-legged black beetles live in one of the driest places on the Earth, where it may not rain for years on end. They manage to find water by standing tail-up, head-down in the pale morning fogs wafting in off the Skeleton Coast of the South Atlantic, and condensing tiny droplets on their backs, which then trickle down to their mouthparts. This behaviour, combined with a tough, water-retaining cuticle and long legs to keep the body away from the scalding sand, enables them to live in one of the most ferociously hot and dry landscapes in the world. Similar darkling beetles are features of hot, dry habitats all around the globe.

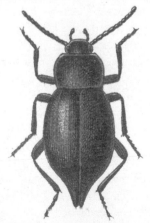

There is no evidence that the cellar beetle fog-bathes in the same way, but it will if disturbed dip its head down and stick its pointed

Cellar beetle *Blaps mucronata*

tail into the air to exude a droplet of foul-smelling, liquid faeces. Its desert-dwelling, drought-resistant heritage, though, has allowed it to survive in the bone-dry underfloor spaces of old houses. Its English name is a bit of a misnomer, because although it does occur in cellars, even some damp ones, one of its main habitats is underneath our floorboards. Anyone who has ever crept into this space, between house and earth, to lay electricity cables or inspect the floor joists, knows that it is far from moist, and is usually chokingly dusty. But the cellar beetle ekes out a slender living down there.

What it feeds on (as both adult and larva), like any scavenger, is whatever it can get, and this means meagre crumbs of dry food dropped onto the floor above, then knocked or brushed down between the gaps in the floorboards. It is, to use one of the jargon words introduced above, a commensal; it doesn't really do any harm to us, or our belongings, food or homes, but it's a definite trespasser.

In houses old enough to have proper cellars – dry places where food was stored, not dank holes where bicycles and old tools are left to rust – the cellar beetle lurked in dark corners, nibbling at spilled grain or scraps of bacon rind that fell to the floor. My grandparents' Kent farmhouse had an ancient subterranean cellar full of bottles, jars and an old meat safe (a wooden construction covered with fine metal mesh to keep out any blow flies) and a healthy cellar beetle colony that fascinated me as a boy. I'm rather pleased to have found the beetle under the floorboards in four of the many houses I've lived in over the years. This actually says something about the parlous state of my residences – a run-down student house in Brighton in the late 1970s, a semi-derelict 'fixer-upper' and an 'unmodernised' terraced house in Nunhead in the 1980s, and the semi-detatched house I still live in, in East Dulwich, described at the end of the 1990s as 'having great potential' in the estate agent's blurb.

Today's homes, of course, more often than not do not have gaps for food to drop through. The gaps were either filled with silica-gel sealant when the floorboards were sanded and polished (I'm guilty of this, I'm afraid), or they have been covered by lino, vinyl, carpet, laminate flooring or any other fashionable and hygienic barrier. This, and a propensity to vigorously spray chemical insecticides everywhere under the floorboards at the first signs of woodworm (not guilty), has meant a drastic decline in the cellar beetle in many developed countries during the last 75 years.

This has been followed by an even more pronounced decline in a large sleek, smooth black beetle, the house ground beetle *Sphodrus leucophthalmus*, which is a predator specialising in attacking cellar beetle larvae. Never common, but at least widely recorded in cellars and houses across much of England, the house ground beetle is now possibly extinct in the UK – it was last recorded, in Cornwall, in 1979.

As a naturalist, I feel a frisson of sadness that these two handsome

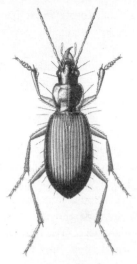

The house ground beetle
Sphodrus leucophthalmus

insects are now so reduced – the house ground beetle to the point of being critically endangered. But synanthropic species carry no nature-conservation value (after all, they do not occur in 'natural' habitats), and since many household creatures are regarded as pests, most people are trying to eradicate them anyway. In Britain, at least, it is clear that neither is a native species. Neither has an independent existence in some natural habitat. This begs two questions – where did these species come from, and how did they get here?

As in the case of so many species, we do not know precisely; we have to make some guesses. Another sleek black ground beetle, *Laemostenus complanatus*, a close relative of the house ground beetle, also sometimes occurs in cellars; it probably lives a similar life and attacks cellar beetle larvae. Very occasionally it is found outdoors, but always near houses, usually near ports – a pretty clear indication that it too is not native here. However, a third predatory ground beetle, *L. terricola*, does occur 'in the wild', and is found in rabbit, fox and badger burrows, where it attacks nest scavengers, quite likely beetle and fly larvae. It sometimes also occurs in rock crevices and caves.

The temptation to hark back to Neanderthals and Cro-Magnons must, however, be resisted. It's fascinating to contemplate when the cellar beetle, probably a generalist scavenger in Neolithic Mediterranean rock crevices, and the house ground beetle, probably an animal-burrow predator, first attached themselves to humans. Evidence for them is scant, but because of the cellar beetle's large size and distinctive shape, it is generally accepted that Pliny the Elder, in the 1st century AD, was describing it (thinking it was a type of cockroach), when he wrote: *blatta odoris taedio invisa, exacuta clune* – 'having an unpleasant smell and being pointed at the tail end' (Beavis 1988). It was presumably well established in Mediterranean houses at the time, and since the Romans are usually claimed to have invented world trade, the natural assumption is that they spread it, along with underfloor central heating, in their empire-expanding endeavours. It's as good a guess as any.

HEAT – COMFORT WARMTH AND COMFORT FOOD

In many cases of household invasion it is not possible, despite my earlier assertion, to divorce dryness from warmth. There is clear evidence that large, heated commercial buildings like hospitals, hotels and office complexes are increasingly invaded because of their all-day and all-year-round central heating, allowing what are really tropical and subtropical species to become established. This is the case with several 'tramp' ant species that have accidentally been introduced to northern latitudes, well away from their subtropical origins.

The pharaoh ant *Monomorium pharaonis* is a prime example. Although the ants are tiny, with workers only 1.5–2mm long, colonies of 350,000 can be a major problem in inaccessible wall spaces and narrow voids. From here long trails of ants set out on foraging expeditions, leaving a pheromone scent to guide them back on their return, and to recruit extra foragers when a good food source is located. The ants do not cause structural damage to buildings, do not bite or sting humans, and are not seriously implicated in the spread of diseases, but they cause upset when found infesting food in hotels and restaurants, or

The pharaoh ant *Monomorium pharaonis*

wandering over supposedly sterile medical dressings in a dispensary. Thankfully, I've never had this ant take up residence in my house. I did, however, come across a few crawling over some typewriters and fax machines in an office-supply shop in Chelsea many years ago. The salesman wasn't very impressed when I popped one into a small glass tube 'to look at later'.

The pharaoh ant was given its name in 1758, from specimens found in Egypt, and for many years it was thought to have originated in North Africa. This had more to do with its name than with any real biogeographical study. By, say, 1890, when burgeoning interest in natural history had started to unravel world faunas of many groups of insects, including ants, it was already known from Europe, the Americas, South-east Asia and Australasia. It had been carried inadvertently by the shipment of goods all around the world. Its world spread is nevertheless recent, and is still ongoing. Its sweep across the USA occurred mostly between 1900 and 1940, and it is still spreading across northern Europe; it only arrived in the Mediterranean islands of Cyprus, Sardinia and Sicily in 2004 (Wetterer 2010), a highly unlikely late arrival if it were truly an African ant.

In cooler zones the pharaoh ant is tied by its tropical ancestry to heated buildings, but in warmer climates it can survive outdoors, although it rarely ventures far from human habitation. It is apparently becoming feral in Florida, USA. There is, however, one region where it does often occur under logs and stones, well away from buildings – South-east Asia, including Malaysia, Indonesia and the Philippines. This, then, is likely to be the ant's original ancestral home, and its spread across the oceans was likely mediated by trade several hundreds (but maybe not thousands) of years ago.

Central heating has warmed humans ever since the Romans started building hypocausts, the underfloor venting through which heated air from a fire was fanned. Today central heating allows many creatures like the pharaoh ant to survive well outside their normal comfort zones, but even when houses were fitfully heated by smoking open fires, they provided sanctuary for warmth-loving visitors.

The firebrat *Thermobia domestica* is named after its close association with fires. It belongs to a group of primitive wingless insects, the order Zygentoma, sometimes called bristletails because of their long tail bristles, or silverfish because of their metallic silvery appearance and fish-like sleekness. In temperate countries the firebrat has long been known to occur around ovens, heating furnaces and boilers, hot-running machinery, including that using steam, and laundry machines. It comes out at night to scavenge on spilled food and crumbs, but also damages fabrics (silk and linen) and paper; it has a special liking for wallpaper, which it grazes through to get at the starch or flour used in the paste beneath.

The heat tolerance of the firebrat is a sure sign that its original habitat (its eubiocoenosis) was also hot – and dry. Although a really rather minor household pest, this creature has been intensively studied

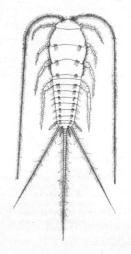

because of its ability to absorb water vapour from the atmosphere, rather than having to drink it or get it from moist food; indeed, it can take water out of quite a dry atmosphere. How it achieves this is still being researched, but it seems to occur in the hindgut. Air is taken in through the anus, and water, at the molecular level, is driven across the gut membranes by a biochemical physiological shunt, rather than by some passive process involving osmosis or diffusion (Noble-Nesbitt 1969). This is quite some achievement, and the implication must be that the firebrat originated in the hot, dry, semi-arid lands of North Africa and the Middle East.

The firebrat *Thermobia domestica*

In our homes today, we separate heat for cooking and heat for warming ourselves. Despite the Romans' architectural skills in the creation of hypocausts, there was a time not too long ago in historical terms when fire was just fire, and its purpose was manifold. However, its use for cooking was of key importance.

Cooking is so mundane a procedure, yet it is one that has transformed humanity and is arguably one of the great cultural advances of humankind. Quite how it arose is a mystery that will most likely outlast us as a species. Speculation is rife, but for the purposes of this book it is enough to know that cooking is ubiquitous across all human societies.

One of the most important benefits that fire brings is the improvement of the nutritive value of almost all foodstuffs through cooking. At the very least, complex molecules begin to be broken down by heat, making their digestion easier in the human gut. Heat also makes unpalatable things positively tasty. Plants like kidney beans and cassava are poisonous (deadly even) unless soaked and cooked. Raw meats become a dangerous gamble within hours of animals being slaughtered unless they are cured or cooked (refrigeration is only a modern alternative). Cooking changes simple, staple, sometimes barely edible ingredients into an infinite variety of delicious feasts. Fire, when it first arrived in the human home, must have seemed like a miracle.

One of the consequences of having fire in the home and cooking on it was that food obviously had to be brought into the home too. This was just begging for trouble.

FOOD – LOADS OF IT, EVERYWHERE

Hunter-gatherers hunted and gathered. Presumably, from very early on this habit brought them into conflict with various pest animals. The very first hunted carcass brought back for butchery and cookery would have had plenty of scavengers in tow, from hyenas to blow flies. The first meagre handfuls of nuts or armfuls of fruit set aside in a corner to be nibbled later in the week would soon have attracted other nibblers.

Today, still, animals coming indoors in search of food are the greatest source of our frustration with domestic pests. This is partly due to a degree of squeamishness, of not wanting to share our foods, usually with creepy-crawlies, or to have them crawling in our food when we finally get around to eating it. Partly it is down to a realisation that so much hard work collecting the food (whether we hunted or foraged for it, or farmed it) is wasted if we open up the store to find it half devoured already and crawling with vermin.

Until the advent of refrigeration meat storage involved short-term hanging of animal and game carcasses to tenderise them, keeping butchered meat in a cellar meat safe (as did my grandma), and long-term storage by salting, smoking and curing. Without being too literally pedantic, whatever the meat, hunter-gatherer humans started bringing home the bacon. Enter, stage right, the bacon beetle *Dermestes lardarius*.

When I moved into my current house in south-east London in 1999, the decor was tired, to say the least. The sculpted flock wallpaper in the bedrooms, harvest-themed bathroom tiles and heavy purple curtains in the sitting room were all very 1970s. Perhaps the strangest discovery was a thick shag-pile carpet in the small kitchen. Originally pale pink but now faded to a grubby beige, and widely stained with suspicious spills of various brown liquids, it had to go, but when I finally got around to pulling it up, it revealed a horrible secret. Crawling beneath it, as it sat heavily on the solid concrete floor, were thousands of bacon beetles and their larvae. This was not a minor infestation, the result of a single pregnant female flying in through an open window and taking advantage of a temporary lapse in hygiene; it was a mature ecosystem, and it had obviously been thriving for years.

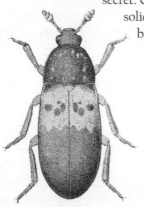

Along with the bacon beetle were the closely related spotted larder beetle *Dermestes maculatus*, black larder beetle *D. haemorrhoidalis* and Peruvian larder beetle *D. peruvianus*.

Bacon beetle *Dermestes lardarius*

As their name suggests, larder beetles (including the species supposedly more attached to bacon than the others) are well-known pests of stored food. In the days before refrigerators and plastic packaging they would attack bacon hanging in the cellar, barrels of flour in the bakery, and cheese and milk in the dairy. They don't need much to scrape a living, and will quite happily breed in food slops spilled down the back of a cooker, crumbs knocked under kitchen cabinets and even dried milk dregs at the bottoms of abandoned milk bottles (another of my student houses in Brighton, this one).

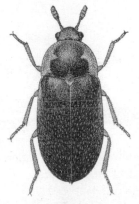

Spotted larder beetle *Dermestes maculatus*

In the 18th and 19th centuries larder beetles were also important pests of bones, when these were a major industrial source of glue, and they damaged stored furs, bath sponges and dog biscuits. Such was their destructive power in one 19th-century London leather warehouse that £20,000 was offered for any available remedy (Butler 1896). If wooden boxes become impregnated

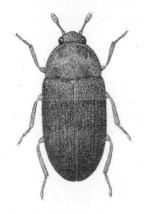

Brown larder beetle *Dermestes ater*

with animal oil or fat, the larvae will burrow into the woodwork. There is a well-documented account of *Dermestes* larvae nearly sinking a ship in 1593 because they reduced the hull timbers to honeycomb; the nearly ill-fated cargo aboard the vessel was a heavy load of dead, possibly rancid penguins (Hinton 1945).

It is these historical accounts that give an indication of where larder beetles originally started off in the natural scheme of things, before humans gave them larders to invade. And the word 'larder' itself

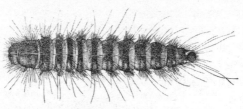

Larder beetle larva

is the clincher. Originally larder did not mean just any old food store; it meant a store of meat (lard is, after all, meat fat). Bread, together with biscuits and other wheat- and corn-based products, would be in the small pantry (from Latin *panis*, or bread) next door – we'll come on to biscuit beetles later. Pickled and other items, stored in ceramic and glass containers, would be in the final kitchen storage area, along with wine and beer. This was the buttery, a corruption of bottlery, sometimes butlery, presided over by the butler.

The dried and cured meat hanging in the larder is really the larder beetles' true niche, because in the wild larder beetles are carrion insects that feed on the decaying remains of dead animal bodies. They are not part of the first wave of scavengers attracted to a fresh kill. Blow flies are the first of the insect clear-up squad to arrive, and there is a mad scramble for the decaying flesh in the first hours or days. Larder beetles, though, play the long game. They arrive once most of the easy food is gone and the carcass starts to become tough and dry, when there is perhaps little left other than bone and sinew, fur and feathers. Again, here is an indication of the importance of the dry quality of human habitations, because it is the dryness of the larder that helps to preserve the sides of bacon and ham hocks that are hanging there. Larder beetles are so good at this final recycling process that the larvae of several *Dermestes* species are still used in museums, laboratories and schools for the final meat-cleaning of animal skeletons to be used in exhibitions and teaching displays (Hall and Russell 1933).

I have no idea what gruesome morsels my personal kitchen colony had been eating under its thick layer of carpet for the last couple of decades. I suspect that, as in the case of the penguin-laden ship which the beetles nearly scuppered, they were now eating the carpet itself, after years of it being soaked with spilled soup, stew and boiled beef. Despite my admiration for the beetles' fortitude, I spent several hours ripping up and bagging the carpet, and disposing of its wriggling contents. Obviously I kept a few sample specimens too.

GET THEE BEHIND ME PARASITES

So many other animals have followed the bacon beetle into our homes, but despite what we might see as a deluge trespassing on our daily bread, it has certainly not been a complete free for all. Those 3,000 or so species might seem like a lot of creatures taking an interest in our sacred spaces, but this is as nothing when we contemplate that there are over 1 million known animal species (mostly insects), and an estimated 10 million more out there (at the very least) waiting to be discovered. Only a very select few ever get past the door – and this is the very secret of their success.

Out in the natural world there are constant ecological checks and balances. In a neat and much-studied checking system, the holly blue butterfly *Celastrina argiolus* lays its eggs on holly and ivy buds. These are common, widespread and vigorous plants, and sure enough within a few years holly blue numbers have increased dramatically. The numerous caterpillars are now easy for a parasitoid wasp, *Listrodomus nycthemerus*, to find. This species lays its eggs inside the holly blue caterpillars, and the hatching maggots eat their hosts alive, from the inside, eventually killing them before they can turn into butterflies. Within a couple of years the parasitoid wasps are very common, but they have now so decimated the holly blue populations that it comes to a point where they cannot find any more caterpillars to parasitise. Their population crashes now too, and this respite allows the scattered holly blue population to recover ... until the next time. The regular cycles occur roughly every six or seven years.

These types of cyclic boom-and-bust population oscillations are commonplace in nature, and although they keep swinging up and down, the populations usually stay more or less within the same upper and lower limits over the centuries, or the millennia. But if an animal is able to leave its natural predators, parasites or diseases behind when it breaks into a new habitat, there is nothing to restrain its numbers and its population can explode. This is exactly what happens when animals invade a new, virgin territory. When North American grey squirrels *Sciurus carolinensis* were either deliberately or accidentally released in Britain in the late 19th century they stepped into what was a land free of specialist predators, parasites and diseases. They spread widely and wildly, and they are still spreading. Crossing the threshold of a human sacred space is a journey into one of the most virgin of all territories.

Inside a home there are precious few dangers, apart from the blundering and largely unobservant human occupants. From the invader's point of view there is a virtually inexhaustible supply of food, and there are none of the usual dangers from predators or parasites. Life is good.

Of course, not everything is actually quite this simple, but a personal exception, I think, proves the general rule. When I was gritting my teeth and getting right into my beetle-infested kitchen-carpet clearance, there was one final entomological delight, right at the end as I brushed the last few morsels of debris into the dustpan. I noticed a tiny insect crawling about in the dust. It was one of the few known enemies of *Dermestes* beetle larvae, a microscopic (2.5mm long) creature called *Laelius* (or *Allepyris*) *microneurus* (there's no common name for such a tiny beast). Under the microscope it resembles a slim, winged ant. In a similar (but not identical) fashion to the parasitic wasp that attacks holly blue larvae, *L. microneurus* sticks it eggs onto the body of a *Dermestes* larva, and the grubs then burrow in and feed on the living larva until they have finally devoured it all, apart from its skin. It's incredibly rare, or at least incredibly rarely recorded. This is partly because, although it might be a 'natural' parasitoid, detecting and attacking colonies of *Dermestes* in the wild as the beetle larvae feed on dried carrion out in the open, it is unable to easily make the jump into our well-defended human habitations.

I fell upon my prize. This was, as far as I'm aware, only the fifth time *L. microneurus* had been found in the UK. On the other occasions it had been found in a presumably equally grubby kitchen in Beckenham (also south-east London), in Kew Gardens, a hotbed of natural scientists, including entomologists, and at the Imperial College's Natural Science Laboratories at Silwood Park, near Ascot, in what was in effect the university's entomology department; a lone specimen was also collected in a flight-interception trap in the gardens of Buckingham Palace. The kitchen of my semi-detatched house in East Dulwich is in good company, and this does go to show that predators and parasites of even the most common domestic pests are almost mythically rare. Despite the dastardly mode of attack employed by *L. microneurus*, the *Dermestes* are still safe.

COSMOPOLITANISATION – IS THAT EVEN A REAL WORD?

The great leap forwards that came with the emergence of agriculture about 10,000 years ago has two features that are easy to forget now, as we look back with slightly supercilious condescension from the highly mechanised modern world. Firstly, agriculture seems to have arisen independently in several different locations around the world – the Near East, the Indus Valley, China and the Americas. It may have appeared at different times, sometimes centuries or millennia apart, but as discussed earlier it was not a sudden, revolutionary new idea, transported by zealous converts throughout the globe, replacing hunter-gathering overnight as it went. It had been going on piecemeal for millennia.

Secondly, almost all of the current farm animals and the crops that we grow today were already being farmed 10,000 years ago. Pigs, cows, sheep, goats and chickens (and many other animals) were being herded and had long been domesticated by then. Oats, wheat, barley, rice, maize, yams, potatoes, beans, cabbages and cucumbers (to name but a very few) were widely planted and were already being improved by breeding selection from the wild strains.

It is not surprising, therefore, to find that many of the domestic pests specifically attached to our stored food were already chewing their way through our larders and pantries well back into prehistoric times. Today, many have become completely cosmopolitan, ubiquitous even, spreading across the globe and vexing widely separated cultures and societies. It is, nevertheless, possible to track some of their histories, as well as those of other domestic pests, guests and visitors, from their natural habitats, their eubiocoenoses. These histories can offer tantalising clues about our own journeys from Neolithic hunter-gatherers to sophisticated urbanites.

III

Shelter:

STORED SUPPLIES, IN THE WAREHOUSE, THE CELLAR, THE LARDER
AND THE PANTRY

*I*t always starts with a casual nose-around. When you're
eying up a new property, the first thing to observe is the
neighbourhood. Is it your sort of place? Does it feel safe?
What are the other residents like? So it is, too, for the
animals looking to move into your home. However, they may
have slightly different criteria by which to judge a particular
home's suitability. Of little importance to them is the number of
bathrooms and bedrooms, the availability of off-street parking
or the colour of the front door. They will find more importance
in the period details — the exact overhang of the eaves, the
detailing of the air-bricks and the fit (or not) of the window
casements.

ike it or not, older homes are more attractive to house guests than new ones, if only because there are more gaps to get in and out by, more nooks to accumulate dust and detritus, and more forgotten corners missed during the last exterior decoration session. Modern homes, and certainly modern high-rise developments, are much more boxy on the outside, sealed against the elements and uninviting as roosts. A rural thatched cottage, on the other hand, is virtually just an extension of the garden hedge; almost anything can get into it.

One of the first ways into any house is through the roof. This is because house builders still have a tendency to regard a roof as just a roughly fitting lid to keep off the rain. There is usually a loft void, or attic, but this is rarely a living space and more usually disregarded as little more than an indoor shed area for dumping unwanted items in uncertain limbo storage for months or years. Ventilation, either through gaps where roof meets wall, or by special vented roof-tiles, is usually important for stopping moisture accumulating, and for keeping things, yes, dry. Lofts are, very much, an invitation to enter.

EAVES – JUST A ROCK OVERHANG BY ANY OTHER NAME

Every year the coming of spring in northern latitudes is heralded by the arrival of charismatic birds wheeling through the clear blue sky. Swifts *Apus apus*, swallows *Hirundo rustica* and house martins *Delichon urbica* fly north from their overwintering grounds in subtropical savannahs and take up residence again under our eaves. All are familiar species (iconic some might say), perching on telegraph wires, swooping high over house tops, and screaming low over fields or down streets in our towns. They are all very much at home around humans,

Swallow *Hirundo rustica*

and have been for centuries, because we provide for them a basic necessity of their lives – places to nest.

Swifts and swallows come right in under the edge of a roof to find a rafter surface or jutting brick on which to make their shallow dish-nest constructions. They are also known to nest in gaps in thatch, in wall holes and on the ledges inside large, old chimney stacks. Swifts catch bits of airborne grass and fluff, and glue them together with saliva to

Swift *Apus apus*

make a precarious, barely rimmed platform for their eggs, but swallows go a stage further and incorporate gobs of mud from pond and stream edges to make a shallow saucer affair.

It is house martins, however, which are most familiar around buildings – a clue is in the 'house' part of their common name and the *urbica* part of their scientific name. These gregarious birds make very obvious nests under roof edges, against corbels or at the top of the window masonry (they were sometimes called window swallows in old books). Theirs are the distinctive mud-daub cups, looking like half-coconuts, wedged in tight against the wood or brickwork,

with just a small semicircular hole for the chicks to peek out of, and for the parent birds to feed them through. The fact that house martin nests are outside does mean that they are sometimes blamed for guano splashes down the walls or on paths beneath, but at least they are not indoors, in the loft, messing the joist spaces with excrement, nest material and bits of food, not to mention old eggshells and the occasional dead hatchling. Swifts and swallows are often lauded

House martins *Delichon urbicum*

for their aerobatic skills, while the poor old house martins are vilified for their toilet habits.

It is pretty obvious where all these birds came from, before humans had invented eaves, rafters or thatch. Quite a few bird textbooks also mention them nesting occasionally on cliff-faces and rocky outcrops. The house martin's closest cousin is the sand martin *Riparia riparia*. In a few very rare instances, sand martins have nested in drainpipes projecting from walls or in holes in brickwork, but they are really so-called for their habit of nesting in horizontal burrows dug into the exposed vertical faces of sand pits, railway cuttings, riverbanks, gorges, canyons and sea cliffs. It seems quite likely that humans have enjoyed the exhilarating sight of these spectacular birds ever since they too took to sheltering in the abris of the Dordogne or indeed anywhere against rocky overhangs.

Eaves are also the easy way in for several other common 'garden' birds, including the starling *Sturnus vulgaris* and house sparrow *Passer domesticus*. The starling is a citizen of the world, the Old World at least, and throughout Europe, Africa and Asia it is intimately associated with all man-made or man-influenced habitats, from garden and meadow, to reed bed and coppice. Likewise, its nesting choices are varied, but it usually selects enclosed spaces, like a disused water spout, gutters, broken drainpipes, holes in walls (including disused dovecotes) and spaces under eaves if it can find a gap in the roof. Away from human habitation it nests in whatever natural crevices it can find, including small hollows in rock-faces and tree-holes, which are almost certainly the bird's original ancestral breeding places.

No such easy observation is available for the house sparrow. Again, this cheeky bird is thoroughly habituated to humans, and occurs throughout Europe and Asia, but it is not immediately clear what its lifestyle might have been before houses were available

Starling *Sturnus vulgaris*

for it. It will nest in any hole in a building, or in creepers and climbers growing up the outside. It will occasionally nest in a tall tree, but only a tree near buildings; occurrences of it nesting away from human dwellings or cultivation, such as high moors or deep forest, are virtually unknown. Here it is replaced by the tree sparrow *Passer*

House sparrow *Passer domesticus*

montanus, although there is wide overlap of habitats. Tree sparrows are also common around rural villages and homesteads, and invade eaves and thatch roofs, and the two species occasionally interbreed.

Genetic and morphometric studies on House Sparrow populations around the world (Felemban 1997) suggest that the species originated in the Middle East, where Arabian subspecies are larger and more variable. Following a theme identified in many animals (Bergmann's rule, after German biologist Carl Bergmann, who described the phenomenon in 1847), they grow larger at higher, cooler altitudes and latitudes. This local variability is taken as a sign of a more diverse gene pool, and thus probably the origin of various colonisation ventures out across Europe and Asia. Here too the birds nest away from buildings, in tree-holes and rock crevices, or lodge in the lower layers of the nests of larger birds like storks and crows. Received wisdom has it that both species of sparrow started their human associations in this area with the birth of agriculture, and spread out with the increasing human dependence on grains.

Sparrows are omnivores, eating insects, worms, buds, fruits and seeds, but their appearance in crop fields and grain stores has brought them into fierce conflict with humans. This conflict can reveal much about the balance that exists between humans and their domestic (or peridomestic) wildlife. Two conflicts in particular illustrate very interesting, but slightly different, aspects of this human/wildlife interaction.

Between 1958 and 1962 the tree sparrow, identified as a major grain stealer, was one of the subjects of the Four Pests Campaign (the others being rats, mosquitoes and flies), which the Chinese government sought to eradicate by mass public involvement. Birds were constantly scared off fields, shot and netted; their nests were pulled down and their eggs destroyed. The population crashed, but rather than increasing grain yield the knock-on effect was that the insects on which the birds also fed now proliferated and locust plagues caused even greater shortage and hardship. It turns out that although perhaps being a bit annoying, the sparrows were already part of an ecological balance that included humans and farming.

The house sparrow is now common and widespread in North America; however, this was not a natural colonisation, but the result of deliberate introductions. The first few pairs of birds were released in Brooklyn, New York, during the 1850s. This was bolstered by further releases on the east and west coasts through to the 1870s (Barrows 1889). The reasons for the releases are variously reported as being to control local insect pests, and out of nostalgia for Europe. The first birds did not thrive; they all died apparently. But such was the Victorian enthusiasm for acclimatising 'good old' species from the Old World to the New, that the releases continued and sparrows were soon spreading. They had found, just as larder beetles visiting the first larders had, that they had been given a new niche to colonise, one well stocked with food, but pleasantly free of predators and parasites. In this case, however, it was not just the new habitat of human buildings they discovered, but a completely new continent.

Today tree sparrows are all but extinct in China, and house sparrows have become nuisance 'tramp sparrows' in the USA and Canada. Ironically house sparrows are declining alarmingly in Britain – a 70 per cent drop in numbers in the last 30 years is reported – making a once-familiar, commonplace garden bird into a species of some conservation importance and concern. The reasons for the decline are unclear and may be to do with the decline of horse-drawn vehicles, dung in the streets and the insects attracted to it, the recent spate of loft conversions or garden-insect pest control. While bird-conservation organisations monitor UK sparrow numbers and try to work out what is going on, sparrows' decline does highlight, very poignantly, the nature of 'pest' status – how it can change suddenly, and that something should not be considered a pest unless it really reaches pest proportions.

THE WELCOME DARK

A trip up into the loft usually involves fumbling in the dark for the inconveniently placed light switch attached to an off-centre joist support or, failing that, trying to find a less than dim torch in a kitchen drawer. Darkness is often portrayed as dangerous, but to most creatures it offers a certain measure of safety, because if you can't see, it stands to reason that you can't be seen – by predators. Lofts and attics are dark places, and this is why they are so attractive to many animals.

Bats, lords of the darkness by all accounts, used to be regular residents of loft spaces throughout the world. They still are in some rural areas, but in developing nations the towns and cities are fast becoming less bat friendly – this despite bats being highly successful creatures.

With roughly 1,000 known species, bats are the second largest mammal group (after rodents). They are the only mammals to have evolved true flight. They have slow growth and long gestation, and give birth to small litters, but they are long lived, with a lifespan of some 20 years; a similar-sized mouse has a lifespan of just one year. They owe their success to the dark. Darkness does not necessarily coincide with the peak availability of food (mostly flying insects, though some bat species eat fruits), but it is the time to avoid birds. According to bat palaeontologists (Rydell and Speakman 1995), the likelihood is that bats evolved flight first, by several million years, but then evolved nocturnality to avoid competition with and, more particularly, predation by much faster flying birds.

During the day bats seek out safe dark places to roost. Apart from the obvious hollow trees and caves, loft spaces are second to none, although roosting in them does have the disadvantage of bringing bats into close proximity with their greatest enemies – people. Bats don't do much real harm; there might be a splatter of bat urine in the loft, and a scatter of small faecal pellets on the patio beneath the small hole in the roof where they go in and out. Technically there is a risk of catching rabies from the bite of an infected bat, but only where the disease is endemic, and only if you can first catch and then pick up a bat. It's the human perception of bats that causes the greatest harm – to bats.

Bats' sinister nocturnal habits, their rapid and seemingly erratic flapping motion, complete with investigatory swoops, and the rather vague misunderstood myths about vampires do nothing to endear bats to us. Added to this, bats are now sufficiently scarce in some

Bats order Chiroptera

countries to merit significant nature-conservation value. In Britain, for example, it is illegal to kill, injure, disturb or even handle a bat unless you have a special licence issued by the requisite government authority. This makes bats supremely inconvenient if they are roosting in the loft that a householder wants to convert to an extra bedroom. There is a real cost implication, in terms of time waiting for roosts to become empty, or expert surveying and monitoring, if bats are discovered in a roof space. This is just another reason why these guests are so unwelcome in the home.

Despite protection, bat numbers have been steeply declining for many years, and it is because their winter rather than their daytime roosts are being mucked about with. Since bats hibernate, a true immobile torpor when the body temperature drops, the heartbeat slackens and the metabolic rate physiologically slows down, their winter quarters (as opposed to their daytime roosts) need to offer long-term shelter over several months. Increasing numbers of loft conversions and roof-insulation schemes, compounded by almost universal central heating in homes, cause constant disruption and displacement of bats at their most vulnerable time of the year. Although bats do not create nests, drop bedding or food, or damage household materials, their presence in lofts is sometimes regarded with suspicion.

Bats can find their own way into the darkness of a loft by actively seeking out entry holes, which they detect by sight and echolocation. Cluster flies *Pollenia rudis* and other species cluster as a result of the thermal qualities of walls and roofing tiles. These attractive, mottled grey, greenish or bluish, medium-sized flies are parasitoids of earthworms, so they are common wherever there is soil, and they thrive in gardens. In late autumn, like many insects, they have a tendency to bask in the slanting rays of the sun, and often choose sunlit south-facing walls and fences on which to warm up enough to fly. As the season progresses, their warming is not quite enough to get them airborne, so their physiological instinct is to hibernate; they begin to crawl upwards away from the cold, damp soil to find a dry nook in which to overwinter. In their ancestral habitat this would have led them up into a tree hole or crevice in a bank or rock face. Now it leads them up the wall or roof, to the small air gaps under the eaves or between the tiles and, true to their name, they cluster together in hibernation immobility.

Knots of cluster flies gather in corners against joists and rafters, and in favourable circumstances drifts of many hundreds or thousands can accumulate. Mostly these clusters go unnoticed, but during the revival of spring the flies can become disorientated. Instead of exiting by the same gaps that they came in by, they find their way down into the living quarters of a building, much to the consternation of the householder, who now finds hordes of stumbling or dead flies littering the window sills and floors.

An alternative effect of domestic roof design encourages another fly, the yellow swarming fly *Thaumatomyia notata*, to cluster in similar large groups. The larvae of these very

Cluster fly *Pollenia rudis*

Yellow swarming fly *Thaumatomyia notata*

small (2–3mm) flies burrow into grass roots, where they feed on other small soil invertebrates, so they are supremely abundant everywhere. During autumn they fly rather ineffectually, and as they get wafted about by the prevailing winds they become trapped in eddies underneath the eaves on the leeward sides of houses. As soon as they regain their footing they scramble up into any available gap to hibernate, and similar mass carnage is revealed when they start emerging from hibernation the following spring.

The chances are that this type of domestic clustering often goes unnoticed, or unreported. It was only because he had a pet entomologist for a relative that my cousin Terry Smith knew someone to approach when he found vast swathes of small black-and-white bugs in the attic of his Kent home. Many hundreds were falling down dead around the house every day, and when they started dropping through the loft-access hatch onto the bed at night, he was forced to seek professional advice. Instead, he approached me. The most unusual thing about this 'infestation' was that the bug in question was a rather scarce species in Britain, without any common name but luxuriating in the scientific name *Metopoplax ditomoides*. It feeds on mayweeds and other wayside plants on road verges, field edges, brownfield sites and wasteland in south-east England, and although it can be very abundant in some localities in this area, it has never been regarded as a domestic pest. It's difficult to make clear deductions from this one-off event, but it seems more than likely that the bugs (of a similar size to the yellow swarming fly) were being blown across from the neighbouring fields and ended up under the eaves of the house.

Metopoplax ditomoides

Until the middle of the 20th century this little bug was known only from the Mediterranean region, but it has spread across northern Europe over the last 50 years (including to the UK). Climate change has been invoked, but it will take many more years of study to test this assertion. It has also been transported to North America, probably in horticultural or agricultural material, and has recently been found 'swarming' in houses in the USA and Canada (Lattin and Wetherill 2002). It won't be long before a common name is coined for it. Let's hope it's a little more imaginative than just 'swarming bug'.

Flies and bugs are apt to get negative responses from householders, but few would take offence at butterflies. In temperate zones several butterfly species hibernate as adults; many also overwinter at the egg, caterpillar or chrysalis stage, but it is as the adults that they can fly into buildings to find winter shelter. In the UK four butterflies are adult during winter. The brimstone *Gonepteryx rhamni* is a delicately pale straw-yellow, and with gently sculpted wings looks like a dead leaf when at rest in a rose or bramble thicket. Three other butterflies, the peacock *Inachis io*, small tortoiseshell *Aglais urticae* and comma *Polygonia c-album*, are brightly coloured above, but dark mottled grey and brown beneath. With the wings clamped firmly closed, they are perfectly camouflaged hard up under the bases of large tree branches, inside hollow trunks or in the dim cool of small caves or shallow rock crevices, so much so that finding them here in winter is a real triumph of naturalist skill and know-how. Less wilderness-tracker prowess is required to find them nestling down for a winter among the curtain folds of a spare room, and sheds, too, are popular haunts. My sister finds small tortoiseshells in her wardrobe every year, shimmying down in a corner behind her wedding dress and party frocks.

The butterflies actually come indoors early, probably through open windows, long before real winter cold sets in, because hibernation is not just for deep winter; hiding is a good survival technique, and getting under cover sooner also means having a

Small tortoiseshell *Aglais urticae*

much better chance of making it through to spring next year. Why court danger from predators by flying around brazenly in autumn when the important biological acts of mating and egg laying will not happen for six months anyway?

Central heating sometimes arouses hibernating butterflies ahead of time, and they can be found listlessly fluttering inside a window in November or December. The best advice is to trap them under a glass with a piece of card and let them go in a shed; they'll soon cool down and settle down again, and wait to be got up at the right time, by natural sun warmth, in March or April.

Ladybirds, too, were unlikely to cause upset if found indoors, but even these familiar and popular beetles are now starting to cause consternation – well, one species is. The harlequin ladybird *Harmonia axyridis* is a native of China, Korea and Japan, but because of its large size and voracious appetite it has been captive bred, then deliberately transported around the world and released as a biocontrol agent. It has been released to control large and hungry aphids, themselves often accidental alien imports, attacking field crops and orchards, and plants inside glasshouses.

Initial reports suggested that this measure was working well. The adult ladybirds and their large, spiky larvae are ferocious predators of aphids and many other sap-sucking insects. The trouble is that they also eat hoverfly larvae, lacewing larvae and the larvae of other ladybird species, all feeding in the aphid colonies. This has led to fears that the newcomers are out-competing and actively destroying the original native wildlife. In the USA many native ladybirds have declined dramatically since the harlequin ladybird become widely established in the 1980s.

The harlequin ladybird was deliberately released in Europe at around the same time, but when it found its own way to Britain, in 2004, it was seen as a potential threat to the indigenous ladybirds, and its inexorable spread has been monitored with awe and concern – it is currently all over England and is making its way into Wales, Scotland and Ireland (Roy *et al.* 2011).

One of the species' most obvious habits is entering houses to hibernate. All ladybird species overwinter as adults, and they usually

seek out a dry chink or cranny on a tree trunk,
plant stem or dead leaf in which to clamp down.
Other useful hiding places include tree-holes,
spaces under loose tree bark, small, rocky
hollows and stony crevices. Several species
congregate in clumps, releasing a safety
pheromone scent to recruit others to the
growing knot. Ladybird warning colours,
often black spots on red, but sometimes in
other striking combinations of black, red,
yellow, orange and white, are a clear indication
to would-be predators (mostly birds) that
these beetles' bodies are packed with bitter
poisons and taste absolutely foul. Numerous
ladybirds huddling together emphasise this
warning; throngs of many hundreds are
recorded – and many millions in one US
species. After they disperse the following
spring some of the safety scent remains, and
although the original creators will have all
died off by the next winter, a new generation is
attracted to the same hollows and crevices. This continues year after
year, in response to the species-specific molecules lingering in the
sheltered hidey-holes.

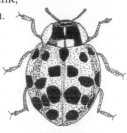

Harlequin ladybird
Harmonia axyridis

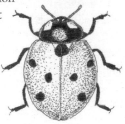

7-spot ladybird
Coccinella septempunctata

Having a few ladybirds tucked up into the edge of the window frame
might be considered a quaint curiosity, but harlequin ladybirds appear
in scores, waddling across ceilings and flying around at head height in
a sometimes alarming manner. Fears over biodiversity loss caused by
them may offend entomologists, but fears of domestic invasion, even by a
pretty ladybird, rank high among many house dwellers where harlequin
ladybirds have started to appear.

Perhaps the most unusual complaints about the harlequin
ladybird have been made by North American wine makers (Pickering
et al. 2004). The problems started when congregating ladybirds were
brought into the wineries while sheltering on the grapes, but wine
manufacturers are also concerned about the insect's habit of venturing

into buildings during winter, in particular into the large warehouses where wineries are operated. Once inside the large buildings the ladybirds nestle together in whatever sheltered corner they can find, including on or in the fermentation vats. It does not take many of the large harlequin ladybird bodies to noticeably taint the wine with their acrid predator-defence chemicals.

CAVITY WALLS – THEREIN LIES DANGER

Loft spaces and spare rooms are at least accessible, and even infrequent visits provide a chance to have a look around to notice potential problems from invading plant bugs or cluster flies. Cavity walls, however, are inaccessible and seldom noticed ... unless squatters take up residence.

Cavity walls, two skins of brick, stone or timber, with an insulating or moisture-preventing void between them, became part of standard building practice from the 1920s, but even older buildings had the necessary air-bricks for underfloor and between-floor ventilation. Air-brick gratings are the perfect size to keep out birds and mice, but exactly correct to allow bees and wasps through.

Social wasps (or yellowjackets), *Vespula* and *Dolichovespula* species, are familiar but much-maligned insects. Having a sting gives them an air of menace, and living in a colony numbering anything up to 10,000 strong can make them seem intimidating. However, these regular lodgers in houses are quite likely to go unnoticed until the floorboards are taken up for maintenance, or deep corners of the loft space are explored during roofing work. Even then, it is usually the abandoned and empty nests that are revealed.

A wasps' nest is started by a single queen, working alone to make a tiny embryo nest the size of a golf ball. She constructs it out of paper chewed from logs and fences, and mulched with saliva to make a paste smeared on and shaped with her jaws. A small, globular roof and 15–20 hexagonal cells is all it takes to get going. She lays the first eggs and forages for food, insects caught on the wing and chewed to a gloop that is fed to the grubs. When the first batch of grubs is mature and hatched out, it forms the first cohort of workers (sterile females), which take over food collection, paper manufacture and nest expansion. By midsummer 8,000 workers may have created a city the size of a beachball, with 6–10 large, horizontal combs each with hundreds of hexagonal cells. The queen is more or less confined to egg laying.

Social wasp *Vespula*

Eventually, at the end of the season, new queens and males are produced. They leave the nest to mate and now the whole thing starts to wind down. Eventually all the wasps die off, except the newly mated queens, which hibernate under loose bark or in a hidden dry crevice somewhere (they occasionally do so in a fold of a curtain). The huge nest is never used again, but remains in place, quietly mouldering, for many years, its only occupants a few dead wasps that failed to emerge properly from their cells, and a few scavenger beetles. (Remember these beetles – we'll come back to them a bit later.)

Most wasps' nests are subterranean, created in a small hole in a bank or mossy overhang, or under the edge of a log, but then actively excavated into a large cavity as the colony enlarges. Because they start with just a founding queen, they are easy to miss at the beginning of the season, so nests in lofts, floor spaces and cavity walls go unnoticed until there is a veritable throng of wasps, with comings and goings every few seconds and sometimes an audible hum coming through a wall or ceiling.

By this time it is hardly worth worrying about. If nobody has been stung yet, the chances are that nobody will be, and the wasps will continue flying in and out, completely oblivious of the human occupants of the house. Of course, each situation has to be judged on its own merits; some people are so ill at ease with the idea of a wasps' nest anywhere in the house that they will have it removed, no matter how out of the way it is, and despite the protestations of any neighbourhood entomologists going on about how good wasps are for gardens, eating nuisance caterpillars, aphids, flies and the like. Unfortunately, much time, energy, fuss and money is spent on eradicating wasps' nests that never posed any problems, and which, in a few weeks, will be empty anyway (Edwards 1980).

Things are not quite so simple when it comes to honeybees. Ostensibly similar to wasps in having large nests and hordes of foraging sterile (and stinging) female workers, there are several key differences between wasps and bees, which are especially important to householders whose houses have been invaded. Whereas wasps are carnivores, hunting insect prey (although visiting flowers occasionally), bees are wholly herbivore, feeding on nectar and pollen. Wasp colonies can reach 15,000 individuals, but honeybee nests can house 100,000 bees. Wasps make horizontal, one-sided combs of hexagonal cells of paper, while bees make vertical hanging combs of back-to-back hexagonal cells from wax secreted from special glands on the undersides of their abdomens. Wasp cells are only ever used for brood rearing, and contain the maggots until they are mature enough to pupate and emerge as new adults, but some honeybee combs are used to store honey; this is where it starts getting interesting.

The western honeybee *Apis mellifera* is native to Asia, North-east Africa and the Middle East, and its honey stores brought it to the attention of foragers way back into human prehistory. At first nests were raided and destroyed for the honey and wax, then bees were kept in hollow logs, clay pots, basket skeps and wooden hives, and their honey was harvested. Waring (2011) and Preston (2006) both give good, readable histories of honeybee domestication and the insects' interactions with humans down the ages. Now, honey is a multi-billion dollar industry, and the bees have been transported far beyond their original natural range right across the globe to places where they never previously occurred – Europe, South Africa, Australasia and the Americas. Today, the honeybee is thoroughly domesticated, in the developed world at least, and kept in man-made hives by back-yard beekeepers or industrial honey farmers. Any colonies found living in natural hollows, such as ancient tree trunks and wall cavities, can only really be described as feral rather than truly wild.

Honey is not just a useful commodity for toast and cakes, adopted as the sweetener of choice by early humans; it is the honeybee's secret of winter survival. Rather than dying out, like wasps, at the end of the year, many thousands of honeybees huddle together in a tight hub at the centre of the combs, using their own metabolic body heat to keep each other warm, and using the honey, a high-energy, pure-sugar solution, as food. The nest survives from one year to the next, and since new queens can be reared

Honeybee *Apis mellifera*

if the old queen dies (workers are constantly replaced throughout the year), the colony is virtually immortal. It will only end if it is destroyed by disease, honey-hunting animals or humans.

Another major difference between wasps and bees is that new honeybee colonies are not created from scratch by a lone individual, but by a form of colony budding. When a large nest gets to a certain size the workers start rearing extra queens, even if their own egg-laying matriarch is still going strong. When the new queens emerge they fight over succession, stinging each other to the death until only one queen remains to take over the colony. Meanwhile the old queen takes off with a large cohort of the existing workers and they swarm – flying through the air in a great cloud, before eventually settling to create a new nest somewhere else. Traditionally this was how beekeepers increased the number of their hives.

This does mean that if honeybees intend to establish a feral colony in a loft space or behind an air-brick grill, their presence is announced by the sudden immediate arrival of several thousand bees. They are likely to be noticed very soon by the home owner. Occasionally they will find a hidden opening and create their new nest out of the way of suspicious eyes. As a boy, in the early 1970s, exploring the South Downs and Weald of Sussex, I was amazed to see an active bee colony high in the bell tower of St Andrew's Church in Jevington, near Eastbourne. It was there for at least a decade, presumably while the vicar and parishioners ignored it or overlooked it.

Honeybees have a good reputation (they are seen as busy, hard-working and industrious), compared with the unjust enmity heaped on wasps. But honeybees are the more dangerous insects to have uncontrolled and away from the beekeeper's eye. For a start they are more aggressive than wasps. If a wasp stings it hurts, but if you flick the insect off and move away from the nest the other wasps will generally ignore you. If a honeybee stings its barbed stinger is prone to get stuck in the skin and ripped out from the insect's body when it is brushed off. The bee dies, but this seemingly suicidal act on her part leaves the muscular venom sac still squeezing the painful poison into the wound; her disembowelment also releases an airborne alarm scent, which quickly alerts and agitates other bees to attack. If you are stung and the sting remains attached to you, you are now chemically tagged as the enemy, and the bees will pursue you much more doggedly than will wasps.

On the whole bee stings are painful but not dangerous, unless they trigger an anaphylactic allergic reaction (which is thankfully very rare). The amount of toxin injected by a bee is minute – 5–50μg (that's micrograms, millionths of a gram), but ten bee stings can make even a healthy adult feel ill enough to need a cup of tea or take a lie-down; 50–100 stings and the victim should probably seek immediate medical help; 300 stings are likely to hospitalise the victim and are potentially fatal.

There are several honeybee races, bred over hundreds of years to produce more honey, to better survive in colder winters in northern climates, to cope with hotter, drier climates, or to be less aggressive or more disease resistant. The most widespread race is the orange 'Italian' honeybee *Apis mellifera ligustica*, transported all around the world from the Mediterranean, but the slightly darker Carnolian honeybee *Apis mellifera carnica* from Central Europe and the Balkans is more hardy, gentle and disease resistant. The traditional northern European bee *Apis mellifera mellifera* is almost black and much more cold resistant than other races. It was probably introduced into Britain from Scandinavia, but was virtually wiped out at the beginning of the 20th century by Isle of Wight disease, caused by a parasitic mite. It was soon replaced by importations of the other European strains (Jones 2011).

During the 1950s an African race, *Apis mellifera scutellata*, was examined because it was high yielding and highly pest and disease resistant. Unfortunately it was also much more aggressive towards any perceived threat at the nest, and once the alarm scent was released by the first sting it triggered very large numbers of other workers to wage into the assault – many thousands are recorded. Carefully quarantined laboratory experiments to cross it with more docile strains seemed to be working well until some 'Africanised' cross-bred bees were accidentally released in Brazil in 1957. They quickly established successful feral colonies and began to spread up through South then Central America, across Mexico and into the USA. Today they occur from California to Florida, their aggressive behaviour earning them the unfortunate title 'killer' bees, since the multiple stings, delivering many times the 'normal' venom dose, make them much more dangerous than conventional hive bees, sometimes fatally so during their massed attacks.

Winston (1992) did much to put Africanisation into bee-history context, and tried to counter some of the needless fears exacerbated by dreadful film plots, but the bees continue to present a domestic problem in Central America. Removing feral honeybee nests is now an important part of the work of pest-control operatives in the southern USA, and a house owner who finds honeybees (Africanised or not) nesting in the fabric of his home would do well to have the nest removed as soon as possible.

FRIENDLY KILLERS ARE ALSO INVITED

Not all killers in the home are a danger to the human inhabitants. There is a time when visitors should be welcomed as guests and made to feel at home. A feature of some traditional barns, now copied by conservationists, is the owl hole, an access gap high on the side of a barn, with a nesting platform provided inside. Unlike buzzards, kites and falcons, which have been persecuted by landowners in the past because of perceived threats to game birds, owls have long been applauded for their control of mice and rats. Their friendly representation in children's literature from Edward Lear poems to *Winnie the Pooh* and Harry Potter has emphasised their benign nature.

Having some predators inside the living area, however, is still a difficult concept for many people, who seem unwilling to share their sacred space with things as creepy or ugly as scorpions, centipedes or spiders. In most of the world the small scorpions that sometimes venture indoors are barely big enough to give a sting like a wasp, but some caution should be exercised if, for the sake of family peace and calm, eviction is the only acceptable option.

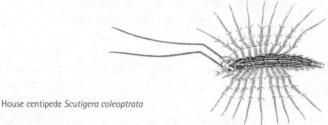

House centipede *Scutigera coleoptrata*

The large (10cm or more), stout centipedes of warm climates are best avoided as they can give a very painful bite if picked up. Centipedes' front legs are modified into powerful biting fangs, which are hollow and through which venom is injected to subdue their prey. These large species can easily pierce human skin, but the most familiar, the well-named house centipedes *Scutigera coleoptrata* (and *S. forceps* in North America), are completely harmless. Their long legs, rippling in undulating synchrony and rapid turns of speed across wall or ceiling, can make them a little startling, but their jaws are just not big enough to get a grip on a human finger or get through tough human skin. They will, however, make short work of mosquitoes during their mainly nocturnal rambles – now that's a consideration worth dwelling on.

A similar plea might be made for geckos, the large-toed, ceiling-gripping tropical lizards. With their bright colours and large eyes, they are decidedly attractive and almost cute. I was quite happy about the small brown gecko living in the wardrobe during my visit to Costa Rica, and in Sri Lanka the night-time squabbling of either mating or territorial pairs in the hotel colonnade veranda at Anuradhapura was an entertaining diversion during an evening. But when I carried a large, bright green and turquoise, bug-eyed specimen in

Geckos
order Gekkota

my cupped hands from the conservatory of a Queensland restaurant back to the table, I wasn't quite sure what all the fuss from my fellow diners was about.

I am slightly more circumspect when it comes to mentioning spiders. There is no getting over the fact that many people just do not like them, no matter how good they are at catching house flies, mosquitoes, beetle larvae, cockroaches and woodlice. The almost primordial fear of these delicate and attractive arachnids among humans causes much unnecessary angst. Luckily household spiders are mostly secretive corner or crevice dwellers, and if they ever come out to hunt they do so at night.

Out of doors the stereotypical spider spins a large, round, carefully engineered web between plant stalks to catch flies. No orb-web spiders regularly come into the house. The indoor webs, if ever found, are untidy messes. The daddy-long-legs spider *Pholcus phalangioides* lives up in deep corners of the ceiling, and makes a gantry of sparse silk strands hardly worthy of being called a web at all. Here it sits motionless, sometimes for weeks, waiting for a disorientated fly to stumble into its trap. Sitting and waiting in a high corner is a useful quality, and one that evolved in the spider's original non-human habitat – caves, rock cavities and hollow tree trunks. Flying insects wafted into the darkness, or emerging into it after hibernation or roost, have a tendency to fly upwards. The spider knows this, and waits.

Daddy-long-legs spider *Pholcus phalangioides*

Meanwhile, on the floor of the cave or stony hollow, or under a log or rock, house spiders *Tegenaria domestica* (and several other species) made their tatty handkerchief webs long before there were houses. Hiding under the pale silk sheet, a house spider waits in a tunnel-like retreat with its feet resting on the web, and at the first feel of vibrations, as a beetle or bug crawls over it, she rushes out and pounces with deadly intent. Nowadays the webbing sheets are mostly made behind furniture, underneath kitchen cabinets and under floorboards, where they are seldom seen. What is seen, however, are the wandering males which, at a certain time in their lives, go off looking for mates. It is these that are seen wandering across the carpet in front of the telly, or getting stuck in the bath when they fall in and are

House spider *Tegenaria* spp.

unable to scale the slippery sides to get out.

The very largest *Tegenaria* house spiders, reaching a body length of up to 20mm and a leg span of 100mm, may just be big enough to deliver a slight nip if picked up injudiciously between the forefinger and thumb. However, body size and jaw size are not precisely calibrated among spiders, so those most famous for biting people are rarely overly large. Most infamous are species like the black widow (*Latrodectus mactans*, nearly worldwide), funnel-web spiders (*Atrax* spp., Australia) and brown recluse spiders (*Loxosceles* spp., North and South America), the bites of which can be extremely painful, and cause swelling, ulceration and occasionally even death. Any textbook of medical entomology will

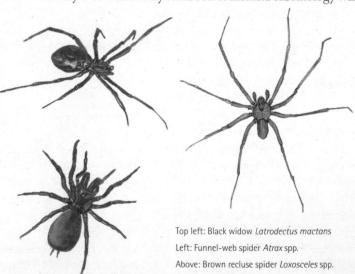

Top left: Black widow *Latrodectus mactans*

Left: Funnel-web spider *Atrax* spp.

Above: Brown recluse spider *Loxosceles* spp.

give full gruesome details of spider bites and the biting perpetrators (for example Smith 1973).

Danger from spiders, however, is greatly overrated, and this is not helped by highly inaccurate identification by victims eager to blame any small scratch, infection, swelling or ill feeling on a creepy-crawly they happen to see somewhere near at the time. Most spider-bite claims presented to medics do not have a captured spider as evidence, and in rare instances when the aggressor has been caught the chances are that it will be a harmless species that got a lucky nip in a sensitive area of skin.

As it turns out, whatever their size *all* spiders are venomous. After all, this is how they catch their prey – by pranging it with their sharp, hollow fangs and injecting deadly venom. But spider jaws are mostly very small, human skin is mostly very tough, and these disparaged arachnids are mostly physically incapable of getting their mouths open wide enough, or inserting their short fangs far enough, to get any sort of purchase to properly bite a person.

Media headlines about spider bites are depressingly predictable; they are all about lurid sensational headlines and panic-mongering text, contain little or no scientific facts, and frequently verge on the rabid. The 'discovery' by tabloid journalists that some small, pretty spiders very distantly related to the black widow could actually puncture human skin to deliver a slightly painful sting, that these spiders could sometimes be found indoors and that they were apparently extending their range across Britain, maybe because of climate change, led to arachnohysteria on an unprecedented scale during 2013. Suddenly false widow spiders *Steatoda nobilis* and *S. grossa* were the new scourge of Christendom, and pictures of them burgeoned on the Internet as frantic householders were desperate to seek reassurance that the spider they'd seen walking across the kitchen floor was not this dangerous beast.

False widow spider
Steatoda spp.

Unfortunately for them it usually *was* one of these distinctive spiders that they saw, because they are very common and becoming more widespread in Britain. Both species have long been known to occur in sheds and compost bins, garages and porches, and to come indoors occasionally. The name false widow still contains the accusing word 'widow', with its deadly connotations, which is a shame because these spiders are much more true to an alternative English name – rabbit hutch spider (guinea-pig hutch spider in my case). This seems an unlikely name to catch on among tabloid journalists, who prefer to emphasise danger in their stories. As I write this in December 2013, the brouhaha appears to be dying down. Perhaps this is because, as one mockingly spoof website correctly put it, 'The number of fatalities is currently hovering near the zero mark'.

There is a time to get annoyed, even aggressively so, with some household invaders, but this anger is wasted on spiders, and is ultimately counter-productive – they are actively helping us to get rid of true life-threatening pests. The real danger from invaders is not from their invasion per se, but from the diseases they might bring with them.

IV

Making a mess everywhere:

MAGGOTS, DIRT, FILTH AND DROPPINGS EVERYWHERE

*T*here is no place for animals of any kind in the modern hygienic kitchen or food store. Cats and dogs may be tolerated in domestic kitchens as long as they stay on the floor and do not jump up on food-preparation surfaces. All other species are forbidden, by law (in the case of commercial premises like restaurants and hotels), custom or squeamishness.

ur understanding of pathogens (be they bacteria, viruses, fungi or protozoa) causing disease is only a relatively recent advance in knowledge. Until well into the late 19th century talk of miasma, effluvia and vague malarial fogs drifting from the stench of decay, to cause outbreaks of diseases from cholera to coughing, was commonplace in general and specialist medical textbooks. It was only with careful observation of disease spread, experimentation on diseased animals and detailed microscopy that the modern notion of germs emerged. Suddenly, scientists realised that micro-organisms well beyond the capabilities of the human eye, and barely visible under the microscope, were causing sickness.

With this realisation emerged an understanding of how germs could be spread by sneezing and coughing, by physical contact between people, and mechanically, by an animal traipsing over our bodies or our food. It seems strange that it took so many millennia to make this deduction. In fact this was really just the culmination of what was already an aversion to animal-soiled food.

It's difficult to be sure what our far-distant predecessors thought about their food quality or its pollution by animals; there are no archaeological clues to tell us whether they were horribly revolted or mildly offended. We can, however, make some educated assumptions.

NOBODY LIKES A MAGGOT – ALTHOUGH THERE ARE LEGAL REQUIREMENTS

In his quaint and curious (and I suspect slightly tongue-in-cheek) booklet *Why Not Eat Insects?* Vincent M. Holt (1885) suggests that the larvae of the cheese skipper fly *Piophila casei* can be safely consumed since they are really all cheese inside anyway. This is one of his less outlandish suggestions; it is perhaps quite understandable why some of his other proposals, like curried cockchafers, moths on toast and wasp grubs fried in their comb, failed to achieve culinary success.

Skipper flies get their name from the bizarre frolics of their small larvae, which can jump into the air. A larva manages this by curling over, gripping its tail in its jaws, tensing its body muscles and suddenly releasing its bite; the flip is enough to get it 15cm airborne, and is perhaps a predator-avoidance strategy.

There are genuine stories of deliberate cheese skipper fly nurture in cheeses to produce a distinctive flavour, not to say texture; *casu marzu* is one such 'rotten cheese' from Sardinia. Today the cheese skipper fly

Cheese skipper fly *Piophila casei*

occurs across the globe, wherever cheese is left out of the refrigerator. When it can't find suitable cheese it lays its eggs in meat, including ham, bacon and beef, and it has been recorded from human cadavers. Since cheese is not a natural product (in that it never occurs naturally, away from humans), this putrescent carrion lifestyle is probably the fly's original habitat. Indeed, rotting cheese is likely to attract all manner of normally meat-based carrion feeders.

I like cheese, and there is a tale, now infamous in Jones history, of an instance when I was forced to keep my very smelly Epoisse de Bourgogne in the small tool shed outside the back door because it stank up the fridge too much for my nasally challenged family. A few days later I fancied some semi-liquid, creamy goo on my digestive biscuits – it took me quite a few mouthfuls to realise that the wiggly lines I could see out of the corner of my eye were not the prelude to a migraine, but wriggling blow-fly maggots lining the inside of the packet. The grey flesh flies I had seen resting on the shed door that week were not sunning themselves after all. They were attracted to the delicate ammonium scents from the ripe cheese – the same ammonium scents that are given off by carrion as it reaches the semi-putrescent stage in its decay.

This is the trouble with maggots in food – they are too closely linked with decay, and a human revulsion of decaying meat is deeply ingrained. This is presumably an evolutionary hangover from a time when pre-human scavengers on the African savannah would have done well to avoid morsels from maggoty, potentially toxic carrion. Blow flies have long been reviled for depositing their eggs on our meat.

On the other hand, we now live in an era of ultra-squeamishness. Finding a caterpillar in a salad is no longer taken as a sign of the leaves' freshness, but rather as an indication of poor hygiene in the supermarket packaging department. When my two-year-old daughter and I found a fat moth caterpillar and large pellets of black frass (droppings) in a packet of basil from Israel in the local supermarket, we were looked at askance by the groceries manager to whom I presented this find. I'm guessing we were being sized up and assessed as to whether we were likely to try and sue the supermarket for negligence. In the end he agreed that I could have the item free of charge, so I could rear the moth in a spirit of scientific enquiry.

There was a time when there was an acceptable level of worminess in food – 10 per cent according to the Baba Batra of the Talmud, where it was decreed that if a man bought 100 figs he had to agree to accept ten that were wormy.

'Worm' would have passed for almost any insect larva back in classical times, when a knowledge of pest animals was utilitarian rather than scientifically correct. We still use the term worm very broadly today for creatures that are not true worms, in names like mealworm, woodworm, glow-worm, wire-worm (all beetle larvae), hornworm, cutworm, bollworm (moth caterpillars) and my own particular favourite, slug-worm (sawfly larva). The next chapter looks in more detail at insect pests in stored food, where it is mainly the larvae (the 'worms') that do the eating. In the meantime, it is worth contemplating the fact that worms (think tapeworm, intestinal worm, liver-worm) are deeply imbued with unpleasant connotations, so much so that they give us one of the most powerful and momentous words we can use when describing pests – from the Latin for worm, *vermis*, we have **vermin**.

DESTRUCTION AND DROPPINGS EVERYWHERE – RODENT HUNGER AND INCONTINENCE

Mice and rats are, despite not being at all worm-like, the archetypal vermin. Today they occur so widely with humans, and so intimately with us, that it is difficult to unpick their history from ours (Berry 1970).

One problem is that fossil and other archaeological remains are rare. Rats and mice are pretty near the bottom of the food chain, so they are usually eaten by something else long before they have a chance to die in a place convenient for later discovery. If they do die, they are likely to be scavenged, bones, fur and all, not least by their own kind.

The earliest fossil mouse remains to date are from India 2 million years ago, and this fits with genetic and morphological studies of worldwide house mouse populations, which suggest that they evolved from a progenitor group (named *Mus linnaeusi*) in the subcontinent, with the eventual appearance of the true house mouse *Mus musculus* in northern India and Russian Turkestan. The earliest remains associated with humans are from southern central Europe 230,000 years ago, but these finds remain rare and enigmatic.

The arrival of human agriculture changed everything. The house mouse now started an inexorable spread around the Mediterranean seaboard, starting in about 8000 BC (Cucchi *et al.* 2005). This fits in neatly with the emergence of grain farming and the rise of sea migration, trade and cultural exchange during the final throes of the Stone Age and the emergence of the Bronze Age (roughly 4000 BC).

Meanwhile house mice also spread east, reaching China and Taiwan, and into South-east Asia through the Moluccas and as far as New Guinea.

To the east house mice settled down with the rice harvest, while in the west they adapted to wheat, barley and oats. This was an easy

House mouse *Mus musculus*

83

transition from their natural foraging habits among savannah and steppe grassland, where they made their ball-shaped nests of tightly wrapped grass stems, and ate seeds (and nuts), making small stores in and around the nests. Many wild rodents, including the common European wood mouse *Apodemus sylvaticus*, continue to live like this.

We'll come back to the niceties of cereal seeds (wild and domesticated), their types, and their harvest and storage capabilities, in the next chapter, when a whole host of other pests gets involved with invading human stores. But remember those early Central Asian mouse prototypes, and their miniature pantries stocked with gathered seeds and nuts.

The final spurt across the whole of Europe occurred in around 1000 BC. The house mouse's arrival in the British Isles is usually blamed, without a great deal of evidence, it has to be said, on the Romans. Intuitively this sort of fits, not just because of Roman negligence when it came to shipboard hygiene, or vague ideas of conquering legions bringing civilisation in the form of sophisticated farming managerial skills, but also because at about this time human population numbers in Europe, settlement sizes and imperial trade routes all conspired to make the increase and spread of mice much easier.

The spread continued. House mice arrived in the Americas with the European adventurers during the 16th century, with stock from various Old World sites. Today in the northern USA and Canada subspecies *domesticus* dominates, having arrived from northern and western Europe, while in the southern states it is replaced by subspecies *brevirostris*, originally from Spain, Italy and southern France (Marshall and Sage 1981).

There is now virtually no place occupied by humans that mice have not invaded. They are recorded in deep coal mines, originally feeding on the spillings from the pit ponies, but now surviving on crumbs of food dropped by miners. The London Underground is estimated to have half a million mice, now genetically different from their above-ground cousins, living between the tracks and eating littered food scraps.

By a delightful serendipity the word mouse and the scientific name *Mus* have remained almost unchanged down the centuries, through the twists and turns of many languages, and can be traced back to *mus* in Latin, to μυς (*mus*) in Greek and eventually to *musha*, from the Sanskrit word meaning 'to steal'. Mice certainly 'steal' the food they take from humans, but their greatest impact is on the food they spoil. This they do by chewing through containers, wrappers and packages (not to mention cupboard doors and floorboards), and by scattering their copious droppings everywhere.

There is a tendency to regard mice as more nuisance than danger, but it can't take many mouse pellets to render a loaf or packet of porridge oats unpalatable, and not many more to make it dangerously polluted. Anything that could help prevent mouse infestation would be a godsend.

CATS – THIS ONE JUST DOMESTICATED ITSELF

The well-known feline statues of the goddess Bastet and mummified cats from Ancient Egyptian tombs have long fuelled the supposition that cats were first domesticated during the pharaonic period about 5,000 years ago. Certainly, the pharaohs held cats in high regard, but felines had been human companions for at least 5,000 years before this. An approximately eight-month-old cat was buried with its human owner in Neolithic Cyprus (Vigne *et al.* 2004).

That date, 10,000 years ago, fits in very closely with the agricultural revolution. The supposition must be that cats first came into contact with humans and were looked upon kindly because of their mouse-hunting prowess around the Near Eastern cornfields, the granary stores or perhaps across the septic, mouse-infested midden. Genetic studies corroborate this idea.

The domestic cat is descended from the wild cat *Felis sylvestris*, and although it is sometimes given the scientific name *Felis catus*, it is usually regarded as a subspecies, *Felis sylvestris catus*. True wild cats still range across Africa and Eurasia, from Scotland, through Iberia, to Namibia, Arabia,

Domestic cat *Felis catus*

Indo-China and Mongolia, so there have been plenty of opportunities for domestication to occur. DNA analysis of wild cats from right across their natural range identified five genetic clusters, closely associated with the five wild subspecies from Europe (*F. sylvestris sylvestris*), the Near East (*F. sylvestris lybica*), Central Asia (*F. sylvestris ornata*), southern Africa (*F. sylvestris cafra*) and the Chinese desert (*F. sylvestris bieti*). The DNA of all the domesticated cats studied, from around the world, was closest to the Near East (*lybica*) cluster, with the most precise matches being to wild cats still living in Israel, the United Arab Emirates, Bahrain and Saudi Arabia (Driscoll *et al.* 2007).

Wild cats are not native to Cyprus, so that a 10,000-year-old cat burial from Shillourokambos, near Limassol, on the southern side of the island, must have been from a population brought over when Anatolian farmers first colonised the area in prehistoric times, perhaps as an early example of biological pest control.

Throughout history cats have been valued as mousers, and despite their haughty independence they remain the most populous pets on the planet. Mice, too, continue to invade our foodstuffs; perhaps our pet cats are just too well fed these days. The last time I had mice in my house I discovered one hiding behind the large packet of cat litter near the back door. Judging from the pattern of footprints, droppings and crumbs, the cats had actually brought this one back alive and released it indoors. For several days it had been cowering in its hiding place, but had sneaked out when the cats weren't looking to nibble some of their cat biscuits from the feeding bowl. I wasn't sure whether to be impressed or outraged. The fact that mice have also been domesticated as pets suggests that away from the food store we are pretty relaxed about them. And it's true, mice really are rather insignificant, compared with our real arch-nemesis.

RATS – THE STUFF OF NIGHTMARE

One species of rat has existed in Europe since before classical times – the black rat *Rattus rattus*. We now have archaeological evidence for it. There was a time, however, when it was thought that rats were unknown to the Ancient Greeks and Romans writing 1,500–2,500 years ago. For example, there was no rat invasion reported in the biblical plagues (Exodus 7:14–12:36); if rats were known in Stone Age Egypt, surely a vengeful god would have unleashed them on the foul Egyptians. The fourth plague is usually represented as being of 'flies' in modern interpretations, but traditional translations have quoted swarming hordes of 'wild animals' roving the country, destroying everything in their path. In this context rats might seem a reasonable choice. Maybe something has been lost in translation.

The absence of specific mentions of rats in classical writings may be down to a practical rather than a scientific knowledge of rodent classification. In those days mice and rats were considered to be very much the same sort of thing, although distinctions were reputedly (Zinsser 1935) made in medieval bestiaries between the large mouse *mus major* and the small mouse *mus minor*, a confusion even apparent today in the unknowing, who still occasionally ask whether a mouse could eventually grow into a rat.

The black rat is rather like a large mouse. It is dark furred (usually, but it does vary considerably), large eared, slim and sleek. Despite assertions of its absence, it appears to have been present in Europe during prehistoric times, albeit in low numbers, and was bolstered by fresh waves of colonisation from South-east Asia in around the 1st century AD. Iron Age agriculture and Roman trade routes are implicated again. A rat skull was found in a timber-lined Roman well in York, and there is evidence that rats were present throughout the Mediterranean littoral quite early in that era (Rackham 1979).

While mice might have been considered a nuisance, rats soon became universally despised. Not only were they bigger (therefore hungrier) than mice; they were much more associated with dirt, degradation and disease. Unlike the small, demure and secretive house mouse,

Black rat *Rattus rattus*

rats are larger and more obvious animals, and with a broader base of scavenging activities they are just as at home in the midden as in the hayrick. The septic fringe was the scene of lawless disorder in many an otherwise well-ordered Roman settlement, and its unpleasant occupants (human and rodent) continued to afflict towns and cities well into the medieval period.

Part of a misunderstanding about the supposed absence of rats in Europe was the later discovery of their association with disease, and a backtracking through history to the 11th and 12th centuries, when returning crusaders were reported to have brought plague back from the Near East. The implication is that infected rats stowed away in the cavalcades of the soldiers and their retinues (Cloudsley-Thomson 1976).

This is more than likely, but black rats were already widespread in Europe by then, and plague (as well as other diseases like typhoid and measles) had been sweeping back and forth across Eurasia for many hundreds of years already. One of the first apparently genuine plague pandemics hit eastern Europe in AD 541–542. Grain shipments from Egypt, imported to the huge metropolis of Constantinople, were the likely source of the diseased rats (Little 2007). Here, as in later epidemics, part of the eventual disappearance of plague (until the next resurgence) was due to the massive die-off of rats, which also become seriously ill when infected by the disease. According to modern epidemiologists the plague bacterium, *Yersinia pestis*, originated in North Africa, where gerbils, which are almost immune to the sickness, are the natural reservoir hosts. It's fascinating to contemplate how human history might have been potentially much more unhealthy had gerbils, instead of rats, become major grain pests in an agriculturalising Near East 10,000 years ago.

The black rat might by now be considered an endemic European rat, but the larger brown rat *Rattus norvegicus* is definitely a more recent colonist. Although sometimes called the Norwegian rat (hence its scientific name), this is a terrible deceit on a great Scandinavian nation; the name was popularised in the middle of the 18th century when the arrival of the rat in Britain, in about 1728, was blamed on Norwegian ships. This was at a time when the rat was spreading across Europe, but it was unknown in Norway at that time. Among some outspoken critics of the monarchy in this period – the eccentric traveller and naturalist Charles Waterton, for example – it was also called the Hanoverian Rat (Phelps 1976). This was in defiance of the elevation of George I of the Protestant House of Hanover to the British throne after the death of Queen Anne

Brown rat *Rattus norvegicus*

in 1714; although there were many other closer blood relatives in Britain, they were forbidden from attaining the crown because of their Catholicism. The rat's arrival in England at this time seemed like a judgement on the religious intolerance of the era.

The brown rat seems to have originated in the plains of northern China and Mongolia, where wild rats still live in earth burrows well away from human activity today, but it spread widely during the expansion of world trade during the 17th and 18th centuries. There is some evidence that it was known in Europe earlier – from medieval archaeological remains, and from a famous description by Swiss naturalist Conrad Gesner who in the 1550s reported albinism, a condition frequent in brown rats but virtually unknown in black rats. Incidentally, this later gave rise to white and piebald laboratory rats during the early 19th century (Donaldson 1915; Krinke 2000).

The major arrival of brown rats in western Europe is well documented during the 18th century. The Russian naturalist Pallas wrote of a vast migration of rats across the River Volga in 1727, which infested houses in Astrakhan before spreading into Russia (Donaldson 1915). This is unlikely to have been the first migration because there are firm historical records of brown rats throughout Europe by this time: in Ireland in 1722, Britain in 1728, France in 1735 and Germany in 1750.

The brown rat is larger, heavier, scruffier, browner obviously and more aggressive than the black rat, which it soon started to displace. It arrived in North America in 1750–1755 and quickly became the dominant species, edging out the black rat that had arrived

250 years earlier. The brown rat edged out plenty of other animals too, and is widely acknowledged as one of the most ecologically invasive animals on the planet. Virtually every remote island on the Earth has been tainted by its arrival with humans, which was followed by mass extinctions of indigenous animals such as the dodo on Mauritius and the giant flightless crickets (wetas) in New Zealand.

Throughout most of its range the brown rat is now the major commensal rat in human habitations, particularly so in temperate latitudes where the black rat is confined to coastal areas, possibly because of subtle temperature requirements. The black rat is still the dominant rat in tropical and subtropical regions, but both are replaced by the Polynesian rat (called 'kiore' in New Zealand), *Rattus exulans*, across much of the Pacific.

The depredations of rats, often in stored grain, but also in a wealth of other stored commodities, have been decried for millennia. As is the case with mice it is not just the 'thievery' in which they indulge that offends and torments, but also their destructiveness to buildings and belongings, the traipsing of dirt and the littering of their droppings.

At least a rat stool is visible to the human eye and can be ejected from the food, or the food thus contaminated can be rejected; other animals do not leave such obvious traces of their toilet behaviour. Take flies, for example.

HOUSE FLIES – THE INSECT MENACE

Towards the end of the 19th century a great change was taking place among entomologists. Where previously they had been happy to contemplate the wonder of nature as exemplified by the supreme diversity of insects, often invoking the Creator's wisdom and artistry, they now became involved with trying to exterminate these noxious pests. It started with the industrialisation of agriculture and the realisation that crops were being decimated by ravenous caterpillars, to be sprayed, dusted, picked off or squished, but attention soon moved on to insects as disease vectors.

Top among these targets were mosquitoes (more of them later) and house flies. House flies have never been exactly celebrated, but they were at least widely recognised and often noted in scientific and educational texts – this, for example, from Kirby and Spence (1815):

> *That active little fly, now an unbidden guest at your table, whose delicate palate selects your choicest viands, while extending his proboscis to the margin of a drop of wine, and then gaily flying to take a more solid repast from a pear or peach; now gambolling with his comrades in the air, now gracefully currying his wings with his taper feet, was but the other day a disgusting grub, without wings, without legs, without eyes, wallowing, well pleased, in the midst of a mass of excrement.*

The tone of the piece is all about the rise from humble maggot, via the marvellous transformation of metamorphosis, to the perfectly formed adult insect; the fact that the grub lives in filth is merely an aside to emphasise its self-improvement, rather than a health warning. At the time the concept of germs and disease micro-organisms was still being elucidated, and although Louis Pasteur had just, the year before, shown that airborne spores were responsible for the spoiling of beer, wine and milk, bacteria had not yet been identified.

A hundred years later things had moved on considerably; bacteria and protozoa had been firmly identified as the culprits causing many infectious diseases, food-poisoning and sepsis. That excrement was a good source of these pathogens was patently obvious, and it was not long before the house fly *Musca domestica* was vying with malaria mosquitoes to be public enemy number one, the source of warning information leaflets, poster campaigns and a nefarious character in books with titles like *Insect Enemies* (Ealand 1916), *The Insect Menace* (Howard 1931) and *The Insect Legion* (Burr 1939).

The exact nature of the threat from house flies is open to debate; choose your statistic with care – more than 100 types of

House fly *Musca domestica*

bacteria, virus and protozoa have been found on (or in the digestive tracts of) house flies (Marshall 2012), a single house fly can carry 6,600,000 bacteria on its body (Hewitt 1914), and house flies have been blamed for countless millions of human deaths over the years. Typhoid, cholera, tuberculosis, dysentery, polio, summer diarrhoea and trachoma (tropical conjunctivitis) are the major pathogens spread by house flies, along with the eggs of parasitic worms and protozoa like amoebae. Many of these are picked up on the adult fly's body and legs when it emerges from its puparium in the manure heap, and passively transferred when it lands on the dinner plate. The fly's mode of feeding makes things worse. The house fly uses external digestion to feed, which means regurgitating some of its stomach contents onto its food so that digestive enzymes can start dissolving nutrients ready to be sucked up again. This also means vomiting up the bacteria festering in its gut, drunk down from its previous meal of faeces, putrescent carrion and any other rotting organic matter. It all makes grisly reading.

The house fly is now ubiquitous and completely cosmopolitan, occurring across the globe wherever humans make their homes. The only region in which it is less known is Australasia, where it is often replaced by the bush fly *Musca vetustissima*, especially around cattle farms. Clouds of these flies can create a serious problem, breeding in the semi-liquid cattle dung that is not being recycled by the native dung beetles, which are evolutionarily adapted only to dry marsupial pellets.

There can be no doubt that the house fly was one of the first domestic pests to make the transition from septic fringe to primitive shelter, very early on during human evolution. The first latrine would have offered exactly the right conditions for breeding, and it is tempting to picture early proto-humans ineffectually waving their hands about, trying to dissuade the flies from landing on any flesh still adhering to the first barbecued mammoth ribs.

This is me getting a bit fanciful, I admit, but human wariness, not to say revulsion, at flies is deep seated, and has been around for as long as we know. According to linguists *dhubab*, sometimes transliterated *zebub*, the Arabic for fly, derives from the root *zbb*, meaning flies in both ancient Hebrew and Assyrian. The cursed name of Beelzebub, or Baal-zebub, god of the Philistine city of Ekron was, of course, the 'lord of the flies' (Cloudsley-Thomson 1976). Whether this was because the Philistines had erected a special god to control the nuisance flies, or because the Israelites were being contemptuous of the fly-infested animal sacrifices, is a matter of continued debate among biblical scholars. Oddly, hieroglyphs of flies in Ancient Egypt are taken to represent impudence and courage; the fly was also an emblem used in a military decoration for courage, and fly amulets abounded (Harpaz 1973).

The truth is that in developed countries house flies no longer present quite the health problems that they used to. Due to food packaging, including plastic film wrap to cover leftovers, Tupperware food-storage boxes and the ubiquity of fridges, food is no longer left out in the open for house flies to traipse all over. Because of improvements in sanitation sewage is flushed away much faster and more efficiently than it used to be, and is dealt with quickly and hygienically in industrial treatment plants. Most importantly, perhaps, horse-drawn transport is now a thing of the past. At its height, at the beginning of the 20th century, many tonnes of horse dung were dropped daily onto the streets of London. Even the smartest areas of the West End were littered with manure heaps as the increasing equine output fell onto the road. With such breeding opportunities house flies could, quite literally, be found in every house, no matter how grand.

Today, many urban areas are virtually house fly free; maybe house flies should really be called farm flies because farm-manure heaps are now the only ready source of excremental breeding materials. In 25 years of living in south-east London, a house fly came into my house only once, in 2013, and I blame the manure-rich guinea-pig hutch cleanings that I had put into the garden compost bin earlier that month.

The house fly should not be confused with the lesser house fly *Fannia canicularis*, although it often is. The smaller, narrower and more delicate lesser house fly does not visit the dinner table for leftovers, but is the small, dark insect making those erratic, apparently random, zigzag flights under the hanging light, occasionally coming to rest briefly upside down on the bulb or on the edge of the lampshade. It breeds in similar substrates to the house fly, or in soil rich in organic

Lesser house flies *Fannia canicularis*

material, but because it is not attracted to human foods it has never been seriously linked with any disease spread.

There are very many species of *Fannia* that do not come indoors. These are often flies of the hedgerow or open woodland; they breed in the soil, in decaying leaves, dung or rotten fungi, but are most often seen flying at about head height in the dappled shade under a spreading tree branch. Here the males have adopted a three-dimensional territory of open airspace, which they patrol by making an erratic zigzag flight back and forth, waiting for females to appear. It seems that our pendant light fittings are merely convenient alternative focal points under which the flies can rendezvous to mate. Lovely.

BAD THINGS COME IN SMALL PACKAGES – THE SECRET OF COCKROACH SUCCESS

Cockroaches, even more than flies, are despised by the householder. These unnerving scuttling dark critters are the bane of many a city dweller, whose only crime is to live within 100m of a cafe, shop, warehouse or anywhere that food is stored, or indeed, anywhere that waste food is discarded – which, after all, is anywhere in a city. Blocks of flats, industrial premises, schools, hospitals and offices – nowhere is immune to infestation. My local swimming pool has been refurbished since, but there was a time when I regularly fished out dead cockroaches floating legs-up from it, as I clocked up my morning 1,000m.

To be called a cockroach is to be insulted far worse than being called, say, a worm, maggot or even leech. Part of this is the association of these awkward but successful insects with poor hygiene, slovenly housekeeping, dirt, grime, and physical and moral corruption. They live in latrines, sewers and drains, and they frequent refuse heaps and overflowing rubbish bins. They then skitter around in the kitchen, scrambling over any left-out food, climbing walls and ceilings to drop into saucepans, and even chewing the toenails, hair and skin of sleepers. Cockroaches are in serious need of some PR support. They're not getting any here, but at least by examining something of their biology we can take a more dispassionate view of why they are so horrid.

Common cockroach
Blattella orientalis (female)

Cockroaches are often depicted in entomological textbooks as being 'primitive' insects. True, they have a rather basic oval insect design, and are flattened, with their mouthparts being tucked under their heads; they have simple long legs and simple very long antennae. Their flat form belies the fact that they have perfectly good wings and are capable of flight, but they keep the wings tucked away, neatly folded under their dark leathery wing-cases. Although this makes them superficially similar to beetles, they do not go through the 'more advanced' metamorphosis from larva, through chrysalis, to adult, and instead grow through an increasing series of non-winged immature nymph stages (usually five to seven) before finally arriving at the fully winged adult. This does, however, mean that, like beetles, they can creep under things to hide without damaging their fragile membranous flight wings, which are protected by the tough wing-cases. Cockroaches may be evolutionarily simple, but this simplicity has not stopped them from being among the most adaptable of insects.

One of my favourite insect jokes is from the Disney/Pixar film *A Bug's Life*:

> *How many cockroaches does it take to change a light bulb?*
> *You can't tell, as soon as you switch on the light, they scatter.*

There are three highly useful behavioural traits at work here: cockroaches hide, they avoid the light and they run very fast. Any of these helps them in the home.

Cockroaches are able to hide so well because of their flattened form and the protection afforded by their wing-cases. They can choose the tightest of gaps under the cooker or between the kitchen units, and cracks in walls and spaces behind skirting boards, in which to secrete themselves. Here they can remain hidden during the day or when the lights are on, only venturing out to scavenge once the room is in darkness.

Emerging at night has obvious safety benefits in avoiding predators, and it is here that the extremely long antennae become useful, as tactile feelers, testing the way ahead through the darkness. Typically, when they hide in a narrow crevice they turn around so that they are facing head-outwards, with their long, thin filamentous antennae projecting just proud of the opening so that they can be sure of quiet safety before emerging. Cockroaches also have sense organs on their tails; called cerci, these resemble short antennae, and are sensitive to movements of air currents and sound vibrations. In a nice example of analogy they have been likened to rear parking sensors on a car.

Cockroaches' simple, unmodified legs are long and slim, but can carry them at startling rapidity. For many years cockroaches were widely quoted as being the fastest insects in the world; with recorded speeds of 1.5m/s (5.4km/h, 3.4mph) they can certainly scamper out of the way very quickly indeed. It was only my quick reaction and an upturned beer glass that allowed me to catch the giant that veritably flew out of a cornflakes packet and dashed along the work surface when we were visiting relatives in Queensland, Australia, many years ago. Everyone else stood transfixed with horror, hands in the air if I remember correctly, as the sleek brown insect raced across the table top at hurricane speed. (It was only recently that an Australian tiger beetle was clocked at 2.5m/s, or 9km/h, 5.6mph, thus overtaking the cockroach's achievement.)

Avoiding humans by running and hiding certainly helps, but cockroach accomplishments in the house may have best been improved by one particularly odd, primitive adaptation – the ootheca. The ootheca is an egg case, a protective, purse-shaped sheath containing the 8–40 (depending on the species) narrow eggs. It is formed by liquid protein secretions inside the female cockroach's body, which harden into a tough, flexible, segmented magazine into which the eggs are slotted. In some species the female carries around the ootheca, half protruding from her abdomen, until near the time of hatching; in other species the ootheca is stuffed

Egg case of a cockroach

into a tight crevice, the female often hiding it with bits of debris or droppings to disguise it, so that it remains camouflaged until the embryos inside have developed enough to hatch.

Other fairly closely related insects like grasshoppers and mantids also make an ootheca, by coating the eggs as they are laid, on a stalk or leaf, or in a hollow in the ground, with a mass of sticky secretions that soon harden into a tough coating. The purpose of these outdoor oothecae is thought to be to give some weatherproofing and protection from egg predators and parasites. Wild cockroaches have a number of parasitic wasps that specifically target these egg pods in which to lay their own eggs; domestic pest cockroaches appear to have evaded most natural parasites by coming indoors and leaving their enemies outside (just like the larder beetles earlier), but the leathery weatherproofing now takes on another function – protection from chemical pesticides.

Hidden away in the deepest recesses of the kitchen or store room, a cockroach infestation is usually dealt with by sweeping and cleaning spilt food residues, then spraying or dusting with insecticides. The problem is that householders are unwilling to tolerate highly toxic and long-lasting poisons in and around food-preparation areas. The quick hit of over-the-counter roach killer may be enough to get rid of the adults, but the ootheca acts as a formidable defensive barrier, keeping the embryos safe inside; by the time the eggs hatch, 3–8 weeks later, the insecticide may have faded away to insignificance. The false sense of success achieved by the sudden removal of all the adult cockroaches is now replaced with despair as the new generation suddenly emerges, giving the appearance of an entirely new infestation.

There are roughly 4,500 species of cockroach worldwide, and most are harmless scavengers living in leaf litter, grass root thatch or low herbage, or under logs and stones. An entomologist would be hard pressed to come up with ten species that ever infest buildings, and even in cockroach monographs (for example Cornwell 1968, 1976) it is usually just the seven most frequently encountered that are listed first, with a few less widespread extras added for completeness. Once those few crossed the threshold, however, they really made themselves at home. Cockroaches have been familiar house-mates all through recorded history, and although they have been confused, at times, with other invaders like house crickets and cellar beetles, there can be no doubt that the dark, scuttling things decried by Pliny, Galen, Dioscorides and Virgil were some of the same species that we still suffer today (Beavis 1988).

A quick look through any pest-control handbook will show that cockroach species are often named after the countries in which they are thought to have originated; thus we have the German cockroach *Blattella germanica*, common cockroach *Blatta orientalis*, American cockroach *Periplaneta americana*, Australian cockroach *P. australasiae* and Madeiran cockroach *Leucophaea maderae*. There is a touch of the xenophobe here, because all of these now-cosmopolitan insects almost certainly started off their simple pre-human existences in Central Africa. Here they were skulking, scavenging creepers through the warm, moist soil and leaf layer of the humid tropical forests.

German cockroach *Blattella germanica*

The German cockroach was one of the earliest known species in Europe. It probably spread from around the African Great Lakes, via Egypt and Byzantine Asia Minor, to Greece and the Caucasus, during the period of Phoenician trade across the Mediterranean in around 1500–500 BC. It was often noted by ancient writers as infesting bathhouses, as well as bakeries and domestic dwellings, no doubt attracted by the steamy warmth reminiscent of its subtropical forest-floor origins.

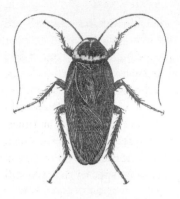 

American cockroach *Periplaneta americana*   Australian cockroach *P. australasiae*

(Indeed, this species especially was often called the steam-fly because of its predilection for steam-filled heating vents, steamy kitchens and engine rooms.)

The German cockroach slowly spread into southern Russia, across Europe and thence to the rest of the world during the period of European imperial expansion and trade in 1700–1900. It was probably brought to the Americas independently but at the same time by an alternative route, during the period of the huge Atlantic slave trade, direct from West Africa. It is reputed to have been introduced in Britain as late as the middle of the 19th century with soldiers returning from the Crimean War. However, by this time it was already widespread across Europe, so it is quite likely to have been transported here from numerous European sources. It was given its 'German' designation by Linnaeus in 1767, when he named it *Blatta germanica* on the basis of specimens not from Germany, but from Denmark. Similar routes out across Europe, Asia and the Americas are also proposed for common, Australian and Madeiran cockroaches, despite the various geographical misnomers by which they are now known.

These few pest species are now almost completely cosmopolitan, occurring everywhere where there are human habitations. There are plenty of others that are occasionally found in houses, and no doubt more in various subtropical wildernesses just waiting for humans to come along and offer them a convenient domestic lifestyle. The

'Japanese' cockroach *Periplaneta japonica* made headline news a year or so ago, after it turned up in New York. This native of the Far East is better cold adapted than many species, so its appearance out of doors in a traditionally snow-swept northern American city led to fears of an imminent invasion and plague from yet another foreign interloper.

The so-called Surinam cockroach *Pycnoscelus surinamensis* is certainly not native to that small South American country. It is likely to have originated in Indo-Malaysia, but was introduced long ago to Africa, probably during medieval Arabian trading across the Indian Ocean, and from there via the usual international trade routes to the New World. It remains mostly a peridomestic outdoor species, living around greenhouses, chicken houses, rubbish dumps and other human debris in warmer parts of the globe, but it is perhaps halfway to becoming a true domestic pest of the future. It has already started to evolve useful adaptations to life among humans.

In the Americas (and Britain) all Surinam cockroaches are female; they reproduce by parthenogenesis, a mechanism whereby eggs develop into embryos without the need to be fertilised by sperm. This is a short-term (possibly only thousands of years) strategy and can cause problems because all offspring are identical genetic copies (clones) of the mother, so all are equally susceptible to natural controls such as diseases or parasites (and chemical sprays, maybe). Lacking the broader genetic variability created by sexual reproduction between males and females, parthenogenetic populations are vulnerable to sudden and complete extinction (a shallow gene pool easily drying up is a good analogy). However, they have the advantage that a new population can be successfully and quickly established by just a single transferred individual of any age, rather than by a fully mature and already-mated adventurer female – a much less likely scenario.

Looking back at worldwide populations of this species it appears that there are at least 20 different genetic clones, indicating that the parthenogenesis has evolved at least 20 times, all in the last few hundred years (Bell *et al.* 2007). The Surinam cockroach's closest relative, the Indian cockroach *Pycnoscelus indicus*, which is endemic to South-east Asia, is identical, even under the microscope, but still completes a conventional breeding life cycle involving males and females. Where their ranges overlap it will interbreed with Surinam cockroaches, producing yet more parthenogenetic clones, this time with different numbers of chromosomes. It all looks very complicated, but the deduction is that the natural native Indian cockroach of the East Indies gave rise to the all-female, globe-trotting forms we now call the Surinam cockroach, and that this creature, freed from the need to maintain the complexities of sexual reproduction, has gone forth and multiplied all the more easily, spread by human trade. Parthenogenesis is fairly widespread among some insect groups, including aphids, many of which have spread worldwide and become notorious pests for exactly the same reasons.

It may only take one cockroach to become the next big domestic pest. My family returned from a holiday in southern France in August 2012, and as we were busy unpacking our bags one of my daughters excitedly called out, 'Ooh, what's this bug?' There, crawling over her bedroom carpet onto which it had just tumbled, was a cockroach. Thankfully it was not one of the big seven major cosmopolitan pest species, or any of the 17 or 77 second-rank potential nuisances. It was one of the other, nearly 4,500 free-living, non-domestic, non-pest species, and one I had regularly seen visiting the flowers in the garden of the holiday house in Provence where, no doubt, it feeds on pollen, petals, dead leaves, seeds and whatever else it comes across. We were lucky this time. But it's so easy ...

A BIRD IN THE LOFT IS WORTH ...?

We can't blame accidental transport around the world for the spread of the urban pigeon, though; we have brought it all on ourselves. Now this may not appear to be a domestic pest to most people, in that it is unlikely to fly into the kitchen and start nesting in the larder, or pecking holes in the packets to get at the cornflakes. However, it is an unhygienic nuisance high up on the list of annoyances for anyone who owns a building with an open canopy (like a railway station), inaccessible ledges (like an office block) or a sun-shade awning (like a cafe or newsagent), or just has a street light outside a shop front, or a loft or roof. Urban pigeons (not to be confused with their wild cousins, woodpigeons, collared doves and turtle doves) are gregarious animals, living, flying, roosting and nesting in large aggregations. And because there are so many of them in an inconvenient location, they become pests (rolling out my personal definition again) simply because they reach pest proportions.

In the 1990s London's Trafalgar Square was home to more than 35,000 pigeons, supported mostly by visitors actively feeding the birds with seed bought from local street vendors. But the swirling, feathery vortices and slippery, guano-sodden pavements did not fit with the West End's image of itself – slick, sophisticated, neat, tidy and clean. Pigeon feeding was banned, seed sellers were banished and professional falconers were brought in to control the unruly flocks, mostly by scaring them away.

Elsewhere across the city billions of small, vertical, plastic, 10-cm, bristle-like 'bird spikes' were glued to every available surface on which pigeons formerly settled, while balconies, nooks, statuary niches and ornamental brickwork were netted to prevent the birds from landing. All-out war was declared on what was one minute an iconic feathery tourist attraction, but the next was seen as a bunch of dirty, smelly, disease-ridden aerial vermin.

Elsewhere in the world similar reversals of fate regularly occur as fickle humans suddenly change their minds about the cuteness of, say, grey squirrels, chipmunks, raccoons or foxes. As these 'wild' animals become habituated to humans and find ready nourishment in rubbish bins, they become more abundant, more brazen and more obvious, and the relatively minor damage they do by burrowing under buildings or strewing rubbish about in the street becomes all the more apparent and annoying. They reach pest proportions, so they become pests.

These are, on the whole, native animals that have made the uncertain transition from wilderness, or at least the septic fringe, to the urban and domestic habitats in which they have flourished. Pigeons, though, were invited into our dwellings – invited and encouraged to breed here.

Today the urban pigeon can at best only be described as feral. These are mixed populations descended from escapees of the doves originally kept for food. When Charles Darwin wanted a useful model to show how humans had created what were virtually new species from a wild type (to demonstrate how natural selection could similarly engineer new species from an ancestral form), he chose the domesticated pigeon. When he was writing in the middle of the 19th century fancy pigeons were all the rage, and there were endless striking forms, from pure white fantails, to fluff-throated

Rock dove *Columba livia*

pouters, tumblers (unable to fly) and homing (racing) pigeons. Today there are reckoned to be more than 1,000 fancy pigeon breeds.

It was Charles Darwin who made the assertion, still supported today, that all these strange colour forms and bizarrely feathered shapes are descended from the rock dove, or blue-barred rock pigeon *Columba livia*. A native of India, Asia, Arabia, Mediterranean Europe and North Africa, a clue to its original native habitat is in its English names – it is a rock dweller, nesting in crevices on sheer rock-faces and cliffs. This was obviously very convenient for early civilisations, which could create or adapt nesting areas by the simple expedient of building nest-sized holes in a vertical wall. Doves have been domesticated for about 10,000 years, and are reported in cuneiform tablet writings from Mesopotamia and hieroglyphs from Ancient Egypt dating to around 3000 BC. The pigeon hole or dovecote reached a pinnacle in medieval Europe, when the building of huge, round tower shapes (*colombiers* in France) was a status symbol controlled and regulated by law.

The doves were farmed on a fairly intensive scale, and although they were technically free to fly away they were 'encouraged' to stay put by the availability of sheltered nest sites safe from hawks and falcons. If some of the more adventurous or flighty pigeons left, then the more sedentary, calmer individuals would have been more likely to stay, and from the very beginning a tolerance and familiarity of humans would have been bred into the birds. The ready supply of eggs, squabs (young) and adults no doubt made a major contribution to the dove owners' (and dove keepers') protein intakes.

There were always escapes, though, and the now-placid, partly domesticated birds found easy nesting around human buildings, even though this might be inside inadvertent nest holes; and they found rich pickings in the spilled food dropped by an increasingly well-nourished human populace.

There remains a certain ambivalence towards feral urban pigeons. On the one hand they are regularly fed by well-meaning (if ill-informed) individuals imagining that they are encouraging wildlife. On the other they are derided by metropolitan authorities and commercial businesses because they make such a mess everywhere with their droppings. Outright claims that pigeons spread diseases may not be fully supported by much evidence, but the move from rock nesting to house nesting brings its own problems of cleanliness and hygiene.

Anyone who has been unfortunate enough to have had pigeons nesting in the attic will know all about the constant early morning and late-night comings and cooings, the slippery grey and white spatters of semi-liquid excrement, and the untidy clumps of dried grass, stems and twigs bunging up the eaves. These are self-evident hazards that can be straightforwardly addressed. What is often hidden, however, is the fact that pigeon nests contain other, surreptitious occupants that we could well do without.

V

Eating us out of house and home:

Many years ago, while looking for insects in an invertebrate survey alongside London's River Wandle, near its outflow into the Thames in densely urban Wandsworth, south London, I scooped out and sieved some old pigeon-nest material from underneath the metal and concrete bridge arches where the river passed under the busy South Circular Road. Along with some bird fleas, a few predatory bugs and general detritivore fly larvae, I found numerous tiny, pale, cylindrical beetles. These were biscuit beetles Stegobium paniceum, but they were not feeding on biscuits.

105

he first time I ever found biscuit beetles, they were floating to the surface of the milk I was pouring onto my breakfast cereal. I regarded the first two or three with bemused curiosity, but by the end of the week I decided to go on a biscuit beetle hunt to root them all out. They were not just in my cereal; they were in the flour (plain and self-raising), cheese crackers, noodles (which looked like ticker tape), lasagne sheets, sugar, pine kernels, sesame seeds, dried beans and cat biscuits, and in the beef-stock cubes, having chewed their way through the tight-fitting metal-foil wrappers. They were everywhere, in fact, necessitating an almost compete clear-out of the shelves, apart from the tinned food.

One or two beetles in my breakfast cereal was neither here nor there, but others have complained about the beetles more earnestly. It may have been this species that naturalist Joseph Banks wrote of during his voyage to the southern hemisphere with Captain Cook. In his journal of 1769 (quoted by Buckland 1981) he wrote:

> Our bread is but indifferent, occasioned by the quantity of vermin that are in it. I have seen hundreds, nay thousands, shaken out of a single biscuit [loaf]. We in the cabin have, however, an easy remedy for this, by baking it in an oven, not too hot, which makes them all walk off; but this cannot be allowed to the ship's people, who must find the taste of these animals very disagreeable, as they everyone taste as strong as mustard, or rather spirits of hartshorn [ammonia].

The variety of the biscuit beetle's infestations in my poorly maintained food cupboard does not make it a thoroughly generalist feeder. As its common name suggests it was traditionally found mostly in biscuits, or taking into account its scientific name, *paniceum*, also in bread (Latin *panis*). The common denominator is, of course, wheat, which is a major ingredient (or a minor one in the case of stock cubes) in so many foodstuffs these days. Of course, it will try anything with starch in it, and has made itself a nuisance in such odd substrates as spices, cocoa beans, liquorice, paper and wooden mah-jongg pieces (it is closely related to woodworm beetles). It is sometimes (especially in North America) called the drugstore beetle, because of its pest status in pharmacies, where it eats stored pills including those containing strychnine, but this is because the major ingredient in any given tablet is the 'filler' made of starch and whey. Wheat is the key nutrient.

Back under the road arches by London's River Wandle, there were no wheat products available. My first thought was that the beetles may have been breeding in scraps of bread brought back to the feral pigeons' nests, but the ravenous birds had eaten every crumb. The ragged nest heaps did, however, contain sheaves of grass stems, complete with very many small grass

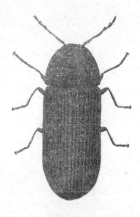

Biscuit beetle *Stegobium paniceum*

seeds, in plentiful abundance. Wheat is, after all, a grass – it has much larger seeds than our wild grasses, expanded by thousands of years of selective breeding, but it is a grass nevertheless. Here was a notorious kitchen pest feeding on its original natural food, in the wild.

Wheat is everywhere now, and the biscuit beetle serves as a useful paradigm for trying to understand where grain pests originated, and how they came to invade the pantry in the first place. There are several variations on this theme.

THE HUMAN LOVE AFFAIR WITH CEREALS

Wheat *Triticum aestivum* is arguably the basis of Western civilisation. It was the cultivation of wheat that transformed nomadic, part-time amateur smallholders into the settled farmers of the Fertile Crescent, resulting in the flourishing of prehistoric cultures such as the Assyrian kingdom and the Egypt civilisation. The initial domestication event is reputed to have occurred somewhere in what is now south-eastern Turkey at least 9,000 years ago. Other cereals are also implicated in the very earliest agriculture hereabouts, including spelt *Triticum spelta*, emmer *Triticum dicoccum*, einkorn *Triticum monococcum* and barley *Hordeum vulgare*.

The appearance of these relatively large grass seeds in the area of the eastern Mediterranean, north-east Africa and Western Asia, now referred to as the Fertile Crescent (also the Cradle of Civilisation), is nothing short of miraculous, but the miracle was not god-given – it was weather related. One of the latest suggestions from palaeobotanists (for example Hole 1992) is that the large grass seeds developed as an evolutionary response to the end of the last ice age, some 15,000 years ago. As the world warmed and the northern ice sheet retreated, local weather patterns were altered and the climate of the area changed from constantly moist subtropical to seasonally dry subtropical.

Seeds are a plant's cold- or dry-season insurance policy, adapted to remain dormant, waiting for the right temperature or soil moisture, for months or years (many survive for centuries). Some plants gamble on success by going for quantity, producing thousands of tiny seeds (this is the way orchids have evolved), but for the grasses of the Near East, larger seed size was the strategy that worked best. For the people living in this area it was a godsend, and humans have never looked back.

Exactly how or why cereal-based agriculture first happened is, however, lost in the dusty murks of antiquity, beyond almost all conjecture. For one thing, even though the archetypal wild cereal seeds grew larger, all those millennia ago, they were still smaller than modern wheat varieties, so that the early farmers must have been scrabbling around for fairly mediocre grains when they first foraged any scattered seeds or harvested their first crops. Grasses themselves have never been a human foodstuff, and are indigestible in the human gut, even when cooked. There are endless theories.

One of the more quirky theories is the suggestion that early foragers raided ants' nests to get at the grain stores. The Mediterranean and Middle East are home to harvester ants, *Messor* and other species; these large, heavily built black ants have massive heads, all muscle to power the jaws they use to carry seeds and hulls many times their own body weights. They drag mostly grass seeds back to the subterranean nests and store them in underground granaries. By biting off the radicle (the embryonic root), the ants prevent the seeds from germinating, and since the evolutionary purpose of seeds is to remain dormant for months or years until suitable growth conditions reappear, these energy-rich, high-protein packages make the perfect food-storage option. This rationale also works for humans.

Harvester ants fascinated the ancients, almost to the exclusion of the many more numerous non-harvesting species. Aristotle, Pliny, Aelian, Plutarch and Virgil all comment at length on the single-minded activity of these marvellous tiny creatures (Beavis 1988). They and plenty of others draw strong moral parallels with the ants, urging tireless and industrious cooperation over shirking lethargy (Aesop is particularly well known for this). In a prehistoric society collecting ant-seed caches might have seemed just as natural as taking honeycomb from a wild bees' nest.

Another interesting idea is the notion that wheat (or barley) was first used not to make bread, but to make beer (McGovern 2010). Often safer than drinking stream water, low-alcohol (by today's standard) beverages made from fermented cereal grains would be mostly free of bacteria and other micro-organisms. Depictions of beer drinking, and recipes and poetry extolling beer's virtues, are known from ancient Egypt (3500 BC) and China (7000 BC).

Whatever came first, the bread or the beer (or the biscuits even), cereal grains transformed human society. And if it wasn't wheat, it was millet (in Africa), rice (*Oryza sativa*, in monsoon Asia) and maize (in the warmish tropical hills of Central and South America), followed by oats and rye in cooler northern Europe. Whatever the proto-farmers did with it, the most important aspect of cereal agriculture was that the surplus grains could be stored for many months to feed the populace outside the initial seasonal harvest glut. Grains could also be moved without them going off in transit, and they could be traded.

All this worked well, as long as the grains were kept dry so they did not start germinating prematurely, and as long as they could be protected from grain pests.

GRAIN PESTS – THE ANCIENT EGYPTIANS PROBABLY HAD A WORD FOR THEM

Despite their pre-eminent place in our cultural understanding of antiquity, we actually don't know much about what the Ancient Egyptians called their grain pests. They certainly had them, and there are plenty of entomological reports from archaeological digs – Blair (1935), Panagiotakopulu (2001), Panagiotakopulu and Buckland (2009). Much to the chagrin of Italian entomologist Anastase Alfieri, his discovery of several beetles in the foods laid out for the afterlife in the tomb of Tutankhamun were considered insufficiently interesting by Howard Carter, who refused to include them in his monograph on the boy king. A disappointed Alfieri had to publish his results elsewhere (Alfieri 1931).

We do, however, have written records from the Assyrian metropolis of Nineveh – the *Har-ra* (or *Hubullu*) tablets, cuneiform texts excavated in the 19th century from the royal library of Assyrian King Ashurbanipal (668–627 BC), which were compiled during the 9th century BC, but are thought to be based on older sources from a thousand years earlier. Written in a bilingual Sumero-Akkadian format, these are the earliest known written records of agricultural pests, listing 33 names of creatures that attacked field crops and stored products.

The Assyrians (together with the Ancient Egyptians, then the Greeks and Romans) were not expert entomologists, and there was no agreed system of nomenclature, but they all adopted a pragmatic approach to naming the vermin they were suffering. The authors of the *Har-ra* tablets appear to have identified three types of insect pest in grain – specifically barley, their crop of choice at the time, rather than wheat, but whether this was because of its use in beer or some other forgotten agricultural choice is unknown. Modern transliterations (Landsberger 1934, quoted by King 2009) give us *uh.še* for an insect pest of the barley field, *uh.še.kú* for one in harvested barley grain and *uh.zí(d).da* for when it appeared in the ground flour.

Languages have changed over the millennia, but those broad concepts of field pests, whole-grain granary pests and milled flour domestic pests remained until the modern scientific age started to use the microscope to establish specific names for specific groups of individuals. Today it is hardly possible to equate ancient words with a particular insect species, especially because they are all relatively small and dark, and similar to the naked eye. Part of the difficulty also lies in the fact that by the time written records start to appear, 3,000 years ago, virtually all of the common grain and flour pests we incur today were already prevalent in granaries, bakeries and homes throughout the civilised world.

An infestation put down to *uh.še.kú* 2,500 years ago could refer to any of half-a-dozen well-known and widespread granary pests, and *uh.zí(d).da* could be one of more than 50 flour or ground-grain pests, including my old breakfast friend the biscuit beetle. Like this species, many of these domestic intruders are thought to have invaded human premises from the grassy steppes of the Fertile Crescent and North Africa, where edible cereal grains first appeared and humans first took advantage of them 10–15 millennia ago. But each has made its own journey from the natural wilderness, the eubiocoenosis, into our warehouses and homes. Levinson and Levinson (1994) give a fascinating account of various ancient granaries and the insects associated with them.

THE LESSER AND GREATER OF TWO WEEVILS, WELL, SEVERAL WEEVILS ACTUALLY

Perhaps the most common, most widespread and arguably most destructive stored cereal pest in history is the aptly named grain weevil *Sitophilus* (formerly *Calandra*) *granarius*. This small (3–5mm), dark, heavily built, cylindrical beetle has a long snout on the front of its head, at the very end of which are its jaws. Using its projecting mouthparts it chews a deep drill-hole down into the centre of the mature grain seed, then its turns around and lays a single egg at the bottom of the hole. Each grain of wheat or barley is large enough to feed one maggot through to adulthood.

The idea of individual grains being devoured by a few maggots might, at first, seem inconsequential, but out of sight and out of mind in a grain bin or silo, it does not take long for a chance interloper to give rise to a serious infestation. Within a few months large numbers of the weevils can occur, and in a discriminating marketplace slight damage can drastically reduce the value of a crop. By the time the processed flour gets into shops and foodstuffs, even a single insect can make a product unacceptable. Typically it took the hardships of war to bring home just how important insect pests could be in the depleted food stores of a nation cut off from its international suppliers. During and after the First World War the Royal Society of London was tasked with reporting on Britain's perilous grain-storage situation, and produced a series of formal, but nevertheless warning, reports about poor warehouse conditions and pest-infestation rates (Anon 1918–1921). Following the Second World War a serious study by the United Nations Food and Agriculture Organization (Anon 1948) suggested that 10 per cent of the world's cereal crop was lost to insect attack, and that the grain weevil was by far the most important culprit. This tithe is still widely quoted (Munro 1966; Buckland 1990).

The empty grain shell with a large chewed hole through which the adult weevil emerges is a distinctive feature of this insect's damage. In archaeological digs the characteristic hollowed grain husks, as well as preserved weevil body parts, are clear evidence of the beetle's widespread occurrence throughout Asia, Africa and Europe, nearly 8,000 years ago, well before writing or cuneiform-impressed clay tablets made comment on them. Because of the beetle's continuing importance as a major grain pest, there has been a lot of interest and study on where it came from and how it came to be so closely associated with humans.

Various studies have tried to map the species' spread across the globe (well, Europe at least), shadowing the spread of arable grain agriculture. Records are sparse, and although intriguing, they remain inconclusive. The earliest known infestations were in what is now Turkey, in 5750–5500 BC, and the Levant (5550 BC), and this fits neatly with the idea of a Near Eastern origin for both cereal and cereal pest, but they were also in Germany in 5140 BC, long before they seemingly arrived in neighbouring Egypt (2950 BC) or Greece (1650 BC). Our ideas of early agriculture are still hazy, but this disparate

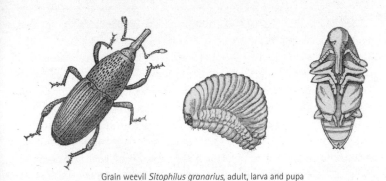

Grain weevil *Sitophilus granarius*, adult, larva and pupa

spread of grain weevil infestations actually gives us some interesting clues (King 2013).

One suggestion is that the grain weevil was already a widespread wild species back in the Stone Age, some 6,000–10,000 years ago, and quickly moved in to take advantage of human stores of grain wherever agriculture was established. This is patently not the case, because the species cannot survive in temperate regions outside heated or at least sheltered buildings, and development from egg, through larva, to adult can only take place at the elevated temperatures found indoors.

An alternative scenario is that it became established as a granary pest somewhere in the warmer climate of the eastern Mediterranean or South-west Asia, and had already, by the 6th century BC, been spread far and wide by trade. Trying to track any prehistoric cereal trade from the archaeological evidence is now impossible, but European trade in other items like obsidian was well established at this time (Gratuze 1999). This is beginning to look like the only possibility.

Later evidence emphasises the trade-route idea. The grain weevil seems to have arrived in Britain with the Romans, in around AD 47 in Londinium, and shortly afterwards in various garrison outposts at Carlisle, Lancashire and Buxton. The military machine offered good conditions for sustaining and transporting the beetle about the country. Notably, however, with the later withdrawal of the Romans, the beetle declined and was apparently absent from AD 400 until the arrival of another mainland European military force with the Norman invasion of 1066 (Smith and Kenward 2011).

The likelihood is that it was climatic factors that kept the species at bay, or at least subdued enough without the Roman trade network to constantly reinforce it (beetle fragments have been found in drowned grain cargoes from Imperial Roman shipwrecks dated to the 2nd and 3rd centuries AD). The grain weevil requires a temperature range of 15–35°C (optimum 26–30°C) to complete its life cycle, but Britain was just at the difficult edge of this natural limitation. Large grain stores, as existed under the Romans, might have helped insulate pockets to this comfortable temperature, but if the popular history books are to be believed, the meagre hand-to-mouth subsistence of the Dark Ages saw them disappear. The species was really a Mediterranean beetle, as was the wheat it invaded.

Even so, the original source of the grain weevil is still steeped in mystery. Unlike the biscuit beetles living in the natural habitat of spilled grass seed in birds' nests (even if they are under the unnatural Wandle Bridge arches in London), grain weevils were never, ever, found outside granaries, even where the original natural precursors of wheat and barley grow wild today. More detective work and hypothesising is required.

In the simplest generalised model of stored seed invasion, a pest burrows into developing seeds out in the fields, and is collected up with the harvest and brought back to the granaries, where it can wreak havoc in the bountiful stores amassed by the unwitting humans. It then flies back to the fields, or is accidentally taken to them when it comes to seed-sowing time again.

Leaving the grain weevil for a moment, the 'bean' weevils, many of them very similar small beetle species in genera like *Bruchus*, *Bruchidius* and *Acanthoscelides*, infest dried beans, lentils and the like, and carry on in just this manner. Their prevalence or importance in the food store varies from species to species, because although some cause great damage once they become established in a warehouse, others need to return to the fields and will only lay their eggs on the developing seed pods, or in the flowers just as the plants' ripe ovaries are being pollinated.

Bean weevils are pretty closely associated with legumes (beans, lentils, peas, carob, peanuts, soya and so on), but will take advantage of whatever crop species is planted. They will also take the plentiful and varied wild legume plants such as broom, gorse, clovers, vetches and melilot. These, then, are the natural origins and constantly renewed reservoirs for bean weevils in the wild.

Bean weevil *Bruchus* spp.

The grain weevil, however, has never been found 'in the wild'. It has also never been found in the barley or wheat fields from which the stored grain is collected. It would be impossible for it to make its way back to the fields anyway, because it cannot fly; its wings and flight muscles have become reduced and atrophied, and its hard wing-cases (which beetles normally flip open to fly) are fused together. It can only move about by crawling, or more likely by being transported about by human travellers carrying infested grain around the world. For an insect already cosmopolitan before the invention of writing, smelted metal or the wheel, this is quite some achievement.

The grain weevil is now truly a wholly obligate synanthropic organism. A bit like silk moths *Bombyx mori*, it can only exist where humans take it, and it no longer occurs as a free-living wild creature. This doesn't stop entomologists trying to figure out where on the Earth it came from in the first place (Plarre 2010).

If the grain weevil did not occur in cereal grains that naturally dropped to the ground in the prehistoric grassy steppes of the Near East, perhaps it started off in the granaries of other animals? Humans are not the only ones to forage and store grain for the winter. The harvester ants that were so enthralling to the classical writers might seem an obvious choice, but although many hundreds of beetle species are known to eke out secret livings by scavenging in various ants' nests, the grain weevil is not one of them.

Rodents also make food caches. Anyone who has read Beatrix Potter's *Tale of Mrs Tittlemouse* will know that this fastidious little animal had several store rooms full of thistle down and cherry stones. Mrs Tittlemouse was a wood mouse (sometimes also called field mouse), *Apodemus sylvaticus*, generally accepted as a sister grouping to the house mouse, and the common ancestor from which they both evolved probably lived in South-west Asia and north-west India, seemingly the hereditary origin of mice. Intuitively, a nice little theory can now be developed along the lines of a progenitor grain weevil, living in Central Asian Tittlemouse nests, and following one evolutionary line of adventurous mice as they invaded human settlements and started to raid human food stores; it is then just a short walk from the mouse's store hole to the village granary.

This still leaves the conundrum that if the grain weevil invaded human stores from its 'natural' mouse-hole origins, it ought to be able to make the reverse transition too, at least occasionally, occurring in rodents' nests or grain caches somewhere in its extensive geographic range. This has never been known to occur.

It is not through the failure of entomologists not bothering to look. The species genuinely does not seem to occur out in the natural world, anywhere, any longer. The exceptions that prove this rule are the several other species of *Sitophilus* known from around the globe. Whereas the grain weevil is primarily found in wheat and barley grains, the very similar-looking rice weevil *S. oryzae* attacks rice and the maize weevil *S. zeamais* attacks maize. Both have very similar life histories to the grain weevil's, attacking stored dry grains, and both are now nearly as cosmopolitan in their worldwide distributions – the difference is that they also occur away from human stores. Both species can fly, and both are sometimes found out in the fields. Maize weevils regularly live in the ripe seed heads still attached to plants, and rice weevils sometimes live in spilled grains scattered along the waysides after the harvest. The transition from wild ancestral rice and maize weevils to the warehouse and silo pests of today is pretty self-evident. The grain weevil, however, is nowhere to be seen out there.

A further pest species, the tamarind pod-borer *Sitophilus linearis*, lives in the mature seeds of the tamarind (or Indian date), a plant native to Africa and/or Asia, and it followed its food plant when it was transported to Mexico and South America by Spanish and Portuguese colonists five centuries ago. Most infestations occur before harvest, while the pendulous seed pods are still attached to the trees; the beetles then emerge when the hanging fruits have been collected and stored ready

for processing. Tamarind still grows wild in
some parts of Sudan, and the weevil is a part
of the natural wild environment there.

Other *Sitophilus* weevils are even wilder;
at least five obscure non-domestic species
feed naturally in the acorns of Central and
South-west Asian oak trees. Holes are drilled
by the weevils' long snouts and eggs are laid
inside the developing seeds when they are on
the tree; the adult beetles emerge from the fallen

Rice weevil *Orazae* spp.

acorns when they drop to the forest floor. Despite
popular etymology linking the word 'acorn' with 'oak-corn', there is
a huge difference between the hard, woody nuts of oak trees and the
cereal grains of wheat and barley. However, they are both types of seed,
containing stored nutrients in dry form ready for germination of a
complete new plant in the right conditions. Acorns are also harvested
by wild animals (jays, woodpeckers, squirrels and mice especially),
and stored in likely dry places as food reserves. Humans, too, used
to eat acorns much more widely than in the niche consumption of
today. The acorns can be dried and ground, and after the soluble bitter
tannins have been rinsed away the resultant flour can be made into
hearty pancakes, biscuits and pastries.

In a series of experiments during the 1960s, when scientists were
studying generation times and nutrient intakes of various storage pests
as a prelude to controlling them, it was discovered that the grain weevil
could develop its full life cycle in acorns, even those from European
and American oaks (Howe 1965). Fewer weevils developed in the
experimental acorn-fed groups than in similar wheat cultures, but
enough came through. They could not seem to live in whole, unbroken
acorns; the hard, woody shells presumably prevented the adults from
gnawing egg holes, but they could develop in broken or shelled acorns.
The rice weevil has also sometimes been found living 'wild' in acorns.

So, one intriguing scenario for the now thoroughly domestic grain
weevil is that it started out as a Central Asian acorn feeder, but not
one that entered acorns developing on the trees – it lived in the acorn
stores of some long-forgotten hoarding animal, then migrated to the

acorn stores of early humans. Buried in the ground or tucked away in root crevices or hollow tree-holes, the implication is that some of the acorns in the caches would have cracked on drying out or getting damp (a natural development in the sometimes long process of quiescence before germination), allowing the progenitor weevils access to the nutrient-rich cores. Since animal-cache sites are regularly reused year on year, and acorns are sometimes moved about by the hoarders, the evolution of flightlessness would not have been a problem for these ancient weevil ancestors. Indeed, losing wings and the ability to fly may have been a useful adaptation to an arid landscape in the often dry valleys south-west from the Himalayas and the Hindu Kush; flying has a great cost in terms of energy use and water loss – plenty of other dry-habitat or desert beetles have also taken this evolutionary route. One of the reasons why grain weevils are so successful in human granaries is because they can develop in the hot, dry, low-moisture storage conditions used to keep wheat and barley; rice and maize weevils need the higher moisture contents of rice and maize respectively.

We are still some way from deciding whether this really was the means by which the grain weevil invaded human settlements during the Neolithic period, but if it was, one question still remains – why do we not sometimes still find grain weevils living in animal-stashed acorns out in the wilderness? The answer may be that this ancestral habitat, probably in the oak woodlands of the Indus Valley and Fertile Crescent, no longer exists. In the last 10,000 years the landscapes of the Near East and the Indus Valley have changed beyond recognition. Climatic changes, even during this relatively short time, have also had their effect on native and cultivated plants in the area. Just as, at the end of the last ice age, the retreating ice cap changed the prevailing winds and produced the dry-season impetus for the evolution of the large cereal seeds that gave humans their newly acquired crops, so too the altered rainfall affected the positions of tree lines in the mountainous landscapes, and the tree species make-up of the forests. The precise conditions under which local acorns were stored by local rodents or birds (or humans), in particular temperature and moisture cycles as the seasons progressed, may now be unreproducible. The grain weevil only has one home now – ours.

THE WAREHOUSE, KITCHEN AND FOOD CUPBOARD
AS ECOSYSTEMS

Grain weevils eat grain, rice weevils eat rice and maize weevils eat maize. This much may be fairly straightforward, but for many household invaders things are far more complicated. On holiday visiting relatives in Florida 20 years ago I innocently picked up a large plastic storage container from the pantry to see what it contained. My host glanced over and announced that it was rice. My eyesight was better than hers and I could see that it was flour. Her confusion arose because the once-smooth self-raising flour now presented a granular appearance against the clear plastic; this was caused by the several thousand beetles living in it.

The horrified householder wasn't much appeased by my forensic interest as I extracted not one, not two, not three, but four different beetle species from the congealed mess: the khapra beetle *Trogoderma granarium*, flour beetle *Tribolium confusum*, saw-toothed grain beetle *Oryzaephilus surinamensis* and a spider beetle of the *Ptinus* genus. There were still some larvae, and it was their feeding in little hollowed-out voids that caused the gritty clumps; there were also living adults and many long-dead specimens, and a good mix of their droppings and remains of their chrysalis shells. It was fascinating. Here was an ecosystem that had been going for several months. The plastic container was well lidded, so I deduced that the infestation had begun either when the new paper packet was first opened, or before, back in the shop from which it had been bought. Who knows?

My delight at the biodiversity I'd uncovered was enhanced by the knowledge that these four species were all from different beetle families; each had its own particular ecology and each had invaded human larders from wholly different evolutionary and historical origins.

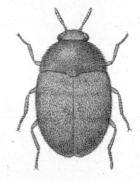

Khapra beetle *Trogoderma granarium*

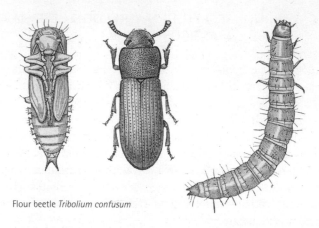

Flour beetle *Tribolium confusum*

The khapra beetle, thought to be native to India, is one of the larder or hide beetles (family Dermestidae) and, like its distant relative the bacon beetle, probably evolved from ancestors scavenging in carrion, or in the feather-and-fur litter of mammal and birds' nests, but later moved on to starchy detritus from seeds and fruits in the host roosts. The flour beetle is a type of darkling beetle (family Tenebrionidae), and is similar to beetles found scavenging in dry, rotten, hollow tree trunks and the fungi causing the decay. Woody cellulose presents a low-nutrient chore, but fungal feeding starts digesting it to more manageable starch products for the beetles. The saw-toothed grain beetle is a narrow, parallel-sided and slightly flattened creature, part of a large family of beetles (Silvanidae), most of which live under dead tree bark and feed on moulds and fungal hyphae that are similarly breaking down the cellulose to more palatable forms. Spider beetles (family Ptinidae) are a sister group to the woodworm beetles (family Anobiidae), but rather than being cylindrical to enable them to bore through heartwood, they are globular and long legged (like spiders), and crawl over the surface and graze whatever mouldy substrate they can find.

It is unlikely that any of these beetles or their progenitors would have been grain feeders or seed feeders originally, although the khapra beetle may have made the jump from scavenging animal nest matter (skin, fur, feathers, bone) to nibbling spilled grains in the nest before

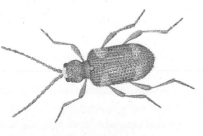

Saw-toothed grain beetle
Oryzaephilus surinamensis

coming indoors. Similarly, the last three beetles prefer ground flour rather than whole grains. Ground-up plant seeds are not a naturally occurring foodstuff, and flour is a completely man-made artefact – nevertheless these beetles have been with us for many thousands of years, and in all probability made the jump along with true granivores like the grain weevil when humans first started cereal-grain storage, and provided the novel ecosystem of the granary. As in all ecosystems, the actions of one species impinge on or enhance the actions of others – it only takes one grain kernel to be broken with chewing to allow other, less vigorous feeders inside it, or to give them access to the powdery leftovers. Mould and decay, which have beset farmers, millers and bakers since the first bread roll was left too long in a cupboard, add to the melange of microhabitats available for invasion.

A theme running through three of these four widespread domestic pests (all four were well known throughout pharaonic Ancient Egypt, Panagiotakopulu 2001) is fungus and mould breaking down the tough, structurally important and complex molecules of woody cellulose into the smaller and more edible molecules of starch. The khapra beetle probably found a route into the first agricultural granaries direct from mammal or birds' nests near human dwellings; the others may have come via similar routes, but only once they had also discovered the nutritional link of mouldy fungal decay, bridging the gap from their probable woodland ancestral homes under rotten tree bark, in fungoid wood or in fungal fruiting bodies, to the festering grain stores of early agriculturalists. They *might* all have come from mammal and birds' nests, but there is another equally plausible alternative – that some of them, or their progenitors, lived in bees' and wasps' nests.

Spider beetle *Ptinus* spp.

IT'S NOT JUST HUMAN HOMES THAT ARE INVADED

Very many species of bee and wasp make nests, larger or smaller, that are invaded by other animals. These other animals are not just badgers or buzzards, intent on destroying the combs to get at the delicious grubs or honey; they are mainly other insects, small and secretive, which have found a specialised niche scavenging in quiet corners of the colony.

Bees' and wasps' nests vary (depending on the species) from perhaps just a handful of small, food-stocked cells in a narrow burrow in the soil, to vast engineered structures as large as fridge-freezers. At the lower extreme, very many species make the simplest of homes, in which a solitary female works on her own to build a small nest and provision the few cells in which she lays her eggs. At the other end of the size spectrum, honeybees and social wasps live in colonies of many thousands, cooperating to make huge and complex nests of wax (bees) or paper (wasps), in which division of labour involves building, foraging, defending, egg laying and brood care by different cohorts of workers, to the ultimate supreme benefit of the colony.

Scavenging opportunities (sometimes bordering on thievery) are available in all sizes of nest, with bees and wasps offering slightly different but nevertheless worthy attractions. Bees, which feed solely on plant materials, store protein-rich pollen and sugar-rich nectar (honey in the case of honeybees, or a cake-like mix in bumblebees and the solitary species). Wasps are predators, feeding the chewed remains of captured insect prey to their grubs. To line their nests and make their cells, bees and wasps variously use wax (honeybees especially) or mud daubs, cut leaves or chew wood pulp to make paper (mostly the social wasps).

In all the comings and goings at the larger nests, things are constantly being dropped and discarded, and this refuse falls to the bottom of a nest. It includes dead bees and wasps, foraged but fumbled food items, faeces and bits of nesting material. The smaller tunnel nests of solitary species are less cluttered, but when completed they are sealed up and abandoned, allowing all manner of trespasser to dig its way in to rifle through the food stores. Empty nests, large or small, soon begin to moulder, and the plant material, whether pollen remnants, leaf fragments or wood pulp, soon starts to rot as those useful and helpful fungi start predigesting the cellulose. And just like human constructions, bees'and wasps' nests are sheltered and dry, either because they have been burrowed into the soil or a dead tree trunk, or because they have been crafted in a natural void like a rock crevice or hollow tree – or the cavity wall of a domestic house (see page 68).

Consequently, bees' and wasps' nests are frequently home to a ragtag of scavengers, squatters and thieves, many of which are the same (or closely related) species that are found in human food stores. *Trogoderma, Tribolium, Oryzaephilus* and *Ptinus* species, similar to those in my unfortunate Floridian friends' flour container, have all been found in bees' and wasps' nests in various parts of the world. So too have the biscuit beetle, larder beetles and a whole host of other familiar warehouse and domestic pest insects.

The similarity between these wasps' and bees' nest faunas, and those found in our homes and warehouses, is striking, as too is the broad range of different groups of organism. This becomes all the more apparent when looking at some of the more obscure and less cosmopolitan species. The Mediterranean flour moth *Ephestia kuehniella* is a major nuisance in grain mills, where its caterpillars spin a silk-webbing protective tube that clogs machinery. It has turned up in honeybee hives, where the same silk tubes hide the moth larvae from the bees. The dried-fruit moth *Vitula serratilinella*, a once minor pest of stored prunes, is sometimes found in bumblebee nests.

Mediterranean flour moth *Ephestia kuehniella*

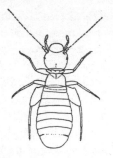

Flour louse *Liposcelis divinitorius*

The flour louse *Liposcelis divinitorius* is also regularly found feeding on pollen stores in bees' nests; this tiny, scuttling, wingless insect is still a regular in my kitchen.

Mould feeders like the rust-red grain beetle *Laemophloeus ferrugineus*, and many species in the highly diverse beetle families Cryptophagidae and Lathridiidae (no common names other than 'mould beetle', because they are all so tiny), are abundant in bees' and wasps' nests. They no doubt evolved from mould feeders that originally lived under dead tree bark, but the same and countless other species in these families are regular finds in mills and granaries, particularly when the main cargo has been shipped and a few dregs are left to go musty in dark corners. The yeasts, moulds and fungi that develop in bees' and wasps' nesting materials are very similar to those found under rotten tree bark, and which invade the less than scrupulously cleaned human granaries. According to archaeologists the earliest grain stores were made of woven straw or reed baskets inserted into the soil and covered by mats, a situation almost designed to encourage them to go mouldy around the edges.

The spider beetles (family Ptinidae) are a large group of general scavengers, some of which have become problem pests in stored human food. The 6-spotted spider beetle *Ptinus sexpunctatus* has the distinction of being the first of these to be discovered in a bees' nest when, in 1872, French entomologist Louis Bedel found it at the entrances of leafcutter bees' nests in France. As their name suggests, leafcutter bees line their small tunnel nests with semicircular portions of leaves that they cut using their scissor jaws. They then provision the small lined nest with stores of nectar/pollen cake for their offspring.

The 6-spotted spider beetle is a relatively scarce UK species, so I have always been pleased to find one crawling about in the bath first thing in the morning. We did at one time have leafcutter bees nesting in one of the narrow, disused overflow pipes jutting from the outside of the wall, so it is possible that the beetles had come from this semi-natural habitat. I always imagined that they had somehow dropped through the light-fitting hole in the ceiling, from the crumbled remains of one of the empty wasps' nests in our cluttered loft. They could, however, have been feeding on any old mouldering rubbish up there, including bird nesting material, and I later found an ancient carton of fish food in the shed that was infested with many hundreds of them. The very similar US West Coast *Ptinus californicus* has only ever been found breeding in the small nests of solitary bees, which burrow into holes in sandy cliff-faces. However, in a nice twist of experimental procedure, it can also be reared in the laboratory on a substrate of cornmeal and other cereal products (Linsley 1942).

Stored pollen, it seems, it very attractive to the same insects that like milled flour, but which are not equipped to deal with whole unground seed grains. So sometimes it is not just the precise nutrient content of the foodstuff that is important, but its size, shape, consistency and granularity. And the migration of insects from bees' or wasps' nests into human houses is not necessarily one way. These nests are ubiquitous in the landscape, although they may often be hidden or unnoticed. Thus there is always the possibility that despite the most vigorous actions by householders, shopkeepers and granary managers, the nests form a constantly renewing background reservoir for stored-product pests, from which new infestation into our homes can occur at any time.

It's at this point that the reader might remember the harvester ants of Aristotle, Pliny and all the other Ancient Greek and Roman writers, and wonder whether their nests, too, might be natural reservoirs for some of our granary pests, even though, as we discovered earlier, the grain weevil has never been found in any ants' nest. It appears that this is not the case, and the reason for this is that ants are better housekeepers than most bees and wasps.

Apart from the nests of honeybees, most bees' and wasps' nests are short lived; they are started, constructed, stocked and used for just one year. Then they are abandoned. One of the usual processes involves mated females (queens) surviving the winter, but everything else, all the workers (sterile females) and males, dying off. A queen then starts a new nest afresh the following spring. Alternatively the nest-building female dies after she has finished construction, but her brood of new males and females emerges the following year; even so the ancestral nest may not be used again, or not for long. It is the ageing or abandoned old bees' and wasps' nests, still with some food stores no doubt, which provide the original homes and the ongoing reservoirs for the various broad-palate scavenger species that may or may not go on to become human food pests.

Ants are different. Their nests, like those of honeybees, are long lived, existing for years or centuries even. As individuals die they are replaced by a new brood, and even the sometimes single egg-laying and controlling queen is replaced if she dies. The colony continues in the same nest; ant hills, for instance, may be the result of decades of work, and the complex network of subterranean corridors and galleries may extend many metres underground. Ants' nests are home to plenty of scavenger species (mainly beetles), but these are now highly specialised, to trick their aggressive host ants using devious scent and tactile mechanisms. These are no longer the generalist feeders that can easily switch to human food if given half a chance. Indeed, many of them only occur in the nests of ants, and perhaps in the nests of only one particular species of ant, with which they have been mutually co-evolving for millions of years. They have swapped general scavenging breadth with narrow niche security.

In such a large and complex community as an ants' nest, generalist scavengers could soon reach pest status themselves, overrunning or at least greatly inconveniencing the hosts. For this reason ants (and honeybees) have evolved very good systems of nest hygiene. They constantly patrol the deepest reaches of the colony, clearing out debris (including their own dead), controlling the internal nest climate through air conditioning, preventing fungal and mould growth, removing stored seeds that accidentally begin to germinate, repelling interlopers and generally defending the nest to the death. We could, as Aesop was so eager to point out, learn a lot from ants.

VI

Eating the house and the home:

WOODWORM, CLOTHES MOTHS AND CARPET BEETLES — THE END OF
CIVILISATION AS WE KNOW IT

Many years ago I was working for the BBC Natural History Unit in Bristol, on the children's wildlife programme The Really Wild Show. Each week a quirky three-minute slot was given over to insects, and one week I was charged with getting some death-watch beetles *Xestobium rufovillosum*. These notorious woodworm beetles are responsible for terrible destruction in old buildings like cathedrals, churches and manor houses, but finding some to order was proving impossible.

fter a day phoning around pest-control companies, university research departments and museums, I went back to the friends' house in the Mendips where I was lodging during the week, and flopped down on the sofa defeated and dejected. I happened to glance down and there, beside me on the chair, was a death-watch beetle crawling across the fabric. The beetle had obviously crawled out from the exposed oak beams in the roof and dropped down onto the furniture below. Immediately I set off on hands and knees, exploring the carpets around the edges of the room, moving cabinets and easy chairs, and within a few minutes I had several glass tubes with living beetles inside them. Success!

Of course, there is nothing surprising about this coincidence. It just so happened that my publishing pal Jony and his textile-conservator wife Fiona lived in an enviably beautiful converted 15th-century lodge house in the charming Somerset village of Banwell, and houses thereabouts were probably crawling with death-watch beetles. This was not because the beetle has a particular liking for the West Country. It's just that any gentrified rural region will have lovely old houses like this one, and it is in such places that death-watch beetles thrive.

At first my hosts were a bit put out. During the relatively recent renovation of the old building they had replaced and repaired much of the ancient roof woodwork, and it had been treated against woodworm. There was more than small concern that the lot might fall down. I did my best to reassure them. My reasoning went something like this.

The death-watch beetle is, at 7mm long, the largest European woodworm beetle, and although its larvae gnaw holes you can lose a biro in, they only do so very slowly. In fact the beetles in Banwell had been chewing away at the rafters for 500 years, generation after generation, and the building was still standing. I reassured my friends that as long as they keep checking every 50–100 years or so, they'll get another 500 years' worth of valuable roof support without too much difficulty. It's not checking for many centuries that has caused structural problems in some of our important heritage buildings.

Death-watch beetles live in the wider countryside, and their distinctive borings are often visible in the exposed heartwood of large veteran trees. However, they do not fly into homes through open windows from old trees outside, to start feeding in the furniture or the floorboards. They hardly fly at all, and many textbooks state (wrongly I hasten to add) that they cannot fly, so infrequently is this behaviour observed. Instead, their ancestors were brought in, unknowingly, by the original builders anything from 200 to more than 1,000 years ago, already living as larvae inside the huge hardwood beams from which the old buildings were constructed.

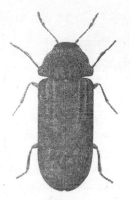

Death-watch beetle
Xestobium rufovillosum

Although the rafters and struts may have looked sound to the architects, there were already pockets of fungal decay deep in the heartwood of the oak, beech, hornbeam and elm when these sometimes medieval trees were felled for their timber. It is only once this fungal association is made in the living heartwood of the original tree that the death-watch beetles can feed. When fully grown (3–12 years recorded), the maggots pupate and turn into adults, but the adults continue living inside the wooden beams, where their gnawings, after many generations, eventually start to create spongy passages, then open voids. It is this insidious inner destruction, across decades or centuries, that eventually reduces the load-bearing strength of the timber to the point of collapse, but it does take ages.

Living inside what can become labyrinthine gaps and crevices within the interior of the heavy beams, the adult beetles need to be able to find one another to mate; this is where their ticking comes in – it is morse code for 'I am here, where are you?' A beetle raises up the front of its body, then drums down with its head onto the hard wood. The tap, which can be mimicked by dropping a pencil point-down onto a table from about 5cm, is actually a series of 11–13 very rapid raps in about 1.25 seconds. There is a gap of 1–2 seconds and it is repeated. Once one beetle starts tapping, others living in the timber reply. Echoing through the wood, the tapping is surprisingly loud for such a small insect, and the eerily repetitive rapping can seem unnerving to the unknowing.

It is easy to see how the beetle got its morbid common name. In an era before clinical hospital death, people died in their own beds, in their own homes. Imagine the scene of a fading life, sick or aged; the person is lying very still, calm but barely breathing under the coverlets, watched over by an anxious parent or other relative. In the quiet gloom a sinister tapping starts up from some secret location, sounding as if it is coming from the walls of the house or the very ground beneath. The slow knocking, like the ticking of some deathly clock counting away the remaining minutes of life, must have seemed a dreadfully ominous portent of the inevitable approaching doom.

WOOD – NOT THE MOST NUTRITIOUS SUBSTANCE, SO WHY EAT IT?

Going back to the myths of human origins for a moment, and the stereotype ideas about cavemen, it's easy to forget that wood is actually the structural material of choice for most of human history. Wood is a hugely useful substrate for building. It is hard, strong, flexible and relatively inert when seasoned, but soft enough to be cut and shaped by simple stone and metal tools. Long before masonry was cut or bricks were baked, wooden branches would have been chopped and woven into hurdles, and used to stretch tenting skins and support thatch for bivouac shelters. Heavier trunks were axed, adzed, cut and shaped for spars, rafters, joists and beams, to build anything from hermit hovels to baronial halls. Unfortunately from many ancient cultures like those of the Egyptians, Maya, Romans and Greeks, all we have left are the fabulous stone monuments of the ruling elites. The vernacular architecture of the average citizen does not last long. It is constantly under attack from a multitude of creatures, eating it away from under the very feet of the occupants.

The power and strength of wood (in the tree that grows it and the use humans make of it) is down to the chemical structure of the plant materials from which it is derived – chiefly cellulose and lignin. These naturally occurring polymers, long, chain-like molecules made up from regular, repeated (many thousands of times) simple sugar units, are cross-linked for added stability and strength, and give wood all the useful characteristics it has for a building and manufacturing material. They also make it relatively unpalatable – trees would not be able to grow very large if they were constantly eaten away by animals. Yet we know that timber is eventually eaten away by wood-boring insects; monographs are written about it (Hickin 1975 is a good start). Why is this?

Wood feeding, although less common than leaf feeding, is a widespread habit. A few vertebrates like beavers, squirrels, porcupines and deer chew wood, but often the chewing is limited to less woody shoots and buds, or living bark. The tough inner heartwood of trees (the 'timber' used by humans) mostly remains the preserve of wood-boring insects, including many beetles, most termites, some ants, a few flies and sawflies (distant relatives of bees and wasps), and a very few moths. Many of these can only attack wood that has started to decay through the natural processes of mould and fungal invasion, when these simple organisms start to predigest the difficult, long-chain cellulose molecules into a more edible, starch-like format. Others have evolved relationships with specialist micro-organisms (symbionts) living in their guts – bacteria, protozoa or fungi – which produce the necessary enzymes to break down the cellulose polymers.

In the natural surroundings of a mature forest, fallen branches and toppled boles are exposed to the elements (and fungi), and start to rot immediately. They may even have fallen because fungi were already at work attacking the living tree, weakening the heartwood to the point of windfall collapse. A tree trunk lying on a forest floor might be expected to vanish, completely eaten away, within a few years, but building timber can remain dry and apparently sound for centuries (not often millennia, however).

Natural wood-feeding insects often have extended life cycles, with large insects like the stag beetle *Lucanus cervus* and tanner beetle *Prionus coriarius* living for up to seven years as fat, pale grubs, laboriously extracting whatever nutrition they can from the fungoid wood before achieving enough body mass to change into adult beetles. Much smaller insects feeding in dry and solid construction timber can also take an age to achieve maturity, despite the help from their gut symbionts. At 3–12 years the death-watch beetle is in the middle ground of this time frame.

Wood really is very tough stuff. Nevertheless, it is perfectly edible for a large number of wood borers; it is their natural food, and just because humans construct with it rather than eat it doesn't make it any less palatable. Another way of thinking about our domestic building timber (and furniture) is that it is simply stored food for woodworms.

The true European woodworm *Anobium punctatum* (*A. domesticum* in some older books) is a tiny beast (2.5–4.3mm) compared with the death-watch beetle, but because of this it is more easily overlooked until it has wreaked havoc in a chair leg, floorboard or stair timbers. Its minute exit holes, about the same size as holes made by darts missing a dart-board, are easily filled with polish or varnish, or a coat of paint, and infestations can go unnoticed for many years before the riddled nature of the woodwork is revealed by breakage or collapse.

The beetle can, however, be accidentally brought in (unlike the death-watch beetle) to create a new infestation – always carefully check any old secondhand wooden furniture you pick up.

European woodworm *Anobium punctatum*

The species is very widespread, and in British house surveys in the 1960s, during the post-war housing boom, it was regularly reported that 50–80 per cent of buildings had the beetle present, rising to 90 per cent in older properties (Hickin 1963). These surveys were carried out by pest-control companies, so there was inevitably some bias; the surveyors were invited in by home owners already worrying that the beetle was present. Nevertheless it does indicate just how common the beetles are. I'm fairly certain that all the houses I've ever lived in have had their grubs chewing away somewhere. Removing multiple layers of lino and carpet, and sanding the floorboards to a shiny, polished finish usually revealed their labyrinthine burrows, like miniature city maps. Today I think they are only in the leg of the old Victorian table at which I work in the kitchen, although all the cat scratchings make the exit holes difficult to see.

Building and joinery timber is different from fresh-cut wood, because it has been seasoned, sometimes for years. This is really a controlled drying out of the heartwood of the felled tree after it has been cut into planks. Wood is not a solid structure, but a sponge- or honeycomb-like structure of microscopic tubules. When the tree was a sapling these tubes transported water up from the roots, but as the tree grew they hardened and stiffened to give support to the tree. Only the tubes near the outside of the trunk under the living bark remained fully active, but the heartwood retained the tubes, and it always contained some water. When a tree is cut down 30–80 per cent of the weight of the wood (depending on the tree species) might be water; this drops to about 15–20 per cent after seasoning, and indoors it can continue to decrease to 5–8 per cent (Eaton and Hale 1993). The natural contraction of the timber as it dries accounts for cracks in planks and shrinkage around joints, especially when old furniture is moved from an unheated warehouse into a centrally heated home.

Heat in itself is not enough to maintain the integrity of seasoned timber. Dampness coming through a wall from soil outside, or due to poor drainage or damaged guttering, can combine with homely heat to reverse the seasoning effects, and actively encourage fungal decay. Damp rot and dry rot are terms guaranteed to upset any home owner. Both types of fungal attack require dampness to get going, but dry rot, as implied by its name, can continue its destruction even after the source of the seeping water has been stopped and the woodwork has been seen to dry out. Both are now likely to encourage a new species of woodworm. Since the 1930s, in the UK at least, reports of domestic timber attack have increasingly implicated the small, dark, narrow, cylindrical woodworm weevil *Pentarthrum huttoni*.

Closely related to the grain, rice and maize weevils of human food stores (see page 111), woodworm weevils were long known to shipping merchants because of their attacks on wooden barrels and casks. The wood of these conveniently rollable transport crates needs to be kept slightly moist, otherwise the curved planks (staves) dry out and leakage cracks appear. In the days of long-haul shipping under sail, barrels were what wooden pallets are today — easily manoeuvrable, storable, stackable and reusable storage containers that could be moved around

Woodworm weevil
Euophryum confine

a warehouse on one side of the world, then manhandled down into the hold and shipped off to another continent at a day's notice.

There is no clear indication of where the woodworm weevils came from originally – they have been moved all around the world and are widespread throughout Europe, North America and Japan. There is a suggestion that this species may have originated somewhere on the Pacific Rim, and it is apparently still spreading in Europe, having been discovered in landlocked Austria as recently as 2005, when it was noted attacking old coffins in the crypt of a historically important Viennese church. The closing of ventilation shafts during the 1940s had increased the dampness levels of the underground vault, reversing the original hardwood's seasoning to the point where the beetles were simply following on after fungal attack (Halmschlager *et al.* 2007).

The multiplying household reports of woodworm weevils from the 1930s and '40s onwards first suggested that the beetle had changed its food preferences, moving from hardwood (usually oak) barrels to softwood (pine and fir) planking used in houses, but closer inspection of collected specimens showed that the majority of household cases now involved a different species. *Euophryum confine* is nearly identical to *Pentarthrum huttoni* to the naked eye; it is a native of New Zealand, but has now become the most common domestic woodworm in England and Wales (Scotland soon, I expect). It only attacks woodwork, often skirting boards and joists, where dampness has penetrated, encouraging fungal rot to start the process of destruction. Apparently the beetles are attracted to α-pinine and 2-pentanone, released by wood undergoing decay (Green and Pitman 2002). The species has also moved out into the wider countryside, and is also now a common beetle that feeds in logs and stumps in natural woodlands.

The importance of dryness in the structural security of human habitation is re-emphasised. The dryness helps to preserve the wood, preventing fungal decay and discouraging associated nuisance wood-feeding insects. It will not necessarily get rid of any wood feeders already living deep inside the wood.

THE WOOD BORER'S WAITING GAME

Just as death-watch beetles were accidentally brought into a building in the structural timbers as it was constructed, plenty of insect species have been recorded indoors that have emerged from wooden furniture, ornaments, rafters and floorboards after many months (or years). These are apt to create anxiety in householders, but most are unlikely to go on to give any future infestation. The wood out of which they have gnawed their way is now subtly but significantly different from the wood in which they started life. The seasoning and drying reduces the nutritional quality of the cellulose even further, and this slows down a wood borer's development to a metaphorical crawl.

Powder-post beetles (small, cylindrical members of the beetle families Lyctidae and Bostrychidae) commonly emerge from cheap wooden souvenirs brought back from overseas (expensive ones too, probably). There was a time when lyctids especially were common domestic woodworms in Britain. They still occur in woodland and in old farm buildings, but are much less common in domestic houses nowadays than they once were, probably as a result of the drying effect of central heating. They may appear, along with a powder-sawdust trickle from emergence holes in a Papua New Guinean wood carving, for example, several summers after an original holiday in the area. It is best to be on the safe side and gather up the offending beetles, but they are unlikely to start attacking chair legs. I never discovered what beetles came from the small, rustic guinea-pig shelter I bought from a south London pet shop a few years ago, but they do not seem to have started work on the rest of the hutch yet. The likelihood is that they will be unable to attack the well-seasoned woodwork.

Even less likely to create a problem, but several orders of magnitude more disquieting, are woodwasps, *Sirex* and *Urocerus*

Woodwasp *Sirex*

species. These large, heavy and loudly buzzing, wasp-like insects are sawflies, so named for their imposing but harmless egg-laying tube, which is tipped with a tiny but tough, saw-toothed cutting edge to drill into a tree trunk where the eggs are laid. The large, fat grubs, reaching 30–40mm long, bore through the heartwood for several years until they eventually transform into adults. These chew their way out, perhaps causing great consternation in the sitting room and dining room.

There are tales of buildings being 'inundated' by apparent mass emergences of woodwasps several years after the construction was completed. In temperate climates the seasonal cold of autumn and winter may further decrease feeding rates of wood-boring insects, slowing development so that it extends over many more years than would be normal under natural conditions.

Perhaps the most remarkable surprise is the occasional emergence of the golden jewel beetle *Buprestis aurulenta*, an attractive metallic greenish-gold insect 15–22mm long. It is a native of western North America, where it breeds in Douglas fir and other pine trees, the timber of which is often cut and shipped to many places.

There are reports of it emerging from furniture made from the wood and exported to various parts of the world, including a 13-year-old cupboard in Germany, and household goods in Australia and New Zealand. For many years during the 1960s and '70s there was a thick, wooden-soled sandal on display in a glass case at London's Natural History Museum, showing a large borehole from which a specimen of the golden jewel beetle had emerged, much to the shock of the wearer no doubt. Indeed, this insect holds the

Golden jewel beetle
Buprestis aurulenta

current world record for the longest known larval development – two golden jewel beetle larvae were found by workers sanding the timbers in a building in British Columbia, Canada, where they had reputedly been quietly nibbling away for 51 years without achieving adulthood (Smith 1962).

Seemingly intermediate between the permanently established, self-perpetuating colonies of domestic woodworm, and the obviously spurious emergence of exotic jewel beetles and random woodwasps, is the bizarre distribution of the house longhorn beetle *Hylotrupes bajulus*. The longhorns (named for their long antennae) form a large group of striking, often beautifully marked beetle species that feed, during the larval stages, in dead wood, bark or sometimes woody plant roots. They are a natural part of any wooded environment, and while the grubs chew assiduously through old logs and stumps, the adults sometimes disport themselves on flowers. Very occasionally a large longhorn beetle will emerge from building timber or chopped wood ready for the log-burning stove, but these are for the most part chance occurrences – odd, but not threatening. We cannot be complacent, however. The Asian longhorn beetle *Anoplophora glabripennis* is increasingly emerging from wooden pallets shipped from China all over the world. It is unlikely to become a household insect, but there are grave fears that it will become a major forestry pest in Europe and North America. The house longhorn beetle, however, as its name suggests, is regularly found breeding in houses.

In the UK this species was never very common, and all the old beetle books state things like 'in old posts, rails and so on'. However, during the mid 20th century there was a spate of records from houses in Camberley, Weybridge and Byfleet in north-west Surrey (Hickin 1947), where the beetle appeared to have become established and was feeding not in old posts and rails, but in modern house-building timbers. It does this elsewhere in the world. The range of this beetle appears to be central and southern Europe into Siberia, and North Africa, but it has also been accidentally transported to Australia, New Zealand, South Africa, China, and South and North America, where it can be an important pest of softwood timbers, mainly because of its large size and the consequent large size of its burrows. In the USA it is ranked second only to termites in the structural damage it does to house timber.

The house longhorn beetle appears to be unique among the longhorns because it will lay its eggs on the dry, seasoned construction timber from which the adults emerge. Most other beetles in this large and diverse family seek out logs, stumps and dead standing trees, where the bark is still attached, attracted by the distinctive resinous scents produced by the cocktails of chemicals in the living, dying or freshly dead parts of the trees. So well established as a domestic wood borer has the species become that natural records of it breeding in the wild are something of a novelty. For example, on Surrey Wildlife Trust's Ockham Common nature reserve, near Byfleet, the house longhorn beetle is actively encouraged, since it was discovered there in the early 1990s, by selective lopping of pine trees to produce dead, standing, monolith-like boles, which it seems to favour. Whether this practice is also encouraging it in Surrey's loft timbers is not yet clear.

Elsewhere across Europe the house longhorn beetle also occurs almost exclusively in buildings and has names that reflect this – *hausbock* in Germany, *capricorne des maisons* (house goat horn) in France and *cerambicido de la madera labrada* (carved wood goat horn) in Spain. I've often wondered whether it was the larvae of this beetle that kept me awake as they chewed their night-time feast in the bedside cabinet of the small family-run guest house I stayed in when I visited the Greek island of Lesvos back in the late 1980s. One table leg had already been reduced to a ragged broken stump and the exposed burrows looked about the right size.

In Britain and other temperate parts of the beetle's range, it is the roof timbers of a house that are often the first to be attacked. One suggestion is that this is because the roof tiles become warmed by the sun, and unventilated attic spaces can become stiflingly hot in summer, benefiting an insect that originated in warmer climes. The useful insulating ability of thatch has been forgotten as this building material has become much less used in recent centuries.

One thing is certain – the house longhorn beetle no longer appears to have a clear endemic range where it exclusively, or at least regularly, breeds in naturally occurring trees, logs, stumps or branches.

However, because of its size and its relatively important destructive power, much laboratory work (Hickin 1975) has been done, studying its development rates under different temperature regimes (28–30°C optimum), the humidity and moisture content of the wood (26–50 per cent ideal) and its egg-laying preferences in different crack sizes (0.25–0.6mm across, extending to 2–3cm into the wood preferred).

House longhorn beetle
Hylotrupes bajulus

In the UK the house longhorn beetle attacks solely softwood (pine, fir, spruce), but in continental Europe it also feeds on broadleaved trees like alders, hazels, poplars and sometimes oaks. At the time of its first appearance in Europe during the last ice age 20,000–25,000 years ago, these woodlands were restricted to the Mediterranean peninsulas of Italy, Greece and Iberia. These subtle clues, together with a look at some of its specialist parasites, indicate that it was maybe once a native of the Atlas Mountains, from Algeria to Tunisia. This now-arid zone was once the site of lush mixed forests, but climate changes after the retreat of the polar ice cap and the end of the last ice age 15,000 years ago, together with extensive felling and sheep grazing in ancient times, have so altered this particular geographic region that it can no longer support the primeval forests where the beetle originated. Instead, it moved into the houses of the shepherds.

TERMITES – THE ENEMY WITHIN

The name 'termite' is laced with connotations of insidious destruction, corruption and decay. Throughout much of the Americas, Africa, Asia and Australasia, termites are reviled for the dreadful damage they can inflict on building timbers, and because they live hidden within their foodstuff their presence is sometimes only discovered when a chance break in the exterior fascia, now a thin veneer of wood, reveals their labyrinthine burrows. Because termites live in large, complex

139

colonies, sometimes numbering millions, the damage can be massive; their excavations can bring whole buildings to the verge of collapse and eventually reduce them to dust.

In Britain we can be pretty blasé about termites. There are none native to the British Isles, nor any serious populations anywhere in northern Europe. Around the Mediterranean there are two native termite species (*Kalotermes flavicollis* and *Reticulitermes lucifugus*, sometimes subdivided into various species sister groups or subspecies), and these can cause minor problems, like any wood borer, but they have never achieved the same notoriety as termites have in the tropics and subtropics.

The Ancient Greeks and Romans called almost any small animal that bored into wood *termes* or *tarmes* (Beavis 1988). Later entomologists used this name in their scientific names for termite species (and *Teredo* for the shipworm genus, burrowing clams), but there is no indication that termites ever caused major problems in Neolithic or Iron Age cultures, and those ancient writers were quite likely to have been referring to *Anobium* woodworm beetles.

Away from Europe, termites have waged war on human civilisation ever since humans became civilised. These tiny insects, sometimes called white ants because of their small size, pale colours and colonial behaviour, are more closely related to cockroaches, demonstrated by subtle similarities in the wings when winged males and females (alates) are produced from the nest. In general, each nest has an egg-laying female (the queen), an inseminating male (the king) and large numbers of non-reproductive workers. Some of the most complicated social structures occur in termite colonies, with different types of individual being produced under complex genetic and chemical control. These can take the form of strikingly different-looking and variously sized individuals, from tiny nest workers to large soldiers. Eaters and foragers chew out the wood, nurses take care of the eggs and the young nymphs, soldiers with large jaws or glue-squirting spouts patrol and protect the nest from attack (mostly from ants), and synchronised production of new males and females can give rise to huge aerial mating swarms at fixed times in the year.

Termites eat wood, although many non-pest species eat other plant material, and they have special cellulose-digesting protozoa

Termites

living in their guts to help them release the nutrients. They variously tunnel out soil or chewed wood to make their nests, and they reinforce the tunnels and outer layers with a cement made from saliva and faecal pellets. The famously huge termite mounds of Africa and Australia are similarly constructed from this tough building material, but these are not domestic pest species. The towers can be several metres high, take decades to construct and may survive for centuries – it is a similar longevity in colony life that causes problems in timber-eating termites that attack buildings. The termites cover over their trails, even constructing free-standing tubular passageways out of faecal cement, so no insects may be visible anywhere on the surface, yet they can be pecking away under the surface of the wood for many years before their presence is detected.

At this late stage the damage may be beyond simple chemical treatment; whole segments of supporting woodwork may have to be cut out and replaced. Entire portions of roofs, walls and floors may have to be rebuilt. In the USA it is not uncommon to see whole buildings draped with specially manufactured plastic tents, inside which poisonous fumigant gases are pumped to kill a termite infestation that might stretch right through the house timbers.

Unfortunately, most of the termites that cause all the fuss in these cases are simply wild-living native species that have wandered in from their natural haunt in the garden or nearby woodland. Some are variously called damp-wood, dry-wood or powder-post termites, depending on their favoured wood-moisture content, and out in their natural biocoenosis they feed on branches, twigs or logs in varying stages of decay, a normal part of the recycling of organic matter. There is not much people living in termite-populated areas can do to prevent the occasional household infestation, other than chemically treating the wood as a prophylactic, and keeping vigilant by regularly monitoring potential invasion points under and around the house. The upside of this is that at least native species will have acquired their own natural predators and parasites over the millions of years that they have been evolving as part of the local environmental community.

Nevertheless, commerce and trade have managed to introduce new species from one part of the world to another, creating potentially much more important pests. The conehead termite *Nasutitermes corniger* (named after its snout-nosed, glue-squirting soldiers and workers) arrived in the southern USA from its original Central and Southern American homelands in 2001, causing some consternation, and has been the subject of various attempted eradication programmes (Scheffrahn *et al.* 2002). The Formosan termite *Coptotermes formosanus* is probably native to southern China, but early in the 20th century it was accidentally introduced into Taiwan (Formosa) and Japan. It has now been spread to South Africa, Sri Lanka, Hawaii and mainland USA, where it is currently ranked as one of the major wood-destructive pests in the country (Messenger *et al.* 2002).

For the last 50 years Paris has been under attack from *Reticulitermes santonensis*, one of the species/subspecies naturally found around the Bay of Biscay. In its natural habitat it is an uncommon insect, but once transported to the shelter of urban buildings it found the ideal foodstuff in the seasoned timber from which many of the city's old buildings are constructed. Traditionally it has been accepted that termites are limited to a tropical and subtropical zone delimited by the

10°C minimum isotherm north and south of the equator, but the heat-island effect of cities (with their huge areas of heat-retaining tarmac, slate, tile and concrete) and permanently heated public buildings has created colonisation opportunities aplenty.

Although no termite species occurs naturally in the UK, we still need to be on our guard. In 1994 an active colony of termites, later identified as *Reticulitermes grassei*, originally from the Iberian Peninsula, was found in a house in North Devon. Speculation in the press blamed a pot plant brought back from the Canary Islands. Immediate treatment by termiticide spraying was followed by long-term monitoring within a 500-m quarantine zone. All was thought to be well when by the end of 2001 no further living termites had been found (Verkerk and Bravery 2004), but in 2010 live ones were found in three closely adjacent baited traps on the property. The supposition is that a few of the subterranean termites escaped the initial chemical blitz, maintaining a microcolony of just a few scores or hundreds of individuals for several years. A ten-year termite-free period is now required to sign off the eradication as successful.

AS SAFE AS HOUSES? ARE BRICKS AND MORTAR ANY BETTER THAN WOOD?

Stone was not a major building material until the end of the 12th century. Before this, of course, fortresses, temples, palaces and mausoleums had been constructed from this durable medium, but cutting, moving and erecting stone was difficult and expensive. Bricks were not cheap either, since they had to be mixed, moulded, dried, then fired, unless they were just air-dried mud, dung and straw, in which case they were useful, but much less sturdy. There were always grand brick and stone structures, from amphitheatres to ziggurats, but the widespread use of brick and stone in domestic houses is relatively modern.

Brick and stone may be impervious to termite and house longhorn beetle chewings, but they still have their detractors. It may not be the bricks or stones themselves that are attacked, but the mortar joints between the Flemish bond or the soldier course are

Mason bee *Osmia tricornis*   Mason wasp *Odynerus antilope*

more friable and crumbly. This is where mason bees and wasps like to dig away. Unlike the social wasps (yellowjackets) and honeybees (see page 68), which build large nests containing many thousands of individuals, mason bees and wasps are solitary species; each of their small nests is constructed by a lone female working on her own. They make a small burrow in soil, a dead tree or masonry, using their small but strong jaws to chew it out, or enlarge an existing hole made by a wood-boring beetle (in timber), or maybe enlarge a shrinkage crevice in brickwork.

Modern cement mortar is quick setting, very tough and has high compressive strength, but traditional lime mortar is a more forgiving, porous and flexible medium. This was (and still is) an important consideration when working with natural stone, terracotta and old bricks, and for combining wooden features. Given the inevitable settling of a structure built (as they all once were) on less than immovable foundations, the relatively flexible mortar can cope with slight seasonal movements of the underlying ground without extensive cracking. It is an easy and aesthetic substance to work with. But it is soft.

Although each female bee or wasp is only making her own nest, a single tunnel lined or divided into cells using mud daubs or leaf fragments, solitary bees and wasps do have a tendency to nest in loose aggregations. In vertical cliff-faces, sand pits and landslips this is because suitable habitat for nesting appears in small, discrete pockets,

Feather-footed bee *Anthophora plumipes* (male left, female right)

so these limited areas tend to become colonised by like-minded bees and wasps. Termed, rather fondly, 'bee villages' by entomologists, this is of no consequence if the nesting insects are digging holes in the steep edge of a roadside verge or railway cutting, but if they take a fancy to the warm, sunny wall of a historically important Oxford college or the teetering chimney stack of a Tudor manor house, there is a point at which they can threaten serious damage by weakening the already delicate mortar seams.

A large number of bee and wasp species nest in loose mortar, but one of the most striking (in Europe) is the feather-footed bee *Anthophora plumipes*. Named for the males' plumed legs, this species is out very early in spring (February to May), and also exhibits a striking sexual dimorphism. The brown males spend most of their time visiting flowers, where they will vigorously defend a territory, waiting for the jet-black females. They are large and furry, and are often mistaken for dark monochrome bumblebees, although they are not closely related. Like most mason bees, they normally nest on exterior walls, but they will also move into the interior brickwork of disused chimneys in old houses. From here they often have a tendency to become disorientated and end up dropping dazed or dead through the old fireplace and onto the living room floor, much to the consternation of the occupants. A specimen given to me was so dusted with grey flue filth that the person presenting it was convinced that it had been frolicking in the bathroom talc.

It will take many centuries of mason-bee excavation to bring down a wall, and for most people having a few fuzzy bees nesting in the corner of the house or in the crumbling garden boundary is a charming adjunct to the nature they are happy to find close to home. But if their mining efforts are ignored in the long term the insects' tunnels can be the first stage in an insidious decay, allowing moisture through, creating crevices for plant seeds to germinate, and generally loosening the mortar enough for wind and weather to start removing bricks. For an old abandoned building, it is just a matter of time.

ATTACKS ON ART AND CULTURE

The luxurious trappings of a civilised life are what raised human existence beyond crude Neolithic subsistence and into the sophisticated era of art, literature, music and science. The right to a quiet enjoyment of private life and the possession of personal belongings is enshrined in the laws of most countries and cultures, but household invaders are not likely to be bound by these legal strictures. Termites and woodworm do not stop at undermining the floorboards. Paper, being just wood pulp with only minor chemical changes, is equally palatable to them.

When termites arrived in Paris some 50 years ago, it was their demolition of historical documents and archived paperwork that caused some of the greatest destruction. Unlike a building, bits of which can be replaced, once a unique handwritten parchment is gone, it is gone forever. There are still regular tales of termite catastrophe in the tabloids, usually involving key legal documents like wills or leases, or wads of cash stuffed under a bed. These are particularly the case in the slightly more northern edges of the termites' ranges, where there has not been a tradition of keeping a watchful eye on things, and where previously wooden boxes were perfectly acceptable storage vessels, but where metal trunks might now become necessary.

You can always recognise old books that have travelled to the tropics. Stacked however neatly together on a bookcase, such books have often been the sorry targets of many wood- and paper-eating pests. Termites will hollow out a volume completely, leaving a dust-filled cavity between the leather-bound boards. Silverfish making an expedition from the kitchen have been known to chew off book labels to get at the glue beneath, or to graze on the starch size, the thin gelatinous solution used in paper manufacturing to get a smooth finish. Bookworms are usually similar to woodworms, the larvae of what are normally wood-boring beetles that tunnel, sometimes through an entire shelf of books, leaving a series of neat, circular or oval holes in the pages. It doesn't take many generations of bookworms to render a book unreadable, making it wholly (holey) beyond repair.

Throughout history, wherever natural materials were used in manufacture, natural feeders came along to digest them. Wood carvings and wooden musical instruments have been disfigured or rendered useless by woodworm burrows; instrument strings of sheep intestines (often mislabelled as catgut) were cut by larder beetles; pigments from wall murals and paintings show the sure signs of having been nibbled off by ants; treasured heirlooms of carved wood, cloth, bone, fur and feather have all suffered, and the few that make it into modern museums are all the rarer for having survived by some quirk of damage evasion. Once inside the museum they are not guaranteed future survival, unless the curators show equal vigilance to the previous proud owners.

During the early 20th century a new assault on Western civilisation came with the fashionable emergence of cigarette smoking. The new-fangled, white, paper-enclosed tobacco products were all very elegant, but they tended to show up the tiny exit holes made by a beetle, *Lasioderma serricorne*, soon named not inappropriately as the cigarette beetle. Although long known previously as a nuisance pest of stored dried tobacco, its damage was much less obvious in the all-brown cigars that had been the fashion to date, although the holes did prevent the smoke from drawing.

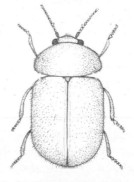

Cigarette beetle *Lasioderma serricorne*

Related to the woodworms (*Anobium* species) and biscuit beetle, the cigarette beetle was thought to have come originally, along with tobacco, from the subtropical Americas, but by the time entomologists started to officially catalogue things with scientific names in the 18th century, it was well established in Europe and Asia. A change of opinion occurred when, during the 1960s, dead specimens were found in old cloth rags used to stuff an ancient Egyptian mummy. This led to all manner of debate about the possible Old World origins of the beetle, and also about the possibility of tobacco trade in ancient times. It was only through retrospective detective work (Buckland and Panagiotakopulu 2001) that it was discovered that the mummy in question had previously been opened at the museum, and partly restuffed, after treatment with nicotine used as an insecticide to control larder beetles and other carrion pest insects that could attack such popular museum exhibits. For a time opinion switched back to the idea that the cigarette beetle really was a New World species, but recent monographs point to the diversity of other closely related species in the genus, which probably arose in the Balkans and around the Mediterranean.

The link between the cigarette beetle and tobacco may well be spurious and completely coincidental, the beetle having easily switched its food choice from its original but unknown dead leaf to another. I've found the beetles flying towards my lighted kitchen windows, and I live well away from tobacco plantations and cigar-rolling factories. The cigarette beetle obviously has a wide food choice and has also been found infesting raisins, rhubarb, cayenne pepper, ginger, dried fish, ergot, turmeric, gun wadding, liquorice and saffron.

Most supposedly specific feeders will, on occasion, choose a foodstuff that is completely out of the ordinary. When pest-control officers were called to a beetle-troubled drug-enforcement office in Arizona in 1979, they found that the store room full of several tons of confiscated cannabis bales was home not to any marijuana beetle, but to confused [sic] flour beetles *Tribolium confusum* breeding in the seeds (Smith and Olson 1982). The bales were also infested with various mould- and fungus-feeding beetles; apparently the Mexican smugglers were less than fastidious when it came to storing the drugs out in the open air before they were shipped across the US border.

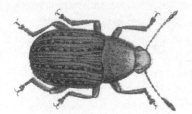

Coffee weevil *Araecerus fasciculatus*

Bamboo borer *Dinoderus minutus*

As civilised advances (and luxuries) come along, it seems that there is always some organism waiting to take advantage of them. Thankfully, tea has remained remarkably pest free, but coffee is attacked by the coffee weevil *Araecerus fasciculatus*, originally an Indian insect and a pest in nutmeg. Chocolate (and cocoa) is devoured by the cacao moth *Ephestia elutella* when it isn't feeding in tobacco. Occasional fashions for bamboo furniture bring in the bamboo borer *Dinoderus minutus*, one of several East Asian species that bore into bamboo stems, reducing the cores to dust.

Early in the 20th century the telephone was surely the height of modern living, but some exchanges were plagued with problems when telephone wires started to knit across US streetscapes. It soon transpired that a native wood-boring beetle, *Scobicia declivis*, had taken to boring into the lead casings of the telephone cables in various Californian suburbs. Normally this small (5–6mm) insect is a wood-boring beetle, but the density and texture of the lead must have mimicked the timber, because the beetles were trying to chew egg-laying tunnels into something patently not edible to any resultant larvae. The small hole, just 2–3mm in diameter, was usually burrowed adjacent to a cable-support ring, an attachment fixed to a building, and this support point offered the beetle purchase to get the necessary leverage to bore into the relatively soft metal. Although the seemingly small amount of damage was

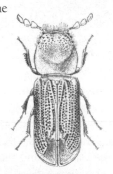

Short-circuit beetle
Scobicia declivis

done between June and August, when the adult beetles were emerging from their natural habitat in timber planks and logs, it did not become apparent until the first rains. Water getting into the tiny holes caused electrical interference, each putting 50 to 600 telephones out of order, and soon earning the species the name short-circuit beetle (also lead cable borer).

There do not appear to be any genuine insect computer-eating bugs yet, but 'crazy' ants will take up residence in computer housings if given the chance. The oddly titled Raspberry crazy ant *Nylanderia fulva* is named partly for its deranged, circling, zigzag gait, and partly after the Texas pest exterminator Tom Raspberry who first noticed that it had become a problem. Originally a native of South America, the species appeared in the USA in 1931, but did not become a nuisance until the 1990s; it is now widespread in Texas, and turning up in Mississippi, Georgia and Florida (Gotzek *et al.* 2012). One of its main nuisance behaviours is nesting inside electrical appliances, but whether this is because it is attracted to the magnetic fields of the wires, or warmth associated with electrical resistance, is still being studied. It

has, however, found notoriety in the press as a computer bug. The use of the word 'bug' to mean a glitch in a computer program is more than just for the convenience of newspaper subeditors. There was a genuine original insect computer bug.

Raspberry crazy ant *Nylanderia fulva*

On 9 September 1947 US Navy computer scientist Grace Hopper noted in her journal that an actual moth had been found stuck in the relays of the Mark II she was programming, causing it to stop working. Although the idea of 'debugging' the system was already in use, this event more or less cemented the term we use so readily today. The noctuid moth, still taped to the log book in the Smithsonian Institution in Washington, was probably attracted by the light from the valves, but then fried by the exposed electrical connections. There is now some evidence that electrical fields (rather than hot wires) can attract cockroaches, silverfish, firebrats and earwigs, suggesting that anecdotal reports of these insects targeting and infesting electrical appliances and outlet sockets are real enough, and not the disgruntled complaints of proud owners frustrated by the damage to their new mod cons. Quite what Mr Raspberry's crazy ants are after in the laptop is still unclear.

COLD COMFORT INSECTS – EATING THE SHIRT OFF YOUR BACK

Unlike their brightly colourful, day-flying relatives the butterflies, drab nocturnal moths have a sinister reputation. In reality, they are sorely misunderstood. Eerie flutterings at a porch lamp or against a lighted window seem to imply that they are set on invading the home, desecrating the sacred space to which they are closed. This is confounded by the knowledge that some moths attack our clothes, and the tiny culprits fly off in mad, tight spirals (well depicted in cartoons) when a cupboard is opened to reveal holes chewed in the favourite old cardigan or the antique silk wedding gown.

Of the more than 160,000 species of Lepidoptera (butterflies and moths) known around the world, the vast majority have the well-known life cycle, familiar to most of us. Tiny eggs are laid on a food plant; they hatch into a cylindrical leaf-eating caterpillar; it spins a cocoon and makes a chrysalis; then comes the astonishing metamorphosis into the winged aerial adult. The Lepidoptera are one of the great hyperdiverse animal groups in the world, with a bewildering array of sizes, colours, shapes and patterns, but of these perhaps only a dozen or two species have successfully made it across the human threshold.

Some species, like the Angoumois grain moth *Sitotroga cerealella*, rice moth *Corcyra cephalonica*, Indian meal moth *Plodia interpunctella*, Mediterranean flour moth *Ephestia kuehniella*, nut moth *Paralipsa gularis* and cacao moth, feed in our stored food. They have had to make the same ecological jump, from wild seeds and nuts into the dry storage conditions

Rice moth *Corcyra cephalonica*

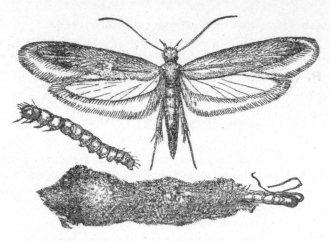

Common clothes moth *Tineola bisselliella*: larva, case with empty pupa shell, and moth

of human granaries and warehouses, as did the many stored food beetle pests that are still attracted mainly to seeds and nuts. Greenery is the caterpillar foodstuff for the majority of butterflies and moths, but in the wild environment larvae of some species also feed on flowers, in buds and fruits, in stems or roots, under tree bark, in heartwood timber, in leaf litter and in fungi. The clothes moths of cartoon infamy, however, have made a different ecological transition; they do not, as intuition might suggest, feed on plant-derived clothes like cotton jeans or linen blouses, but attack fabrics of animal origin – wool and silk.

The two main protagonists are the common clothes moth *Tineola bisselliella* and the case-bearing clothes moth *Tinea pellionella*. The adult moths are slim and cylindrical, with the narrow wings tight furled around the body. The common clothes moth is more or less uniform pale brown or beige, while the case-bearing clothes moth is slightly silvery-grey with three small dark flecks on each side. Their erratic twisting flight depicted in cartoons is accurate, but even though they can fly, these moths prefer to run; left to their own devices they will seek out dark crevices in which to hide. This is a natural adaptation to finding the most secret spot in the wardrobe.

It is the small, pale caterpillars that do the feeding and growing, so it is they that do the actual cloth damage. The common clothes moth, sometimes also called the webbing clothes moth, makes a loose, tubular silken retreat in which to hide, using its own silk spun from spinnerets at its mouth; this is similar to the silk that all moth caterpillars use to make their cocoons. In heavy infestations

Case-bearing clothes moth *Tinea pellionella*

the tubes of several caterpillars mat together to form the rough web of its alternative name. Caterpillars of the case-bearing clothes moth make their own portable silk tube, a bit like a body-sock, which they drag about using their front legs that, along with their jaws, just project from the entrance. Both species also incorporate some of the fibres from the fabrics they are eating, sometimes creating bizarre multicoloured cases that look as if they have tie-dye effects.

The evolutionary switch that precursor clothes moth caterpillars must have made when they stopped feeding on plant material and started to digest animal proteins happened many millions of years ago. We know this because although there are only a very few domestic clothes moth pests, plenty of their close relatives feed on similar animal materials in the wild. They find sustenance in mammal and birds' nests (Woodroffe 1953), where they feed on moulted fur and feathers (and possibly the remains of dead nestlings). Others are found in owl pellets, which are really just the regurgitated fur and feather remains of the prey that owls cannot digest, and in wasps' nests, where they feed on dead insect remains dropped into the bottom of the colony by the wasps. Yet further related moths feed in leaf litter, on dead leaves, and some feed in fungal fruiting bodies, in particular the tough fibrous bracket fungi that grow on dead tree trunks, stumps and logs.

The proposed evolutionary path from plant to animal foodstuff is thought to have occurred when scavenger caterpillars, eating dead leaf, twig or fungal material, first came into contact with mixed-in fur and feathers in these animal nests. Occasional nibbling gave an advantage to any caterpillars more able to digest keratin, the major constituent of hair and feather. Like cellulose, keratin is a polymer molecule with long chemical chains, which needs to be broken down into simple digestible and absorbable nutrients. The exact mechanisms of keratin digestion are still being studied, but once they had evolved in moth caterpillars, they opened up a new niche from which moths had previously been excluded.

Hair, feathers, wool and silk are natural products, but clothes made from them are decidedly modern artefacts. Their origins are lost in prehistoric myth, but the use of wool from the sheep and goats domesticated at the dawn of agriculture about 15,000 years ago, first as complete skins, then as felted and woven coverings, is easily imaginable. Silk manufacture is thought to have begun about 5,000–6,000 years ago. Chinese legend has it that silk thread was discovered by Empress Lei-zu, wife of the Yellow Emperor Hwang-ti, during the 27th century BC. She was said to have dropped a silkworm *Bombyx mori* cocoon into her cup of tea, where it started to unravel. Whatever silk's beginnings, certainly in China where the silkmoth originated, the polymers that give silk its strength are similar enough to keratin molecules for clothes moth caterpillars to get stuck in immediately. Pure cotton and linen weaves are unattractive to clothes moths, but many modern fabrics are now mixtures of fibres, and clothes of different fibres are often folded and stored together, so almost any cloth seems fair game.

In middle-class Britain (and probably elsewhere in the industrialised world) clothes moths are enjoying something of a renaissance. Traditionally a nuisance of old clothes bundled up and forgotten about for years, all species underwent a significant decline in the last half of the 20th century. Several factors were involved, not least the appearance of easily available commercial insecticides like DDT, the ascent of inedible (to caterpillars) man-made fibres like rayon, nylon and polyester, and the increasing use of dry cleaning. The removal of many chemical pesticides because of the environmental dangers, and a retreat to more 'natural' fibres like cotton, wool and silk, have reopened the door to moth invasion.

We also have so many more clothes now than did our forebears even a generation or two ago. Our wardrobes are full to the point where instead of having 'best' and 'work', winter and summer clothes, we have so much stuff that we leave the clothes hanging, or pushed away in a drawer, for months on end, years even. This is just perfect for the moths, which creep in and find a ready food supply left undisturbed for several of their brief but destructive generations.

There has been a tendency, in some of the more disreputable rags of the tabloid press, to link an increase in clothes moths to the burgeoning numbers of charity and thrift shops selling secondhand clothes on high streets. It's easy to detect a snobbish and patronising undertone here. As someone who has bought secondhand clothes for all of their adult life, I can personally attest to the nonsense behind this pompous fear. You're much more likely to get an infestation of the moths from the felt hammers of an old piano you bought in an antique shop.

Not all clothes moths are increasing at the moment; the tapestry moth *Trichophaga tapetzella*, distinctively bicoloured mottled black and white, like a bird dropping brought to life, has hardly been seen in the UK in the last 50 years. Its larva also lives in a rough silk tube, but it prefers heavier and coarser materials. These were sometimes used in traditional hanging tapestries, but were more commonly utilised in the form of unspun wool, horsehair and feathers. Long ago these may have been common materials in rural hovels, but nowadays they are mainly likely to occur discarded in farm sheds and barns.

One area of domestic wool use that is increasing every year is in carpeting. Although coconut coir and synthetics like polypropylene are also popular, wool maintains a certain status in the carpet industry as being luxurious, hardwearing and 'natural'. Clothes moths make no distinction between natural woollen fabric draped in a cupboard and

Tapestry moth *Trichophaga tapetzella*

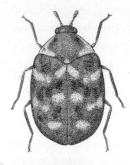

Varied carpet beetle
Anthrenus verbasci, and larva

natural woollen fabric placed over a floor, so their larvae are also sometimes carpet pests. Here they are joined by several other denizens of the thick pile, notably varied carpet beetles *Anthrenus verbasci*.

Small (1.5–3.5mm), squat, short-legged, domed to the point of being almost spherical and covered all over with pretty mottled scales, varied carpet beetles and several other similar species look fairly innocuous, and so they may be – as usual, it is the larvae that do all the eating, and therefore all of the damage. The similarly sized grubs are also short and squat, but are armed right across the body with long and short bristles, which stick up and out in well-ordered tufts. Resembling an animated boot brush, they go by the quaint (and some might say overly cute) title of 'woolly bears', quite a bizarrely endearing name, given their depredations.

Fitted carpets are a comparatively modern commodity, but rugs and tapestries have been around for longer. Even so, it is curious to contemplate what varied carpet beetles were up to before humans started laying down food for them. They are closely related to *Dermestes* species larder beetles, but instead of invading the kitchen for fallen food scraps, they made straight for the Axminster in the sitting room. They did, however, probably evolve from the same original stock of scavenging beetles that, way back in prehistory, fed on whatever dead animal matter they could find in carrion, or in mammal and birds' nests. What is most fascinating is the idea that they made a slight detour on the way into our homes.

Dermestes and *Anthrenus* larvae are superficially similar – just what you'd expect from them sharing a common carrion-scavenging ancestor many millions of years ago – but *Anthrenus* grubs are more jerky in their movements, and more densely and tuftily bristled, and the hairs are tipped with tiny barbed points, like miniature spearheads. Just as the long, sharp, brittle hairs of some butterfly and moth caterpillars are a good defence against being eaten by birds, so too the bristles on a woolly bear (and its erratic twitching movements) are a foil against spiders.

In the living room this characteristic may be useful against roving house spiders, but there are also several non-domestic *Anthrenus*-like beetle species that live entirely among spider webs (Hinton 1943). Here they nibble, undetected by their hosts, on the remains of other dead insects – the spiders' previous meals. These are not in the large orb webs spun between tall flower spikes in the garden or against the hedge, but in the tangled sheet webs made by the multitude of secretive spiders that live under the loose bark of old trees and logs. These spiders specialise in waiting for insects to hide in the dry nooks and crannies provided by large or veteran trees. Feeling the vibrations as the hapless prey walks in the darkness across the silk strands, the spider runs out from a tubular tunnel retreat and pounces.

Most spectacular among the web scavengers is a very close relative of the varied carpet beetle – *Ctesias serra* (no common name, I'm afraid, but we might call it a web beetle I suppose). Its larvae are even more bristly than those of the varied carpet beetle, and it looks like a demented toothbrush. Its thick coat of spiny hairs is enough to keep even the most determined spider at bay, but it hardly needs to, because spiders cannot find it. At its tail end it has two horizontal clusters of much longer bristles, which it can vibrate to a blur. These appear to set up the equivalent of jamming signals across the web, confusing spiders in the pitch black under the bark, and leaving *Ctesias serra* apparently immune to assault. The species was regarded as being quite scarce in the UK, but this may be because the adult beetles are short lived. The larvae, on the other hand, can be found readily and are easy to rear – just keep a bit of the loose bark in a jar and occasionally throw in a dead fly.

Once these facts were discovered, it also soon became clear that other similar species were living in the tangled matted bark webs, feeding on the dead insects left by spiders, including, yes, several species of *Anthrenus*. In what might be a curious case of throwback behaviour, entomologist Dafydd Lewis was bemused to find several woolly bear larvae feeding on dead flies at the bottom of an electric insectocutor in a store room. Presumably the smaller adult beetle had managed to fly in and miss the lethal electrified bars to lay eggs on the insect remains of the unlucky larger flies.

That *Anthrenus* should feed on dead insects is no surprise to entomologists, because these species have also long been known to them as museum beetles. *Anthrenus museorum* is one such, although the varied carpet beetle is equally abundant. Museum beetles can attack and damage stuffed animal and bird exhibits, but the greatest danger is if they get into insect collections. Pinned or glued onto small cards, the insect specimens housed in museums are generally stored in cork-lined boxes or glass-topped drawers in cabinets. Because there are so many, only a tiny fraction are ever on public display at any one time, leaving most of them to be examined by visiting experts as time and inclination allows. This means that some drawers, of the more obscure groups, can remain shut up for years on end. If a single museum beetle gets into a drawer and starts laying eggs, by the time that drawer next gets opened, months, years or decades later, all that may remain is an array of pins and data labels amid a sea of chewed insect dust. Every museum in the world will have tales of unique and irreplaceable specimens, whole drawers of them, destroyed by this tiny fiend. For a museum curator, or an entomologist, that really is the end.

VII

They're after us:

BLOODSUCKERS

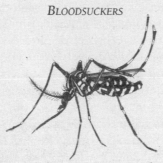

It is perhaps one of the supreme ironies that humans created their shelters not just to escape the weather, but also to get away from hungry carnivores, only to find that they had created the perfect microhabitats for a new band of secret microcarnivores – the bloodsuckers. Blood had been sucked before, often enough – mosquitoes, midges, ticks and leeches were but a few of the many attackers to have targeted humans and prehumans long before caves or bivouacs had been contemplated. But the false sense of security imparted by the sacred space has opened up humans to even more frustrating attack.

uman blood (indeed all mammalian and avian blood) is a useful high-protein nutrient; it is conveniently liquidised for easy consumption, uniform in consistency and biochemical make-up for easy digestion, and readily discoverable by virtue of the copious animal scents and smells given off by its owners. It is no surprise that bloodsucking has evolved on more than 20 separate occasions in insects, and also in ticks, leeches and vampire bats (Lehane 2005). Nevertheless, this is quite some achievement, because drinking blood is not just a passive puncturing and lapping up; it is inserting a delicate hypodermic needle and having to prevent the very capable anti-bleeding effects of the host's clotting mechanisms from immediately blocking up the attacker's mouthparts.

Human blood clotting is a complex business, but because it is so important in medicine it is rather well understood. Briefly, damage to the capillary blood vessels exposes a 'tissue factor', which activates tiny circulating blood cells called platelets. The platelets bind to the underlying tissue of the damaged area, changing shape as they do so from smooth spheres to long-tendrilled mop-heads, and creating a tangled primary plug. Meanwhile circulating 'clotting factor' proteins bind to the platelets to strengthen the clot. It's all very biochemical bricks and mortar, but there are countless different chemicals involved in a veritable physiological cascade. It all happens in milliseconds, and it is very effective, otherwise we'd quickly bleed to death every time we nicked ourselves shaving or slipped with the bread knife.

In order to take a swig of human blood an attacker initially has to locally disable the clotting system, and this always involves injecting anticoagulant chemicals of its own first, before it can take down its bloody draught. It is the human body's immune response to these alien proteins that causes the allergic reaction of the itchy spot, and in some people a more ferocious reaction causes a swollen bite mark as big as a hen's egg. This is annoying enough at the time, but the real impact of bloodsucking comes later. Along with the anticoagulants, to keep its mouthparts clear the bloodsucker can inject much more sinister substances, most notably the spores (technically called sporozoites) of malaria, sleeping sickness, Leishmaniasis and Chagas diseases; the microscopic bloodworm larvae that cause elephantiasis; bacteria like Lyme disease, plague and typhus; and viruses like yellow fever, dengue and encephalitis. For humans the importance of bloodsuckers is not in the tiny drop of blood that they remove, but in the legacy of the diseases that they can leave behind.

Different bloodsuckers have evolved relationships with different diseases. Quite often it is only one particular species or closely related group that is implicated, and the species involved vary from one part of the globe to another. *Anopheles* mosquitoes can spread malaria, whilst *Aedes* mosquitoes are vectors of yellow fever and dengue. Ticks are carriers of Lyme disease. Fleas spread plague. Body lice carry typhus. Many of these formerly dreaded diseases are now understood, and some have been eradicated or at least are controlled in parts of the world.

Ague, the traditional English name for the endemic malaria of East Anglia, disappeared from the UK in around 1900, and was gone from southern Europe and the USA by the 1950s. Malaria is still extant in many tropical countries, but has long been treated with quinine and other antimalarials. This is fine for wealthy Western tourists, but expensive enough to be out of the reach of many, and malaria still kills roughly 700,000 people a year, mostly children in Sub Saharan Africa. Plague is now the stuff of history books and nursery rhymes (unless you live in India, Africa or Madagascar). Typhus is merely a dark memory from the itchy days of lice-infested clothing; nothing to do with head lice, thankfully (except, perhaps, in Ethiopia or Peru). It is too easy to be smug, especially in the comfort of our civilised homes. In the West we may have conquered many of these diseases, but there is still opportunity for the same painfully biting bloodsuckers to visit us, and the diseases they carry have not stopped evolving.

THROUGH THE CURTAIN – THEY CAN SMELL US IN OUR SLEEP

Anyone who has wandered marshes on a warm, sunny day will know how quickly mosquitoes appear, and hover in a cloud around the head. In the open they, together with horse-flies, cleg-flies *Haematopota pluvialis* and other biting flies, are attracted to your silhouette presented against the open sky. This is, after all, one of the best ways of finding a cow or horse, or other blood-filled animal, out in the fields. This strategy does not work inside a building, but mosquitoes have another prey-detection method – smell.

Humans, like all mammals and birds, breathe out carbon dioxide, a gas that mosquitoes can detect at very low concentrations with special chemoreceptor organs on their antennae. They can also distinguish between a constant low-level background concentration, such as that given off in general decay from the soil and leaf litter, or from fires, and the characteristic regular pulses given off during animal breathing. Again, like silhouette hunting, this is a long- to medium-distance detection technique working best out of doors, but carbon dioxide also acts as a trigger, enhancing a mosquito antenna's sensitivity to human skin odours.

Humans (and other animals) give off many different aromatic chemical signals, although they may be imperceptible to us today, after we are showered and bathed clean at regular intervals. Our noses are no longer the most sensitive organs anyway. If we take a big sniff of purified skin chemicals collected in a laboratory vial, we might just about notice a hint of fruity musk, but insect antennae work at the level of detecting just a few airborne molecules. Despite soap, eau de toilette, deodorant and expensive perfumes, it is by smelling us out that mosquitoes can find us indoors, in the dark, when we sleep. Once inside the house, finding us to bite is relatively easy; it is finding a way in through the doors in the first place that was their greatest ecological jump.

Mosquitoes lay their eggs in fresh water – rivers, ditches, lakes, ponds, puddles – and their wriggling larvae feed on tiny morsels of decaying organic matter in the murk. When they hatch into adult flies, the males are happy to visit flowers to drink nectar for energy, but the females must take a vertebrate blood meal to get enough protein for the eggs developing in their ovaries. Finding a natural marshland animal like a buffalo or horse by its silhouette and carbon dioxide puffs is easy enough, so why venture into the dark confines of a human shelter? This, at first, seems unlikely behaviour for a swamp-inhabiting fly.

Mosquitoes, however, are a widely diverse group (Jones 2012), with many thousands of different species around the world, and although most live and bite outdoors, there are plenty with alternative behaviours. Away from the marshes a few species lay their eggs in the flooded rot-holes in old trees, where a branch has fallen and the heartwood has rotted away to form a dark cavity that fills with rainwater. Others will utilise small puddles, water-filled hoofprints, ruts, drains or blocked gutters. Some species feed during the day, others roost in sunlight, seeking out a rock crevice, small cave or dark shade from hanging leaves and dense branches under which to hide so that they can feed at night. Similar dark, dry spaces offer overwintering sites to adult mosquitoes. In the end it is no surprise that among all their variety, some inquisitive mosquito species were ready to fly in through an open window into the interior darkness as soon as houses were built.

Instinctive house-entering behaviour is under genetic control. In East Africa the yellow fever mosquito *Aedes aegypti*, a major vector of dengue virus, is very common and widespread, living near human habitation and also well away from it in the wilderness. Laboratory breeding and release studies showed that domestic larvae collected around buildings, living in water dregs in old pottery, tin cans and animal troughs, produced adults more likely to enter buildings to feed; feral larvae collected from tree-holes in the jungle were less likely to do so (Trpis and Hausermann 1978). The clincher is that peridomestic larvae, living in between, in the steps cut into the trunks of coconut palms, were intermediate in their behaviour and may be genetic hybrids. There is no simple on/off switch for house entering; like most complex behaviours, it is under the control of many genes, the understanding of which is still some way off. Nevertheless, there is often a close link between a mosquito species being an indoor biter and breeding in small water pockets close to human habitation.

It is tempting to suggest that the arrival of pottery in human prehistory, around 10,000 years ago, could have been a major advance for mosquitoes, as they found discarded broken but flooded receptacles in which to lay their eggs right on human doorsteps – in the septic fringe rubbish midden perhaps. This much is speculation, but in a strange twist, a possible recurrence of these potential human/mosquito relations is going on in modern-day Queensland, Australia. A decade of droughts has encouraged householders to store rainwater in garden containers, and this has increased the numbers of mosquitoes breeding there (Trewin *et al.* 2013). There are fears that this mirrors the container-breeding fauna when the yellow fever mosquito was more prevalent in the area, particularly from 1904 to 1943, when dengue epidemics occurred.

During the malaria and yellow-fever reduction campaigns of the early 20th century, mesh screening of water tanks and the removal of rubbish from the streets was a key tactic to reduce the availability of mosquito breeding sites in disease-oppressed towns and cities (Boyce 1910). Flooded tin cans littering the streets are still a minor problem in some places today, and water slops in secondhand tyres could herald a major disease epidemic in the 21st century. The Asian tiger mosquito *Aedes albopictus*, named for its pretty banded patterning and aggressive biting behaviour, has been spread from its original native range in South-east Asia, into southern Europe and much of the USA, and it is making inroads into South America and West Africa. Its aquatic larvae have been accidentally transported about the globe in the rainwater accumulating in secondhand tyres (Hawley *et al.* 1987). There is a major world trade in reusing and remoulding the tyres, but because they are hardy and non-perishable, they are liable to be left on docksides, uncovered, in all weathers. They soon accumulate pockets of rainwater and are easily accessible to egg-laying mosquitoes.

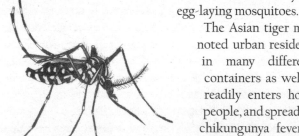

The Asian tiger mosquito is a noted urban resident, breeding in many different flooded containers as well as tyres. It readily enters homes to bite people, and spreads dengue and chikungunya fever, and West Nile virus – all debilitating and sometimes deadly maladies. At the time of writing this book Australia

Asian tiger mosquito *Aedes albopictus*

and New Zealand are on full Asian tiger mosquito alert. The mosquito has been intercepted at several seaports, and has already become established in the Torres Strait Islands just off the Queensland coast (Ritchie *et al.* 2006).

Litter in the form of flooded pots, tin cans, broken jam jars, tyres and other rubbish is not always necessary to sustain populations of house-invading mosquitoes. Throughout the world some species are generally more prone to come indoors than others, and almost inevitably many have acquired major importance when

Anopheles maculipennis

it comes to biting humans and spreading human diseases. Detailed study of British mosquitoes during the 1930s showed that what was at first thought to be a single species, *Anopheles maculipennis*, was actually a group of closely related sister species. Two species were virtually identical as adults, but could be distinguished by the patterns on their floating egg masses. One form, *A. messeae*, laid its eggs in inland pools, hardly ever bit humans and was not a disease carrier. The other form, *A. atroparvus*, laid its eggs in coastal marshes, often came into houses to roost, frequently bit humans and was historically responsible for spreading ague (malaria) in lowland England (Edwards *et al.* 1939).

The sinisterly named *Culex molestus* has taken indoor biting to an extreme. On the face of it almost identical to the globally common and widespread *Culex pipiens*, even under a microscope, this ferocious biter first came to the attention of medical entomologists when the beleaguered citizenry of London took to sheltering in the deep railway platforms of the London Underground to escape the night-time bombing during the 1940–1941 Blitz (Shute 1951). DNA studies show that it is distinct from the surface-dwelling *C. pipiens*, and has adapted to breeding in the rainwater puddles along the subterranean

Culex pipiens

rail lines. Such is the isolation of different populations in the tunnels that different branches of the underground railways are now evolving genetically different strains (Byrne and Nichols 1999).

C. pipiens normally feeds on bird blood, but *C. molestus* bites mammals – the mice and rats infesting the tunnels, and the daily herds of human commuters and shelterers. It also breeds all year round in the mild, temperature-stable tunnels, rather than just in summer, a characteristic also noted in similar *C. pipiens/C. molestus* species complexes in Croatian cellars, Portuguese caves and several other metropolitan subway systems in North America, Japan and Australia (Merdic and Vuljicic-Karlo 2005). There is more to this behavioural plasticity than mere annoyance at yet another human-biting mosquito species. Intermediates between *C. pipiens* and *C. molestus* occur where the populations overlap. The exchange of one type of host (birds) for another (humans) may just be enough to transfer blood-borne diseases, too. *C. pipiens* is a major vector of bird arboviruses; Japanese encephalitis and West Nile virus are arboviruses from this same group, and they have recently become important human diseases.

THE BED BUG – IT BITES US IN OUR BEDS, OBVIOUSLY

Bed bugs do not spread human diseases, but they cause no end of headache. *Cimex lectularius*, to give the aptly named bed bug its modern scientific name, is a broad, round, flat, reddish-brown wingless insect. It is also called wall-louse (for its habit of hiding under wallpaper), red-coat (for its blood-filled colour), crimson rambler (likewise) and mahogany flat (it is, indeed, very flat).

This is the notorious bloodsucking bug that infests cheap hotel rooms the world over – and some not so cheap ones, as I discovered in the elegant but faded grandeur of a hotel in the Sri Lankan capital Colombo some years ago. It hides during the day between the planks of a bedstead, or tucked into the folds of sheets, but sneaks out to bite at night. Its presence is usually only detected the morning after a stay in a room where it is present, when the red welts left at the puncture wounds or some spilled blood on the bed sheets are discovered.

At only 5.5–7mm long, the bed bug is quite small, but it can drink a huge amount of blood in comparison to its body size. An adult female weighing 6mg unfed was able to consume nearly 14mg of blood (Goddard 2009). She could do this because she has an enormously flexible body. Although flat to start with, the abdomen of the bed bug has wide, elastic membranes between the hard armour plates. As the bug feeds the abdomen swells grossly into bloated satiation.

The main medical (and veterinary) importance of bed bugs is in the sheer volume of blood extracted, with victims living in highly infested conditions (5,000 bugs per bed have been reported) receiving many hundreds or thousands of bites nightly. In one particularly gruesome account a homeless semi-destitute man was living in a single room alive with many thousands of the bugs, some of which were lodging under his uncut curled toenails and between his toughened and filth-impregnated toes (Burgess and Cowan 1993). Blood loss can become very significant, leading to iron deficiency and anaemia, not to mention irritability from disturbed sleep. The emotional distress can be misdiagnosed as neurosis, or it can lead to costly lawsuits from disgruntled wealthy guests of luxury hotels. How things have changed.

Bed bug *Cimex lectularius*

When my father, aged 14, manhandled a secondhand bed through the bombed-out streets of Shepherd's Bush and Paddington on a borrowed costermonger's barrow in

1944, he was pleased with his thrifty purchase, but not at all surprised when blood spots appeared on the sheets a few days later. Unlike the surgical precision of a mosquito, bed bug feeding is a brutal and imprecise action, and repeated probings with the rather stout, blunt stylet mouthparts often leave a trail of adjacent small bites before the true feed puncture is made. Instead of panicking or trying to sue someone, my father and his mother set about stripping and dismantling the bed, cleaning it and removing the vermin. In a time of hardship and deprivation, this would have been completely normal.

Bed bugs went through a bit of a slump in the second half of the 20th century, and a nuisance insect that everyone had heard of, even though they may not have necessarily been pestered by it, appeared to be in terminal decline. A modern lack of public awareness and the insects' resistance to chemical insecticides may explain why the bugs are making a comeback today, but it is their evolution in the long term, how and when they first started biting human beings, which is even more fascinating. For whether they are hidden in the plump mattresses of five-star hotels, or in the cramped palliasse in a wayside tropical camp, one question keeps arising: where did bed bugs live in the first place, before we humans offered them our blood, and before we had beds to sleep on?

John Southall, writing his *Treatise of Buggs* (1730) thought he knew – they lived on trees, more particularly 'Firr' trees, and he assured his readers that the sap of deal in particular was 'one of their beloved foods'. Nonsense, of course, but Southall had his reasons for stating this. He was shamelessly advertising a concoction to destroy the bugs – his 'Nonpareil liquor' – and by way of self-promotion he wrote his pamphlet about their life cycle, their increasing numbers, their destruction and, most intriguingly, 'when and how they were first brought into England'. He pinpoints their arrival directly to the 1670s, blaming the traders whose ships daily sailed into British ports bringing 'chests and casks, linnens and paper' riddled with the insects. He makes the astute observation that port towns and cities are thick with bed bug infestations, but villages further inland are less troubled, if at all.

There were certainly widespread reports of bed bugs in and around the metropolis in the decade following the Great Fire of

London, in 1666, and one of the usual stories has it that they arrived with building timber (notably deal) imported from the Americas. The bug's arrival in the 1670s is now well established, but this was not the first time it had appeared in England. Remains of bed bugs were dug from a pit dated to the 2nd century AD in the Roman town of Alcester in Warwickshire, and there is a tale (though highly likely to be apocryphal) that King John (1199–1216) was troubled by them at Kingsclere in Hampshire.

The first real evidence of bed bugs' occurrence comes from the writings of Thomas Moufet (sometimes Moffet or Muffet, stepfather of the Little Miss of nursery rhyme curds-and-whey fame), who clearly and accurately describes the 'wall louse' in his *Theatre of Insects* published posthumously in 1634. It recounts how the bugs were troublesome to two ladies of a noble family at Mortlake, Surrey, in 1583. The high status of the victims' family is no mere name-dropping snobbery on the part of Moufet. Their social standing says much about the fact that bed bugs need the warmth of a well-heated house to breed and multiply to pest proportions; and at this time they were unlikely to be found much in the unheated hovels of the English peasantry.

There seems little doubt, now, that bed bugs had probably crept into Britain since time immemorial, but that they did not become established enough to warrant major pest status until the late 17th century, when John Southall patented his liquor.

An American or at least a Caribbean origin of the bugs is hinted at by Southall, who claims to distinguish between American and European bugs – the former slightly larger, the latter a smaller degenerate form. The New World source of the bed bug suited Southall's New World Nonpareil Liquor. He was able to charge two shillings a bottle for it, enough to treat a 'common bed'. That was more than the weekly wage of the servant who might be applying the treatment.

However, contrary to Southall's supposition, bed bugs were firmly rooted in the Old World. They were recorded from Italy and Germany in the 11th century, and France in the 13th century. They were well known in classical times, when they were called *koris* (a name still used for many plant bugs today) and *cimex*, the official scientific name entomologists now apply to bed bugs. The bed links to the bloodsucker were already known to the Ancient Greeks five centuries before Christ, and are discussed by Aristotle, Aristophanes and others (Beavis 1988). Bed bug remains have recently been found in archaeological excavations in Egypt. Beyond Ancient Egypt written records are lost and subfossil remains are scant, but an extrapolated history of the bed bug can still be guessed at by examining the modern insects and their relations to other, similar species.

Although *C. lectularius* is the human bed bug of choice in temperate latitudes, it is replaced by the very similar, but subtly different, *C. hemipterus* in the tropics. There are also another 16 species (at least) of *Cimex* known across the world, and a further 70 or so bloodsucking bugs in the bed bug family Cimicidae. They all have similar broad, round body shapes, all are wingless and all feed by sucking vertebrate blood. More particularly they attack bats and birds. Even more particularly, they attack bats, pigeons, swifts, martins and swallows – birds that, as already noted, originally nested in caves and on rock-faces, long before humans had emerged and built the first houses or laid down on the first beds. Caves, it seems, are where humans (and birds) first picked up these bugs, and it is likely that bats are the original hosts. Incidentally, bats are also blamed for being the original hosts for the fungal diseases of ringworm and athlete's foot. But it is their gift of bed bugs, however, that we should most resent.

It's temping to speculate that for millions of years progenitor bloodsucker bugs feasted on the blood of the bats that roosted in a roughly weathered rock cavern somewhere in the East African savannah, when one day a tired primate shuffled in and slumped down onto the floor. To the bugs it was just another food source to be exploited. They have continued to exploit it to this day – it's just that now, rather than scuttling off into rock crevices, the bugs find perfect shelter in the joints of bedsteads, the cracks in floorboards, and the tight spaces behind peeling wallpaper and loose skirting.

BUGS AND BUGBEARS – NIGHT-TIME NUISANCES, PAINS IN THE BUTT

In a nice etymological, rather than merely entomological, twist *C. lectularius* was the first insect, courtesy of Mr Southall's informative pamphlet, to achieve the common English name 'bug'. Nowadays almost any insect, or indeed any invertebrate from giant squid to bacterium or virus, can loosely be called a bug, but to entomologists true bugs are really only those insects, with sucking rather than chewing mouthparts, that are in the order Hemiptera. This is the group that includes shieldbugs, stinkbugs, water boatmen, pond skaters, aphids, leaf-hoppers and scale insects. Most of these are plant feeders, using their tubular mouthparts to suck plant sap, but a large number have evolved predatory behaviour, skewering other small insects and sucking out their innards. Not surprisingly, the Hemiptera have also produced bloodsucking insects like bed bugs. This probably arose from insect-feeding bugs living in animal nests where they fed on fly maggots, flea larvae, beetle grubs and each other, but occasionally taking an exploratory poke at a nest owner's flesh, almost by accident, in the darkness. A small relative of the bed bug, the debris bug *Lyctocoris campestris*, lives in barns, haystacks and the odd grain store, feeding on the other insects in there, but can give a sharp nip if picked up (Busvine 1976).

Before Southall, the term 'bug' really meant a bugbear, similar to bogeyman (sometimes bogie or boggart), and usually referred to some ill-formed neurotic worry or night terror, although it was sometimes personified into the shape of a hobgoblin. Whether Southall picked up his usage from reports of night-time feeding of the bed bug is not completely clear, but it is during the night that humans are most susceptible to vampire feeding. Vampire bats, three species in the Central and South American family Desmodontidae, occasionally roost in decrepid old buildings, but they mainly feed on wild and farm animals. Human victims are usually limited to the unfortunate homeless poor, or campers sleeping out in the open. However, there is a group of true bugs for which the term 'vampire' is much more appropriate.

Fly bug *Reduvius personatus*

The assassin bugs are a large and diverse group of Hemiptera, well named for their aggressive predatory behaviour. They are often large and stoutly built insects, with long legs to move stealthily and grip firmly, and powerful stabbing mouthparts. Most feed on other insects, caterpillars, maggots or worms, but several have adapted to sucking the blood of birds and mammals, including humans. The widespread European species *Reduvius personatus*, often called the masked hunter or fly bug, occurs in old houses and also some commercial premises, and although it mainly feeds on other household insects (bed bugs are a favourite), it can give a painful bite if carelessly picked up, and will also take advantage of the sleeping human form to drink down a little of the body's red liquor.

Elsewhere in the world larger and even more aggressive assassin bugs can become a real problem. In Central and South America several species of *Panstrongylus*, *Triatoma* and *Rhodnius* are called kissing bugs because of their habit of biting the faces of human sleepers, especially near the eyes. They hide during the day in crevices around a bed, or in the folds of bedclothes. Their bite, or resultant swelling afterwards, is very painful. This is not just down to the irritant prick or injected blood anticoagulants. The bug's faeces get rubbed into the wound, or into the eyes (notably in children) causing the eyelids to swell – Romaña's sign, named after the Argentinian doctor who first noticed the phenomenon.

Kissing bugs also spread the parasitic protozoan *Trypanosoma cruzi*, known as Chagas disease after the Brazilian physician who first described it in 1909. Once injected into the body the parasite multiplies in the lymphatic nodes and muscle tissue, causing glandular swellings, fever, fatigue and body aches. Then large numbers of infective stages are released into the bloodstream, for another assassin bug to pick up for onwards transmission to yet more victims. Although people can live apparently symptom free for many years, chronic infection can lead to serious disorders of the heart and digestive tract, and may eventually be fatal.

Kissing assassins cannot always get a human blood meal. They have been found in the burrows of various native rodents, such as house mice and black rats; others live with communal hole-nesting birds like pigeons. The broad, flat young (nymphs) are covered all over with a sticky substance, and they disguise themselves by coating their bodies with sand, dust, fluff and other debris – a good technique to enable you to hide if you are living right inside the den of your victim.

Sleeping, far from being the restful recovery we might expect, can be a dangerous business. At least rough beds raised above the dirt give some protection from attack (although bed bugs and assassin bugs are good climbers). In areas of tropical Africa, maggots of the deceptively cute-sounding tumbu fly *Cordylobia anthropophaga* and the Congo floor maggot *Auchmeromyia luteola* come wriggling out of the bare, dusty ground looking for a tasty mammalian meal. The adult insects, about the size of blow flies, lay their eggs in the soil, especially if there is contamination with faeces, but also in damp clothing or bedding.

The tumbu fly grub will, if it has a chance, burrow into the flesh of the cheeks, arms, lower back or buttocks, causing a boil-like swelling in which it feeds for two weeks before popping out and pupating. The congo floor maggot prefers to pierce the skin and drink the dribbling

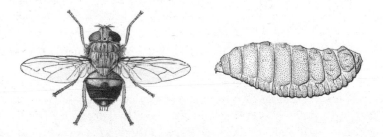

Tumbu fly *Cordylobia anthropophaga* and maggot

blood. It is well adapted to its intermittent feeding opportunities and has the accolade of being the fly larva able to withstand the longest fast between meals, surviving 48 days in laboratory tests (Garret-Jones 1951). The original hosts for both species were probably wild animals, particularly burrowing warthogs, aardvarks, hyenas and wild pigs, but they now commonly attack dogs and chickens, so the flies are often near domestic dwellings. It is us humans, literally being eaten alive, who are generally regarded as being the primary hosts today. The rest of the world should be perennially thankful that neither the tumbu fly nor the congo floor fly followed humans on their long migrations out of Africa.

VIII

Hangers on:

FORGOTTEN FRIENDS, CASUAL VISITORS AND A RAGTAG OF OTHER
UNINVITED CALLERS

*H*umans have only been human for a million years or so, and have been building houses for only a few thousand years. This is nothing in the unimaginably long evolutionary timescale over which animals on this planet have been slowly and subtly changing and adapting. In the last few centuries, a mere twinkle of time for them, humans have made the greatest changes to human society, in terms of urban living and modern house design. By rights we ought to have outwitted common nature by now and left it behind, but our homes are still invaded or intruded upon.

he same attractions that enticed visitors over the threshold countless thousands of years ago still hold true today – shelter, warmth, dryness and stored food (be it meat, vegetables, grain, wood or human blood). There are some old favourites that have been with us since the beginning, but things constantly change. The household visitors of today are subtly different than they were even a generation or two ago. Fashions in household accoutrements, furnishings, food items and clothing have all had an effect. Among the grain weevils and bed bugs that have been with humans since the Neolithic period, new interlopers still appear, while others that were once apparently commonplace are now in decline.

THE LOSERS – SHOULD WE FEEL SORRY FOR THEM?

Throughout the literature of archaeological entomology, one species keeps cropping up again and again. *Aglenus brunneus* is a minute (1–2mm), cylindrical brown beetle lacking eyes and wings, and although it is fairly widespread in the world, it is secretive and rarely found. I'm very good at finding insects, and I've never found it. Its natural habitat is the leaf litter in European forests and woodland, where it occurs sporadically just above and just below the soil level, under logs or against old roots. It can also sometimes be found in manure heaps, hotbeds and mouldy haystacks, and although it does sometimes turn up in cellar refuse or in the mouldering remains at the bottoms of old corn-storage bins, no modern book on domestic pests (other than this one) would give it page space. Yet its remains are among the most common finds in archaeological digs from the Romans onwards (Kenward 1975; Buckland 1981).

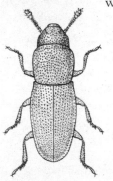
Aglenus brunneus

Its body parts are regularly unearthed (sometimes in large numbers) in digs throughout Britain and the rest of Europe. By the end of the Roman period it was to be found in obscure regions of Egypt and the Middle East; it seems to have arrived in Iceland in the Middle Ages, and has been widespread in North America since European colonisation. Being blind and flightless, it has relied on human travel and trade for its distribution, but its zenith in medieval times has passed. The reason for its rise and fall is probably all to do with changes in household hygiene.

Until well into Elizabethan times the usual domestic floor was bare dirt, trodden down solid, but scattered with dry straw or cut rushes, which could periodically be cleared out and replaced. Sweet-smelling herbs like mint were strewn to cover the smells, as all manner of household refuse (and probably animal dung) were dropped. This would have created the ideal habitat for blind, flightless, scavenging *Aglenus brunneus*; even when it came to a spring clean, a scratchy besom broom of twigs would have missed tiny reservoirs of infested decay in the corners of the rooms. The change came with the modern fashion for suspended floors of wooden boards. With the rush and straw coverings now gone, *Aglenus brunneus* retreated back to the woodland, with just the occasional colony surviving in a compost bin or beneath an abandoned hay bale.

Soon rugs, then carpets took over, and although we still suffer those carpet beetles and wool-eating clothes moths in them today, they too have suffered from the invention of another new-fangled fashion – the vacuum cleaner (which also did for fleas). Infestations, although still present, and sometimes replenished by new beetles and moths flying indoors from neighbours' houses, are much less common than they were even half a century ago, when many houses still relied on a less efficient push-pull carpet sweeper, or a dustpan and stiff-bristled brush, to keep the carpets clear of mud.

I doubt whether anyone will mourn these carpet eaters, but a tiny dark fly once also found in these houses may be on the way out too. The window fly *Scenopinus fenestralis* could be thought of as a beneficial insect, since its narrow, snake-like predatory larvae seek out and eat house-moth caterpillars, carpet-beetle grubs and the maggots of any

Window fly *Scenopinus fenestralis*

other domestic pest they can find. It is only ever discovered when it has completed its development and the adult emerging flies waddle around on the inside of a window pane trying to get out. I used to find it regularly on the kitchen windows when I first moved into my south London house 15 years ago. I have no doubt that the flies were breeding in that disreputable kitchen carpet, the one which was grubby not only in the sense that it was stained, but also in the sense that it was infested with larder beetle grubs. Here was a plentiful food source for the window fly, until we cleared them all out. I've not seen it since.

Being one level further up the food chain from the beetles has an important consequence for the window fly. First, its populations can only really survive if it has a good supply of food, meaning a healthy colony of carpet beetles and clothes moths to feed on. If, as has been happening, its prey is being systematically eradicated by disgruntled vacuum-cleaning humans annoyed that holes are appearing in their rugs, the prey density falls below a level viable for the window fly larvae to survive. Second, with prey populations being extinguished, the chances of recolonisation from the house next-door also fall.

Each small window fly population, barely surviving, becomes like a small island in a large, hostile sea, with other suitable islands nearby all slowly vanishing beneath the waves. Eventually all the remaining islands of prey are just too far from each other to allow any recolonisation at all. At this point the window fly ceases to be a domestic denizen. It may revert to a sparse natural human-free existence, like its very close relative the ironically named forest window fly *Scenopinus niger*, which lives in ancient woodland where there are no windows, but where its larvae can feed on beetle and fly grubs living in the dusty rotten hearts of veteran trees and fungoid stumps.

Another one-time irregular passer-by at the window casement is a small, slightly hairy metallic blue beetle, the blue clerid beetle

Korynetes caeruleus. It is one of a series of scavenging carrion beetles that also used to feed on old bones (when they were a commercial commodity in the glue-making industry), but which would sometimes occur in old houses. As an alternative to chewing dried sinews, it was also predatory on the larvae of window flies, house moths, woodworm and death-watch beetles. Like the window fly and for the same reasons, the blue clerid beetle has all but vanished from domestic houses now. The last time I saw one it was many years ago; it

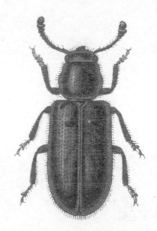

Blue clerid beetle *Korynetes caeruleus*

was crawling on a window sill in the National Trust's Knole House, near Sevenoaks in Kent, when some renovation work was being done in one of the royal bedrooms, and the ancient, worm-riddled wood panelling was being removed and repaired. In ridding the building of the death-watch beetle, its predator was also being extinguished. The beetle still lives as an uncommon outdoor carrion feeder, but its domestic association has all but ceased.

And whatever happened to the house cricket? All the old books, not just entomological textbooks, but books by authors from Shakespeare to Dickens, constantly allude to the cricket chirruping in the kitchen or around the hearth. It was never really considered a major nuisance; unlike its relatives the locusts, crickets have a much better public image. Jiminy Grasshopper just doesn't sound right. When, in 1850, Miss L. M. Budgen wrote *Episodes of Insect Life*, a popular (and slightly patronising) series of general essays to 'instruct' the reader, she chose for herself the light-hearted and unassuming pseudonym *Acheta domestica*, the scientific name of the house cricket. Among a certain strata of society it was considered undignified for ladies to stoop to the commercial lows of publishing, and her choice might appear odd, except for the fact that there has always been a fondness for these seemingly gentle and musical creatures.

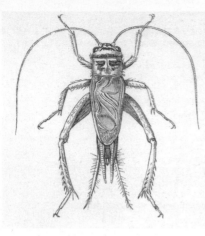

House cricket *Acheta domestica*

Nevertheless, like cockroaches, crickets are omnivorous, scavenging on raw and cooked meat and vegetables, bread products, leather scraps and other insects. In northern temperate latitudes they only occur in or near houses, although they will take up residence in rubbish dumps where fermentation in the heaps raises the temperature above the cold cut-off point below which they cannot breed.

In the Far East many different cricket species were kept as singing pets in small wire cages, and long before modern systematicists allocated scientific labels to them they were given friendly local names like 'golden bell', 'weaving lady' and 'singing brother'. It's quite likely that the now-cosmopolitan house cricket originally started its human association in South-west Asia or India, an early household visitor once human agriculture was established.

I once heard what I thought must be cricket singing in the back garden of a neighbouring south London house late one summer evening a few years ago. Whether it was truly the house cricket, I never found out. Certainly it would not have been the only other UK species – the critically endangered field cricket *Gryllus campestris*. It could, however, have been an escapee from a packet of the insects readily available in pet shops or via online stores, which supply various unnamed live crickets for enthusiasts to feed to their pet lizards and tarantulas. A word of caution here to any pet owners who feed their exotics with live crickets – do not on, any account, deliberately release the insects into your garden. In September 2013 an Oxford plant scientist released 1,000 crickets he bought on the Internet, because he liked the sound they made, which evoked memories of the tropics. His actions contravened UK wildlife laws, which prohibit the release of alien species that might become invasive or negatively affect native plants and animals. He was issued with a police caution, and ordered to trap and remove them all.

So a few household critters are on the wane. They are in a minority compared with the hard core of permanent house dwellers that have been the subjects of previous chapters. There is also a multitude of borderline oddities, a weird selection of creatures that have dropped in, stayed for a while maybe, but which have never quite made that jump to full and complete domesticity. Or perhaps some are on the cusp – they could be the regulars of the future.

PART-TIME LODGERS – THEY COME, THEY GO, THEY LEAVE A MESS

Watching wildlife in the garden is all very well, as long as it stays there. The sacred space of the house remains inviolable. This includes any attic and the underfloor area too. Because of the need to ensure ventilation beneath the roof, vents are common under the eaves of buildings. In the UK most traditional brick homes have an underfloor subspace accessible only through the occasional perforated air-brick. Elsewhere in the world (Canada and the USA in particular) timber-framed houses often have large, open gaps between the floorboards and the ground beneath. This is extremely helpful when it comes to installing and maintaining electrical wires, plumbing and air-conditioning ducts, and it makes a useful storage space for the lawnmower or children's bikes, but it also gives easy access to inquisitive animals.

In the UK foxes and badgers already share an ambivalence from householders when it comes to garden visits. On the one hand they are cute and fluffy and true wildlife, on the other they dig things up, chew garden toys, defecate everywhere and spill refuse from dustbins. Having them excavate dens under the fabric of the building would almost inevitably be too much. Thankfully, this type of intimate household association is rare.

In North America, however, the standard building techniques often allow easy access under the house to the local fauna. Striped skunks *Mephitis mephitis*, spotted skunks *Spilogale putorius* and North

American porcupines *Erethizon dorsatum* might be as endearing as foxes and badgers, if it were not for their remarkable defence mechanisms. The infamy of skunks is such that they barely need to use their foul-smelling anal spray glands; the distinctive aroma follows them about and a house owner will know that they have been scratching around in the rubbish, because the scent lingers in the air when they have passed by. Although unlikely to take up nesting behaviour under an occupied house, skunks and porcupines are inquisitive animals and are often attracted to buildings to scavenge (skunks) or chew wood (porcupines), particularly garden-implement handles, tools and furniture impregnated with sweat.

Raccoons *Procyon lotor* are definitely more cuddly, and their appealing face markings, pert, cat-like ears and delicately prehensile paws often encourage people to hand feed them in parks and gardens. Becoming increasingly acclimatised to humans, they are now familiar urban animals throughout metropolitan North America, and there are introduced colonies in Germany, Bellarus, Azerbaijan and Japan. Originally woodland animals adapted to tree climbing, they are very capable of finding their way into disused barns and attics, where they can make a considerable mess when they create dens. Although unlikely to attack and bite humans, they (and skunks) carry and can spread rabies.

Lofts in the UK are only really likely to be invaded by the birds mentioned earlier (see page 56), or maybe squirrels if your cottage is thatched – unless you live in the Chilterns. If you do own a house in one of the charming villages in these picturesque limestone hills north and west of London, you might find the night-time scrapings there are made by the edible or fat dormouse *Glis glis*. Related to the common or hazel dormouse *Muscardinus avellanarius*, which is a widespread denizen of hedgerows and copses, the edible dormouse is 'fat' because it is much larger, like a small squirrel, and also because it was once fattened up for eating. Famously the Romans first brought edible dormice to Britain 2,000 years ago, keeping them in special terracotta pots called *dolia* until they were plump enough for the table.

Edible dormice did not survive in Britain during the Dark Ages, but Lionel Walter (Lord) Rothschild of Tring was an enthusiastic and very wealthy Victorian naturalist, and he kept some as a minor part of his large private museum and menagerie until they escaped in 1902 (Thompson 1953). There are now reckoned to be more than 10,000 living in the area, and as well as having a penchant for loft living they like chewing electricity cables, so their presence is often betrayed by the lights going out. Dormice, like the squirrels to which they are related, are tree-dwelling animals, and make their nests in the crooks of large

Edible dormouse *Glis glis*

branches, hollow logs, dead trunks and log piles. Climbing into the loft is an easy transition.

For such a relatively small animal edible dormice are remarkable noisy, as I can attest from their occupation of the attic above the Provencal gite in which I stayed recently. So as not to upset the sensibilities of the regular English visitors, the owners' guide to the house insisted on calling the dormice by the French name *loirs*, rather than risking any idea that there might be rodent vermin in the roof.

It is ever the lot of the slightly relatively unusual house guests, like mouse-like dormice, to be mistrusted beyond their rightful measure. This is simply down to the fact that they are not quite familiar enough to us, or that we confuse them with other creatures. We are not used to them, so we don't understand them; if we don't understand them we fear them, and if we fear them we will not tolerate them. That unfamiliarity breeds unnecessary disgust and loathing for many other slightly out of the ordinary household visitors.

Hoverflies ought to be praised, some for their aphid-feeding larvae, most for their pollination efforts and all for their striking and attractive forms. However, their bee- or wasp-mimicking colours can cause some concern. These are outdoor insects, but several of the largest, most boldly patterned species regularly turn up indoors. Here they can

Hoverfly *Volucella zonaria*

cause unwarranted anxiety. These are members of the genus *Volucella* and they normally breed in bees' and wasps' nests, their short, thick, wrinkled maggots feeding on detritus under and around the combs, and also on some of the host brood.

The large flies buzzing, rather lazily it has to be said, around the ceiling or windows, are apt to get thrashed by a rolled up newspaper because they resemble hornets *Vespa crabo* or large wasps, but they are completely harmless. And they have usually not come indoors from the garden, but are probably trying to make their way outside. The usual scenario is that the adult flies have emerged from their pupae in the host bees' or wasps' nest in the loft or inside a cavity wall, but have taken a wrong turn through a duct, crack in the ceiling or gap in the skirting boards. Their large size and out-of-context unfamiliarity makes them seem dangerous invaders, to be (hopefully) ejected or (sadly) swatted. Having the heavily built, fat, corrugated grubs wriggle across the floor looking for a likely spot to pupate is not for some people either.

Volucella maggots might also be competing with the odd scuttling larvae of a bizarre tapered, long-legged and feathery antlered beetle, the wasp nest beetle *Metoecus paradoxus*, in the old wasps' nests. This unusual, fly-like beetle lays its eggs on or in rotten tree trunks, but the tiny active hatchlings (called triungulins) do not feed on the wood; instead they rear up whenever another insect lands nearby and try to grab hold of it. A very few of the lucky ones catch hold of the legs of a wasp visiting the

Wasp nest beetle *Metoecus paradoxus*

184

dead tree to chew wood pulp for its paper nest. The hitchhikers are taken back to the nest where they set about digging into and eating wasp grubs in the brood comb. The beetles, when they finally arrive at adulthood, must exit the nest and find their own suitable oviposition site on a tree. Their emergence in a house can cause considerable but unnecessary concern to householders because of the unfamiliarity of the beast. This is what happened to the parents of entomologist Joseph Parker, who thought it was bad enough that the wasps had constructed a nest inside the light fitting in their toilet, without diabolical-looking beetles shuffling about on the floor as well.

Conversely (and perversely actually), earwigs (*Forficula auricularia* and related species) ought to be extremely familiar and therefore not at all bothersome to anyone. However, because their ecology and behaviour are so poorly known to non-experts, they can cause upset simply because nobody seems to know what these remarkable insects are going to do with the strange forceps structure at the tail end. Confusion with scorpions is rife,

Earwig *Forficula auricularia*

even in Britain where scorpions don't actually occur. Despite many a local belief or folk fiction, these forceps have no sting and are nowhere near powerful enough to deliver a nip, let alone hurt anyone.

The exact nature of the pincers (called cerci) is debatable. Certainly any earwig picked up between finger and thumb immediately starts to pinch away at the skin, but this gently tweaking is nothing more than a tickle. It may be an attempt to evoke a startle response (it wants you drop it in surprise), or it may be more effective against smaller predators. The fact that the cerci are of different shapes in males (strongly curved) and females (nearly straight) suggests that they may be used in courtship or mating. This is partly borne out by the fact that in both sexes the younger stages (nymphs), which are not sexually mature, all have straight cerci. Some adult males also have much longer (macrolabic) pincers than others. It has also been suggested that the cerci are used to assist in the complex concertina folding necessary to tuck the delicate membranous flight wings away under the short wing-cases. The nymphs do not have wings to tuck away. The evidence is still equivocal.

The connection with ears is most puzzling, but is also international. In French earwigs are called *perce-oreille* (ear piercer), in Danish *ørentviste* (ear twister) and in German *ohrwurm* (earworm). According to dictionaries, earwig derives from the Old English *ear-wicga*, 'ear wiggler', and even without any knowledge of their biology there is a general myth in the wider population that they live in ears. The only reasonable explanation for this is that they do, on extraordinarily rare occasions, crawl into an ear canal if it is available. They are certainly renowned for their knack of crawling into tight spaces to hide, and can often be found under loose tree bark, beneath logs or stones, or tucked up tight into a nook in feather-edge fence panels. A common garden trapping technique for earwigs is to stuff an upturned flowerpot with straw so that they are attracted to hide inside the hollow stems.

There are well-documented medical reports of insects being removed from ears after they crawled or flew in, seemingly accidentally, but if there are earwigs in these accounts they are easily outnumbered by beetles, cockroaches, flies and moths (Kroukamp and Londt 2006). There is a tale, likely apocryphal, that in the early 20th century a 'gentleman of the road' (homeless tramp) called in at London's Natural History Museum specifically to testify to the assembled experts of the entomology department that if one is regularly inclined to lie down to sleep under a hedge, earwigs will, on occasion, crawl into the unprotected ear.

It's one thing for various animals to come indoors and there are lots of reasons why homes are so inviting, but if visiting the human body is disturbing, climbing inside an ear is stretching the concept of house guest too far. It does, however, show that in nature almost anything is possible. Wild animals, particularly those at the smaller end of the size spectrum (that is, insects) are astonishingly variable and infinitely adaptable. They will seize any opportunity to scrape a living, and they have done so in some very surprising places.

THE FINAL ODDS AND SODS – WHATEVER NEXT?

When Yorkshire entomologist Barry Constantine's brother, a coal miner, showed him some tiny, shining spider beetles he'd found at work, they could have been just another common stored product pest finding its way into the canteen space of a commercial enterprise. But Constantine (1994) identified the beetles as *Gibbium aequinoctiale*, a species not known in Britain at the time, and he was even more surprised that these insects had been found 800m underground.

Several closely related species of *Gibbium* are found in stored product handbooks, and like other spider beetle scavengers they will feed on a wide variety of things like bread, flour, cereals, wool, leather, tallow, hay, vegetable refuse and a rubber sponge bath mat. Down in the Silverwood Colliery mine, however, they were feeding on human excrement.

Coal mines are unusual working environments; they do not have the usual facilities associated with workplaces above ground. During the arduous shift work there is no time to visit the toilets back up in the offices; instead disused tunnels no longer being worked are unofficially allocated as latrines. Understandably the miners take their meal breaks well away from the latrine areas, so there is no chance that the beetles are feeding on food debris. When deposited, the dung is not treated to any conventional sewage disposal, nor is it broken down and recycled naturally by coprophagous insects like dung-beetles and dung-flies. Instead, it slowly desiccates in the cool but dry subterranean atmosphere until it reaches a consistency not unlike stale cake. At this point its dung-like qualities (wet, fragrant, clagging) are gone, and what remains is merely a dry organic material probably little different in its nutritional make-up from the meals that produced it. *Gibbium aequinoctiale* was right at home.

How it got there is still a bit of a mystery. It is flightless, so must have been carried down into the mine by accident. Until the late 1960s pit ponies were kept underground, and animal feed and straw were brought down for them. This seems the likely origin of the spider beetles, which have also been found in similar mines in Staffordshire and Durham. As far as I know, though, the beetle has not yet been found in any location above ground in the UK.

Spider beetle *Trigonogenius globulus*

There are not many deep mine tunnels under most homes, but unusual insects still turn up in the weirdest of places, including semi-subterranean drains. The most unassuming household guests have got to be moth flies (also called owl midges) of the family Psychodidae. These tiny (wingspan 2–6mm), pale, fluffy, round-winged flies flit around the taps and up on the wall, after emerging from the overflow hole at the back of the kitchen sink or bathroom wash basin. Here the microscopic larvae feed in the scummy slime of algal growth, congealed fat and rotting, not-quite-flushed food particles trapped on the inside of the pipework or in the U-bend (Withers 1989). They are quite harmless, are not attracted to food and do not spread disease. It's quite something to think of them living perfectly happily in what might otherwise be the most squeaky clean item in the house – the kitchen sink. Outdoors they breed in smelly, stagnant water, drains, ditches, oozing tree-sap runs, fermenting and stinking compost heaps, and animal dung. Perhaps the kitchen sink is not quite so clean after all.

Of course, anywhere in the house that is not scrupulously clean can always acquire an interesting patina of mould, and this can attract all manner of minuscule scrapers of fungal hyphae. Somehow a tiny (1.5mm), slim South American beetle, *Adistemia watsoni*, and a small (3mm) but stout spider beetle, *Trigonogenius globulus*, eked out a living on the mouldy toilet walls in the old and decrepit (now demolished) offices in High Holborn, central London, where I worked in a small antiquarian booksellers in 1982. Mould feeders account for a large number of the smaller and more obscure insects used to pad out pest-control handbooks (Hinton 1945, my favourite); most (like my Holborn beetles) are rather inconsequential, but some are very strange.

The bristly millipede *Polyxenus lagurus* is, at 3mm, Europe's smallest and squattest myriapod. With its bristly body and tufted tail, it more closely resembles a carpet-beetle larva (for which it is sometimes mistaken), but rather than being found on the floor, it seems to have a predilection for ceilings, where it finds inaccessible (to the home owner's mop) mould to its liking. Away from houses it inhabits old tree trunks in ancient woodlands, lichen-encrusted boulders in quarries and dry-stone walls, and vertical cliff-faces close to the sea. It is a marvel, since it is wingless (like all millipedes), how it manages to colonise a new ceiling. Must it crawl in through an open window? Here is a mystery in need of some more research.

Thirty years ago at a dinner party at a friend's flat in West Hampstead, north London, I spotted a tiny fly walking across the ceiling high above us, waving its distinctively 'Y'-banded wings like semaphore flags. I suffered some good-natured mockery for my geekiness as I named it to species without even getting up from my chair, *Toxoneura* (now *Palloptera*) *muliebris*. I knew this pretty little insect from the ancient broadleaved woodland of the Sussex Weald, where the larvae are probably predatory on other small insects under rotten bark or in hollow trees. I assumed it had drifted in from outdoors, but it now turns out that other entomologists have on occasion found it inside houses, and the balance of opinion is that it attacks carpet-beetle larvae there. This is still very much a casual visitor to the home, though, and cannot really be considered a house guest quite yet.

One of the most obscure domestic animals is surely the beer mat nematode *Panagrellus redivivus*, a nematode worm that was first noted (Cobb 1914) as occurring 'in the felt mats on which the Germans are accustomed to set their mugs of beer, and has been found in no other habitat'. It was later reported from rotten peaches and appears to be slightly more widespread than just in the bierkellers of Bavaria and Alsace. A link to acetic acid (vinegar), a by-product of alcohol oxidation, has been mooted, with the suggestion that the beer mat worm is the same as the vinegar eelworm of previous centuries. Such is the complexity of nematode systematics (Ferris 2009 took great delight in the beer-mat connection) that the species' identity and name is now in doubt. It is just as likely to be one of the paste eelworms, so-called because of their appearance in pastes made from wheat, potato, rice or other glues; its occurrence in sodden bar mats is not altogether unexpected.

Sweetgum shot borer *Cnestus mutilatus*

Another mystifying culprit was eventually identified boring tiny holes, 2mm in diameter, into three large plastic jerry cans in a Louisiana garage in 2011. They were chewed by the sweetgum or camphor shot borer *Cnestus mutilatus*, a tiny, bark-boring weevil originally from Asia. The beetles (all females) had successfully bored into and through the tough plastic containers, which were half-full of petrol, or petrol-and-oil two-stroke mix, so that when the cans were tipped up the fuel leaked out through the many holes (157 in one container). Under normal conditions the female beetles chew a short tunnel into tree bark in which to lay their eggs; the developing larvae then bore outwards, eating the bark as they go. It seems that in this case the female shot borers were responding to volatile chemicals, like ethyl alcohol, leaching out through the plastic, attracting them to what they imagined were gently mouldering and fermenting logs (Carlton and Bayless 2011).

Curious and intriguing as are these spider beetles, nematodes and shot borers, at least they have found a secret living in something vaguely appropriate to their natural origins. There is precious little to link the tiny scuttle fly *Megaselia scalaris* to some of its strange food choices. Boot polish is at the sensible end of its peculiar diet. This was discovered in 1944, when the wax and lamp black were mixed with stearin, a rendered derivative from lard and thus an edible animal fat in some sense. Finding it breeding in a tin of blue emulsion paint is something else, and an observation unequalled anywhere else in the insect kingdom (Disney 1994). A total of 355 larvae, pupae and dead adults were found in the tin, presumably the offspring of one founder female. Larvae and adults had blue pigment in their guts, proving that they had been eating it. The paint mix comprised 33 per cent pigment (phthalocyanine blue), 43 per cent solvent (water with a little alcohol), 23.5 per cent binder (vinyl acetate, dibutyl phthalate and wetting agents) and preservative (diphenyl mercury dodecenyl succinate), not the most appetising menu.

The phthalocyanine blue has a molecular structure of nitrogen and aromatic groups surrounding a copper atom, and as synthetic as it sounds this is thought to have been the metabolic energy source for the maggots. The dibutyl phthalate acts as a plasticiser in the paint, but is also used elsewhere as an insect repellent. This is a seriously weird fly. And as if to confirm this status, it has also been reared from a museum snake specimen preserved in alcohol and from a jar of beets pickled in vinegar. Nothing is safe.

Scuttle fly *Megaselia scalaris*

The list of animals found inside homes increases year on year as new and unusual finds are reported. Some are animals that are being misdirected by their senses, mistaking smelly petrol cans for sweetgum tree trunks, others are simply taking advantage of our carelessness as they breed in beer-slopped table mats or feed on our mouldy ceilings. Some are simply adventurers accidentally flying in through the window. The large, flat violin beetle, a *Mormolyce* species, which had squeezed its way under the glass of a framed map of Singapore hanging on the wall of the Raffles Hotel, was not the vanguard of an assault, leading its brethren from their normal habitat under loose tree bark, but a one-off and had dead-ended, quite literally. Likewise there was a YouTube video doing the rounds recently of a two-year-old puma that had found its way into a Santiago kitchen in Chile. It took umbrage at the Venetian blinds and ended up trashing the place. It was most likely an escaped or deliberately released pet, and not likely to be a portent of other feline invasions to come.

Many other animals are introduced innocently, living inside the fruit and vegetables brought back from supermarkets. Despite worries about deadly hairy spiders in the bananas, most stowaways are unable to become established, and if they survive being squashed by terrified shoppers they will find nothing to eat and nowhere to live in the new home in which they find themselves. The Mediterranean fruit-fly *Ceratitis capitata* has been transported all around the world in infested fruits of one form or another, and has become a major orchard, berry and vine pest in

Australia, and North and South America, but it is an outdoor breeder, not a domestic animal. Few of these animals will ever make a real alternative home in our houses. Once in a while, however, something extraordinary happens and the irrevocable link between once 'wild' animal and human dwelling is forged. Sometimes a new pest is revealed, while at other times serendipity throws a blessing in disguise.

EPILOGUE – THE SILVER LINING OF ONE INFESTATION

Not everyone has a pet giant African millipede *Archispirostreptus gigas*. At 300mm long, 15mm in diameter and sporting something in the region of 250 legs, I picked up Millie from a livestock dealer at an entomological trade fair for £10. My then five-year-old son thought she was dead cool, but the rest of the family were singularly unimpressed. Millipedes are not the most exciting of animals to domesticate. Mostly she burrowed into the shallow soil of her fish-tank home and we hardly ever saw her. We did see her house guests though.

Millipedes eat dead and decaying plant material, so we fed her cut slices of apple, slightly squashed grapes and the browning bits of anything rapidly approaching its bin-by date from the fruit bowl; what she did not eat was soon colonised by fruit-flies. These tiny, dumpy flies, species of the genus *Drosophila*, are nowadays a minor indoor nuisance, but only really if you are in the habit of keeping over-ripe bananas on display in the living room.

Aristotle knew fruit-flies; he muddled them with mosquitoes and midges, but described them clearly enough as vinegar flies (Beavis 1988) and, sure enough, they are also attracted to the delicate scents of acetic acid and the many complex esters in the bouquet of fine and not-so-fine wines. More than once I've been delivered a lunchtime glass of claret, obviously from a bottle left open behind the bar from the night before, with one or two dead fruit-flies floating in the deep red liquid.

Millie's tank was clearly a good source of fermenting fruit, and for some months we had to clean her out much more vigorously than suggested on the care sheet we'd been given, and hang copious flypapers over her tank to try and manage the floating hordes. It was something of a relief when, after 18 months, she reached the natural end of her myriapod life and popped her clogs, all 250 of them.

It must have been a similar infestation that came to the rescue of Harvard University biology professor William Castle in 1900. He was looking for an animal model that his students might study. He needed something cheap and easy to breed, and that had a short generation time to fit tight academic schedules and research against the clock. His associate Charles Woodworth

Drosophila melanogaster

suggested the exceedingly common garden and domestic species *Drosophila melanogaster* as the obvious answer. Hundreds could be reared in a fortnight using just an old milk bottle and half a rotten banana.

For nearly a decade the small and rather boring fly was a perfectly good biological workhorse in the department and in other universities, but one day in 1909 one of Castle's colleagues at New York's Columbia University, Professor Thomas Hunt Morgan, noticed something odd. The story goes that he set some *Drosophila melanogaster* free in the classroom to demonstrate positive phototropism, the movement of an organism towards the light. Sure enough they all flew over to the window and ran around on the glass. As he was pontificating about light sensors in the eyes and mouldy mangoes on the dark forest floor, he noticed that one of the flies he'd reared had pure white eyes, instead of the usual brick-red ones. He quickly bottled it back up again. Within weeks he was rearing and crossing white- and red-eyed flies to see what would happen. What happened was a revelation.

Drosophila melanogaster has now been the leading genetic tool, model, demonstration organism and biological paradigm for over a century. After white-eyed mutants there came orange eyes, brown eyes, no eyes, long legs, short legs, short wings, curled wings, four wings, yellow body, black body, humped body, legs for antennae, and hundreds more distinct and discrete mutations, which could be identified and tracked down the generations. More importantly, experiments showed how the genes for these physical characteristics were connected one to another along the chromosomes, how they were turned on and off, how they were controlled or emphasised, how they produced all the physiological chemicals, enzymes, hormones and proteins for the entire animal, and how they controlled growth, development, behaviour and metabolism. *Drosophila melanogaster* revolutionised the study of genetics, and in 1933 Morgan was awarded a Nobel Prize for his discoveries.

It soon became clear that understanding what happened in the genes of a small fruit-feeding fly could be extrapolated across the entire Animal Kingdom, and even to humans. DNA sequencing has now detailed the entire genome of the fly, and it is no surprise that 75 per cent of human disease genes have a recognisable match in the *Drosophila melanogaster* genome, and that 50 per cent of the fly's genes have a close equivalent in mammalian tissues.

Drosophila melanogaster is still the genetic model of choice in academic studies. I well remember breeding dozens of tubes of them when I was at university, then analysing and counting the resultant offspring and trying to use statistical tests to see whether traits were dominant or recessive, sex-linked or cross-over recombinations. It was all very complicated, but great fun. Sometimes the flies would escape. Sitting in the refectory one lunchtime a familiar pale fleck floated across my field of vision and I looked up to see my genetics tutor sitting further down the table. I could swear she had a loose halo of them flying around her head.

Unfortunately, there is no clear record of how Charles Woodworth, now largely relegated to a footnote in biological history, first came across *Drosophila melanogaster*. All the biographies of his more famous colleagues credit him by name, but then state things like 'apparently the first to cultivate *Drosophila* in the laboratory' (Brown 1973), or 'it appears that *Drosophila* was first bred in quantity by ...' (Anon 1965).

I doubt Woodworth had a pet giant African millipede, but it is tempting to imagine him, or his wife, muttering about the useless damn flies constantly floating in through the window and settling around the apples, cherries or pears on the dining room table. Useless they may have seemed then, just another annoying critter violating the sacred space of the family home.

IX

To live and let live?
Or squish 'em?

HOW TO DEAL WITH YOUR OWN VISITORS

*T*his is not a pest-control textbook, so do not expect lists of poisonous chemical sprays, recipes for mosquito or louse repellent, or contact lists for termite or woodworm eradication specialists.

he first rule of dealing with any potential household pest is *don't panic*. Unlike, say, a flood or a fire, domestic pests and guests are unlikely to do any serious harm overnight – or even, say, by the middle of next week. They were probably around for some time before you noticed them. Obviously shooing a wasp out of the window is quickly and easily done, but dealing with a problem wasps' nest is not to be rushed at. Similarly, coping with mice in the larder, beetles in the pantry or ants in the dispensary is something to be done calmly and carefully.

The second rule is to correctly identify what it is that you're dealing with. Are termites really dismantling your house mouthful by mouthful? Or are some pale-coloured woodlice just sheltering from the storm? Those holes – were they made in a circle by trigonometrically trained woodworm, or has some careless darts player just removed the dartboard from the back of the door?

Although I say so myself, somewhat patronisingly perhaps, the first rule is easy to master: do some deep breathing and some meditation, and get some help if need be. The second rule is somewhat more troublesome, unless you have a resident naturalist or pest-control operative to hand. I'm making a bit of an assumption here that it will be insect and invertebrate visitors to the dining room or kitchen that will be causing the confusion, rather than more easily named birds or mammals. It's all very well knowing a porcupine from a pigeon, but distinguishing a 2.5-mm biscuit beetle from a 2.5-mm pollen beetle that just happened to fly in through the open back door might cause the average observer some difficulty. And I have to say, even more patronisingly I'm afraid, that the average observer's powers of observation can be notoriously poor.

IDENTIFY THE VISITOR – DO IT YOURSELF OR
EMAIL A FRIEND

I hope that the identification guide (see page 205) is useful. It cannot include everything likely to be found indoors, because so many things can casually fly in and out again. But it will be a start. Good luck. If, however, you're not sure, or you need firmer evidence, you can take things into your own hands.

In this day and age most people have access to a digital camera. Even a picture of potential pest taken with a phone is a start. However, it has to be a photo of something other than a dark blob. You have to get close enough to show at least some detail. You have to make sure you have enough light. The photo really needs to be in focus. You may have to steady your hand by leaning your wrist on something as you press the shutter. Take several images, and take them from different positions. If you have captured the offender in a food container or beer glass, move it to where there is more light – not direct stark, shining sunlight, but diffuse light outside, which is better than artificial light indoors. Try and include something to give a sense of scale to your image – a coin works. Now send your images to someone to have a look at.

In the UK (and with increasing worldwide users), I always recommend iSpot. Formerly at ispot.org.uk, it now redirects you to ispotnature.org but either will get you there. Organised by the Open University this site allows users, after a simple registration procedure, to upload photographs of animals and plants for identification. Experts and enthusiasts regularly trawl through the latest images looking for unusual things, and at the same time naming the easy things. Identifications normally take hours or sometimes days, but rarely any longer. As time goes on these identification/nature-recording websites are going to proliferate, so have a quick search for something local to you.

If you know what type of beastie it is (a beetle, fly or bee, for example), try looking for special-interest groups or forums where research notes are exchanged, species identifications are confirmed or pretty pictures are posted. Even closed groups (to stop spammers) usually have contact details for you to make a genuine plea.

If you have a local natural-history society, museum, Wildlife Trust or nature-conservation body, try asking them. They may not be able to help with a straight identification, but can always offer suggestions as to who to contact next. Email your pictures to friends, family and Facebook acquaintances. Tweet your pictures too. The wider you disperse them, the more chance you will have of getting some sort of answer.

Do not send your pictures to a pest-control company – unless you are going to hire them to do some work. These professional people don't have the time to answer random queries from the general public. They will often come round in response to a concerned call about domestic invasion, but they may have a call-out charge, or expect you to buy their spraying or eradication services.

Even better than looking at a photo, especially when it comes to small invertebrates, is to have an expert look at a specimen. Preferably several specimens. People making academic studies of particular animal groups, or monitoring them for nature conservation, are often happy to receive specimens to look at, but always check with them by letter, phone or email first. Hopefully in your initial photo-dissemination exercise someone will come up with a suggestion along the lines of 'This is a larva of one of the larder beetles. Why don't you send it to so and so to have a look at?', or 'Looks like a moth caterpillar – try the such-and-such moth-recording group'.

Again, make contact with hopefully helpful people first; don't send anything out of the blue. Don't necessarily expect a firm answer straightaway. Even experts don't know everything, and they may be unable to give an exact species identification from, say, a slightly squashed larva or a few battered moth wings. They should, however, be able to give you a start, something you can look up and use to start assessing whether you have a worrying pest or just a slightly nuisance guest.

You will have to decide whether you need to kill your specimen, or whether you will ship it alive. This is an ethical quandary for some. To send a live insect or spider through the post you will need to pack it in a non-crushable container like a small plastic snack box from a child's lunch pack, a small bottle that once held herbs or spices, a tin that came with fancy peppermint mouth fresheners, a urine medical sample tube – whatever you can find. It needs to be big enough for the animal to crawl around in it comfortably. Put the creature in with a few leaves to give it something to crawl over, hold on to or hide under, and to keep it moist, and also a twist of tissue to prevent it from getting sodden or too shaken about. Don't worry about air holes; unless you're sending a giant locust crammed into a cigar tube, there should be plenty of oxygen. Wrap the container in padding or in a padded envelope, and send it by first class/next day/rapid post. If you want the specimens (or containers) back, it would be courteous to include stamps for the return postage.

To be honest, it's easier to mail a dead bug. Use a similar container to those listed above, and put it in the freezer overnight. This is the most humane way to kill an invertebrate, and one recommended by all entomologists and entomological societies. The cooling will gradually slow down its metabolism, through hibernation-like torpor sleep, to a dead stop. The specimen can then be put into a much smaller container (still something solid, though, like a Tic Tac mint box, or a couple of jam-jar lids taped together) to prevent crushing, and wrapped in a bit of tissue to protect it from vibrations. Don't just put the specimen in a piece of tissue and stick it in an envelope. On more than one occasion I've been asked to identify what has become dust sent like this through the highly mechanised, crushing, roller-powered franking and sorting postage service. Your small parcel still needs to be slightly padded to protect it in the post, but can now be sent by less urgent and less speedy mail.

ONCE NAMED – THEN WHAT?

It's a bit like getting the diagnosis for a disease. Once you know the name of the critter, you have to decide what to do next. The two big options are to ignore it because it doesn't really matter, or to destroy it now.

In reality, 'destroy it now' can be subdivided into an infinitely subtle series of gradations from flicking a critter out of the window every time you see one, to major emergency fumigation of an entire building. This is the decision you always have to make when deciding whether a creature really is a pest.

My dispassionate advice stands – it's only a pest if it reaches pest proportions. That judgement is different for each of us.

Despite the availability of endless chemical sprays, dusts, powders, vapourisers and insectocutors, the obvious low-tech solution is to physically remove the offenders. This is the 'hygiene' mentioned in all the old textbooks, and it means more than just keeping something clean; it means sweeping out the nuisance, along with whatever it is that it is feeding on.

When I found biscuit beetles in the food cupboard, I simply cleared out all the infested foods, had a good clean around with dustpan and brush and vacuum cleaner, mopped the floor, and wiped down all the shelves and surfaces. They were gone that afternoon, and they never came back. I suppose better kitchen hygiene in the first place might have prevented the infestation. It would not have stopped the first beetle flying in through the window though.

General cleanliness is much more achievable nowadays than it was in the long-distant past. Smooth vinyl, lino and polished wood floors are much easier to mop than medieval mud and rush; wipe-clean surfaces can be quickly wiped clean. Vacuum cleaners have probably done more for removing household pests than any other household implement in the last 100 years, and the widespread decline of human fleas, carpet beetles and house moths is down to this labour-saving gadget.

Barrier methods also work. Mesh screens over windows stop flies (including mosquitoes) from coming indoors. Chicken wire stops other birds too, and will prevent sparrows, starlings and pigeons from getting in under the roof. Refrigerators, Tupperware and cling film keep flies and cockroaches off our food.

I've always been rather sceptical about repellents. At least deet (diethyltoluamide) has been measured in tests against mosquitoes and other biting flies visiting bare arms and necks, but you can't douse the whole house in it. Notions of lavender keeping scorpions at bay outside the window, or essential oils keeping you safe from clothes moths, all seem a bit too whimsically mythical for me. Even the tried and tested traditions of camphor-wood chests probably have more to do with tight-fitting lids than insect-repelling resinous scents.

I was once very intrigued to hear about an ant repellent propounded by someone who lived on the edge of Ashdown Forest, a high sandstone ridge of woods and heaths in Sussex. The ants he suffered from were the local wood ants *Formica rufa*, a large and aggressive forager that makes massive heap nests of pine needles and leaf litter. He claimed to have stopped them by drawing chalk lines across the doorstep where they came in, arguing that it interfered with their ability to follow scent-trails laid down by returning scavengers. I remain unconvinced; it sounds like magic to me. The wood ant is not at all an indoor species. I suspect his visitors were just a few explorers, but they got bored and soon went elsewhere.

Hygiene is also about frequent looking and checking. Modern washing machines and dry cleaning have reduced clothes moths, but we now have so many clothes that all too often they get left unworn or unused for long periods, either in a wardrobe, or stored in bags and boxes in a loft. These are perfect infestation conditions. If you really want to keep everything against some vague future need, at least work out a rota for taking it all out, checking it, refolding it and repacking it, every few months. If a lone moth gets in its damage can be discovered and checked in the first generation of chewing caterpillars, rather than after several more generations of silk and wool carnage down the line.

You can never make your house impermeable to visitors. They will fly under the eaves to hibernate, or fly in through an open window. It is easy to miss a few crumbs falling down the side of the cooker, and who moves the sofa every time they run around with the hoover? The sudden appearance of house moths, woolly bears or bacon beetle larvae is just a reminder to keep vigilant, and to be a bit more vigorous in future.

GETTING MORE HEAVY-HANDED

I don't mean to be dismissive. Attacking a serious pest problem with a duster and a wet mop will not always work. There are times to get tough. If the very fabric of a building is threatened by imminent destruction because termites, woodworm or death-watch beetles have been gnawing it until there is nothing left to hold up the roof, then this is the moment to consider extreme prejudice, either from the nozzle of an industrial insecticide sprayer, or in a cloud of death from a whole-house fumigation exercise. If you have a wasp or a honeybee colony in the cavity wall, it's best to get in someone with the requisite sting-proof clothing to protect against the irate insects once the nest starts getting destroyed. And again, I would suggest leaving general broad-spectrum chemical pesticides to the professionals.

In times past, poison controls were a bit lax. Many an early 20th-century pest-control textbook offered advice on where to get all the necessary ingredients and how to mix them all up in a bucket before liberally applying. Several pages later, in the more thorough guides, there were details on resuscitation and medical treatments should an unfortunate householder become overcome by the fumes. It is no coincidence that Professor Harold Maxwell-Lefroy, founder of the now-international pest-control company Rentokil, managed to kill himself in 1925 in his laboratory at Imperial College when he was developing poisons to rid Westminster Hall, next to the Houses of Parliament, of death-watch beetles. However, there are still some useful domestic alternatives. You can now squirt slightly less toxic over-the-counter preparations into the woodworm holes in the antique chair picked up at a local auction.

Poison against rats is a well-established control technique, but there are all the usual dangers to children and pets. Always follow the instructions on the packet. About the only way to get rid of ants is also by poison baits. It's no good just squishing the foragers visiting the pantry, or spraying their patrol lines along the skirting boards. While these individuals might die, there are thousands more being reared back in the nest. Ant slow poisons work by allowing the field workers to feed on the poisoned bait and then return to the nest. Here they regurgitate their crop contents to the brood grubs, to the nurse workers tending the young, to the soldiers protecting the nest from attack and, most importantly, to the central egg-laying queens. The insidious poison takes time to work as returning workers unknowingly feed their siblings until they reach a fatal dose, but there is no other way of delivering the insecticide to the dark recesses of the hidden colony deep in the brickwork or down in the soil.

Pheromone traps use high-tech chemistry to fool usually male insects attracted to what they think is a species-specific scent signal from a virgin female. In most cases, however, they are not meant as a full control, but as a monitoring system to warn if an infestation is growing. Originally developed for orchard moth pests, they indicated to farmers a peak in numbers, at which time conventional sprayers were brought in. Similarly, these packs are laid down in offices and large buildings, in quiet corners, and checked every so often to see if they have attracted anything that might warrant a call to the pest-control department. They are now also especially marketed for domestic use against clothes moths, and although they might trap and kill many moths, it only takes one escapee to lay lots more eggs. Don't let them lull you into any false sense of security.

Flypapers may sound rather old-fashioned, but they work well enough without polluting either the kitchen or the wider environment. Electrocutors are really for large commercial properties, and although they kill any flying thing attracted to the ultraviolet light, these are mostly non-pest moths and a few flies; but they do not deal with any infestation at its source. Large, heavy-duty, sticky floor traps are also available to cope with cockroaches. These are not for the faint-hearted. Before you put one down, know that you're going to see wriggling and writhing insects twitching their last in glue-smeared semi-paralysis. The occasional mouse or rat ends up stuck too. Sometimes the only sign is a mouse or rat foot where its previous owner has chewed it off in desperation to escape.

Mousetraps are still big business. And they work. But you must decide on spring-loaded, break-neck killer traps, or sneaky 'humane' live traps that close when an animal overbalances the baited box or dislodges the lever and the trapdoor shuts behind it. At least with the traditional trap all you have to do is dispose of a body. With live traps you now have to decide what to do with a live mouse. If you let it go at the bottom of the garden it will be back the next evening. So where can you take it? Off to the park or the local woodland? It will just end up dead by starvation, or dead by owl, fox, cat, stoat or any of a hundred other imminent dangers a domestic animal is not prepared for in the wild.

THAT MORAL DILEMMA IN FULL

What to do about mice really brings home humanity's dilemma when it comes to how we deal with invaders of the sacred space. We might want these animals out, but we might also be unwilling to face up to the fact that we are mostly not evicting them back to their rightful place; we are not translocating them to a better place, but actually sending them to their deaths.

If you see something you don't like in the house, the easiest response is to swat it and have done with it. This is a simple low-tech solution that does not further damage your house or your environment. Most people would not hesitate when it comes to swatting flies or treading on a cockroach. However, in a world of nature lovers this personal touch, fatal as it is, sits ill at ease with many modern sensibilities. Some people are unaccustomed to directly killing things and would rather shelter behind sprays and potions where the death of the organism is not immediately visible, but takes place somewhere else – out of sight.

Mice *can* seem quite cute, really. Compared with rats. Rats are evil. They deserve to die. To the biologist this is absurd nonsense. There are no good or bad animals, just as there are no good or bad plants. A plant in the wrong place is a weed. It might be a lovely wild flower on a country walk, but if it's in among the tulips or the lettuces it gets pulled out by the neck. It's the same with animals; they do not come classified as good or bad, helpful or harmful, just those we like (for whatever reason) and those we despise. They are not in your house as an act of revenge, or to torment you, or to repay bad karma or as an act of god. They are in your house because during millions of years of harsh, unthinking, blind evolution they have become adapted to finding and using something that, just by coincidence, now resides in your loft or your living room.

So when you find that something has been nibbling the skirting board, living in the flour, nesting in the air-brick or scuttling about under the eaves, don't just reach for the pesticide spray or call in the exterminators; actually make a decision about whether it is acceptable or not to share your home, at least for a while.

If you want to live and thrive, let a spider run alive. If you smack it with a slipper, there'll just be another one crawling about tomorrow.

Appendix:

*A*lthough I hope this identification guide will help, it is not fully encyclopaedic. According to several in-depth monographs, 1,500–3,000 animals (mostly insects) are regularly found in human homes, offices, shops, warehouses, cafes and restaurants around the world – and there are plenty more casual visitors. Many of these require specialist knowledge and a good microscope to tell them apart, and any exhaustive list is well outside the scope of this book. Nevertheless, I hope this guide will serve to give a bit more information on the selected species.

MAMMALS

DOMESTIC CAT *Felis catus*

Size: Most adults 20–25cm high, 50cm long, plus 30cm tail, weight 4–5kg, but some breeds larger and heavier, to 15kg.

Description: Lithe, compact, short-necked, short-headed mammal with distinctive broad face and small, triangular ears. Despite age-long breeding of various varieties, most are of similar shape with short, thick fur, although colours and patterns vary from jet black, through tortoiseshell, tabby and marmalade, to blue, white and brown, but not green.

Life history: Litters of 3–8 young (kittens) born helpless and blind, but furred, after ten-week gestation. Weaned after seven weeks; independent after 12. Wholly meat eating; fed by humans, but also preys on small birds and mammals; will eat blowflies, moths and lizards. Sporadically active, usually at night, but much time is spent grooming or sleeping. Buries its dung away from dwelling.

Human/household impact: Associated with humans for at least 10,000 years. Descended from wild cat *Felis sylvestris*. Perhaps tolerated, then lauded for its control of rats and mice. Now celebrated as a companionable pet. Rarely used for fur, and even more rarely eaten by humans. Thoroughly domesticated, but with feral populations, especially in urban areas.

DOG *Canis lupus familiaris*

Size: Adults hugely variable, from 'toys' 6cm high at shoulder weighing 120g, to hunting hounds over 1m high weighing 150kg.

Description: Generally slim and relatively long-legged, short-furred mammal with large mouth, flat tongue and prominent wet nose. Bred to extremes of size, shape and body form, from stunted squat to nearly skeletal, short haired to shaggy, long or short tailed, pert to flop eared. Colours generally variations on black, brown and white.

Life history: Litters of about 4–8 young (puppies), but 2–20 known, after 8–10 weeks' gestation; weaned after 5–8 weeks and independent soon after, but will remain in family groups much longer than will cats. Nominally meat eating, and fed animal-based foods by owners, but generally omnivorous, scavenging scraps, carrion and dung of other animals; will swallow bits of almost anything it can chew, including furniture, clothing and domestic goods. Very active diurnally. Defecates anywhere.

Human/household impact: Descended from grey wolf *Canis lupus*. Associated with humans for at least 30,000 years, although modern lineages derive from domestication event 15,000 years ago. Has been bred for various uses, including hunting, draught, guidance, protection, skins and food. Some modern dogs still 'work', but most are kept for companionship and as status symbols.

STRIPED SKUNK *Mephitis mephitis*

Size: Length to 45cm, plus short tail, weight 2–4kg.

Description: Small, squat, sleek, short-legged animal with fluffy, erect tail. Black, with distinct white face-stripe and prominent 'V'-shaped white marking down back and on to tail.

Life history: Mates in spring; 4–10 blind, naked kits born seven weeks later; suckled for 6–7 weeks. General scavenger; will eat carrion, also insects, fruits including berries, and mice. If attacked can spray foul-smelling jet of acrid-scented liquid from anal glands with good accuracy to 4m, against any would-be predator, or irate householder. North America.

Human/household impact: Does no real damage to fabric of a building's structure, but will squeeze into small hole and take up residence under building, filling entire house with intolerable odour. Can carry rabies. Similar spotted skunk *Spilogale plutorius*, smaller (to 26cm, 1kg), more weasel shaped and with 4–6 broken white stripes down body.

NORTH AMERICAN PORCUPINE *Erethizon dorsatum*

Size: Length 60–90cm, weight 5–14kg.

Description: North America's largest rodent. Large, stout, humped body, with short tail covered all over with iconic sharp spines (quills); variously coloured, mottled, grey-brown to black, sometimes beige or yellowish.

Life history: Mates in autumn; usually one offspring born the following summer. Young remains hidden in burrow; mother climbs trees; weaned at four months. Long lived, to 18 years in the wild. Forages, often in groups; generalist herbivore, but chews bark from trees.

Human/household impact: Often comes near houses to chew wood, plastic and rubber impregnated with sweat. It is after the salt. Will burrow under buildings too.

RACCOON *Procyon lotor*

Size: Length 40–70cm, plus bushy tail, weight 2–14kg (usually 3–9kg).

Description: Long-legged, bushy-tailed and round-faced mammal, with pert ears and prehensile, hand-like paws. Mottled smoky-grey, with distinctive white face, black eye-bands and boldly ringed tail.

Life history: Litter of 2–5 kits born in summer; weaned in 6–9 weeks. Mostly nocturnal; omnivorous, eating insects, plants, berries, mice, nuts and worms. Good climber; often 'washes' food in water. North America, but deliberately released in Central Europe, Transcaucasia and Japan.

Human/household impact: Intelligent, curious and open to hand feeding by humans. Scavenges from bins and will enter unoccupied houses. Can carry rabies.

BLACK RAT (or ROOF RAT) *Rattus rattus*

Size: Length 16–22cm, plus 17–25cm tail, adult weight 150–230g.

Description: Long-bodied, slim, short-limbed, long-tailed mammal, with pointed snout, erect small ears, and short, thick, soft black, brown or dark grey fur.

Life history: Nests in burrow or crevice; 6–8 naked blind young born after three-week gestation. Sexually mature at four months, making them highly fecund and creating massive population explosions if conditions are right. Eats (scavenges) almost anything, especially food left out for pet or farm animals, and in rubbish.

Human/household impact: Major household, agricultural and commercial pest, eating goods, stores and just about anything else. Chews holes to get into buildings, soiling with its droppings and urine. Spreads various diseases including bubonic plague, Weil's disease and toxoplasmosis. Thought to have arrived in Europe, through Egypt and the Near East, from India and South-east Asia during Roman times. Has since been spread throughout the world by travellers and traders, causing ecological harm to many fragile ecosystems. More of a climber than brown rat, and very much at home in roof thatch, hence its alternative common name. Slightly smaller Polynesian rat *Rattus exulans* dominates South-east Asia and Pacific region.

BROWN RAT (or SEWER RAT) *Rattus norvegicus*

Size: Length 21–27cm, plus 16–22cm tail, adult weight 280–520g.

Description: Long-bodied, short-limbed, long-tailed mammal, with pointed head, small ears and short, thick, coarse brown fur. Larger, stouter and plumper than black rat, with smaller eyes and ears, and comparatively shorter tail compared with body.

Life history: Nests in burrow or crevice; 6–12 naked, blind young born after 3–4 weeks' gestation; sexually mature in 2–3 months. Highly fecund. Like black rat, eats anything.

Human/household impact: Major household, agricultural and commercial pest, invading buildings and farmyards, eating everything, and chewing through and contaminating everything else. Spreads diseases including Weil's disease, cryptosporidiosis and haemorrhagic fever. Thought to have originated in China, arriving in Europe in the Middle Ages. Scientific name coined, rather unfairly to Norwegians, because its arrival in Britain was blamed on Norwegian ships in 1728, although it was unknown in Norway at that time. Has now been spread all around the world, causing environmental havoc to countless fragile ecosystems the world over.

HOUSE MOUSE *Mus musculus* (sometimes *M. domesticus*)

Size: Length 7–10cm, plus 9–13cm tail, adult weight 12–28g.

Description: Small, delicate, slim, long-tailed, short-limbed mammal, with pointed snout and large, erect ears. Fur short and smooth, brown to almost black.

Life history: In buildings lives in wall cavities and under floorboards. Nests in nook or cranny; 5–8 blind and naked young born after three weeks' gestation; sexually mature at seven weeks. Reproduces all year round. Eats almost anything, but prefers grain and other plant materials. Nocturnal, agile and a good climber.

Human/household impact: Major household pest, but perhaps more tolerated than rats. Thought to have originated in

Asia, but arrived in the Mediterranean in about 8000 BC, and in the rest of Europe, with increasing agriculture, in around 1000 BC. Now spread throughout the globe. Has been domesticated and kept as a pet, and bred as a 'fancy' show animal and as a laboratory animal for medical models, drug testing and genetic studies.

EDIBLE DORMOUSE *Glis glis*

Size: Length 13–19cm, plus tail 11–15cm, adult weight 70–180g.

Description: Small, sleek and plump mammal, with prominent round ears and pointed, mouse-like snout, but fluffy, squirrel-like tail. Luxuriant fur thick, grey, with a faint yellowish tinge.

Life history: Agile climber; nests in tree hollow or burrow, lining it with moss and leaves. Hibernates September to April. Mates in June to August; 4–6 young born after four-week gestation; adult within three months. Feeds on berries and nuts; also fruits, insects and nestling birds.

Human/household impact: Normally a wild creature of mature broadleaved woodland, native to southern Europe, but spread and introduced to Britain by Romans, who kept it in semi-domesticated form for food. It subsequently died out, but was accidentally reintroduced by escapes from a private zoo at Tring. Generally a secretive woodland animal, but there are many reports of it moving into houses, nesting in lofts, cellars or even remote cupboards, and causing damage by gnawing electrical cables.

BATS order **Chiroptera**

Size: Length to 10cm, wingspan to 30cm.

Description: Small, round-bodied mammals, with membranous wings stretched between long-fingered arms and short legs. Body covered with short fur, wings nearly naked skin. Ears large or small, eyes small; some species with nose flattened and wrinkled, others with snout.

Life history: Nocturnal, emerging from daytime roosts to catch flying insects at dusk. Aerobatic and agile in the air, clumsy on the ground. Use high-pitched squeaks to detect flying prey by echolocation. Long hibernation during winter.

Human/household impact: Creatures of the night, so often viewed with dark suspicion, not helped by myths (ignorance) of vampire bats (rare South American species). Roost in lofts and building voids; occasional night-time scratchings, some messing with urine or droppings. Can carry rabies. Often protected species so inconvenient during loft conversions and other building work. Otherwise charming and harmless. Many similar species.

BIRDS

FERAL PIGEON *Columba livia* var. *domestica*

Size: Length 30–35cm, wingspan 65–70cm, weight 250–375g.

Description: Plump, short-legged bird; generally bluish-grey, with neck especially iridescent greenish-purple; variously marked with large or small areas of black, brown, white or piebald. Rump always with white, and wings most usually with two black bars.

Life history: Nest a rudimentary mess of dry grass stems, twigs, paper and plastic strips, perched on ledge inside derelict building, under bridges, in loft spaces. Two or three clutches of 1–2 round white eggs a year; hatch in three weeks; nestlings fledge in 3–4 weeks. Clusters in large flocks in parks and squares. Male's persistent head-bobbing, coo-laden courtship display observable all year.

Human/household impact: Feral outlaws from escapes of domesticated pigeons, themselves descended from wild rock dove. Originally bred for food (adult flesh, eggs and young 'squabs'), a wide variety of breeds was also developed for carrying messages, racing and display ('fancies'). Now discouraged in urban centres because of droppings mess and potential (although unlikely) disease transmission.

HOUSE SPARROW *Passer domesticus*

Size: Length 15cm, wingspan 21–25cm, weight 25–40g.

Description: Small, pert, inquisitive and active bird. Mostly brown, but flecked or streaked with black, breast pale, grey; head of female buff; male with head warm brown, cheeks pale and chest-bib black. Small or large flocks chatter noisily; incessant squabbling chirps and double-syllable 'phillip'.

Life history: Cup-shaped nest of grass, often domed, in loft spaces, eaves, tree hollows or dense bushes. Multiple broods each year (three in UK), of 5–10 suboval eggs, pale greenish or grey speckled with brown. Incubation 10–15 days; young fledged by three weeks. Omnivorous, eating seed and grain for much of the year, but insectivorous too, eating caterpillars, aphids, grasshoppers and beetles, and also worms.

Human/household impact: Generally tolerated in European towns and cities; even actively fed by householders, and appreciated for its engaging curiosity. Traditionally reviled in agricultural areas for perceived crop-feeding pest status. Once more widespread and common in UK towns and cities, and recent declines are causing concern among conservationists. Introduced into North America in 19th century; an invasive species there, so more denigrated for its pest status.

STARLING *Sturnus vulgaris*

Size: Length 18–24cm, wingspan 30–45cm, weight 60–100g.

Description: Modest, sharp-beaked, short-tailed, sleek avian humorist. Adult plumage more or less uniformly iridescent, almost metallic, blue-black, spangled with pale flecks, especially in winter. Juveniles duller, mouse brown.

Life history: Nests in loose colonies in trees and buildings, often under eaves, sometimes on rock cliffs. Lays 4–9 pale blue eggs in April, which hatch in two weeks; young leave nest at three weeks; sometimes two further broods later in year. Mostly eats insects, worms, spiders and woodlice, but also fruits and bird-table scraps. In autumn and winter huge flocks many tens of thousands strong fly at dusk in smoke-like clouds, whirling and shoaling to give spectacular and seemingly choreographed displays. Song of laughing bubbles, chatters, chuckles and rambling melody of throaty warbles. Mimics other birds and human sounds, from bicycle bells to telephone rings.

Human/household impact: Roosts in very large numbers in trees and on buildings, causing problems with splattered messy droppings. Dirties lofts with cluttered nest material. Often derided as 'bully' on bird tables.

SWALLOW *Hirundo rustica*

Size: Length 17–20cm, of which 3–7cm is long tail, wingspan 32–35cm, weight 15–20g.

Description: Sleek, delicate, fast aeronaut, with long, slim, pointed wings, tiny beak and distinctive long tail streamers. Upper side deep blue-black; belly pale, almost white; dark red to chestnut throat-bib.

Life history: Famously migratory, moving north in summer to build saucer-shaped nests of mud daubs, lined with grass and feathers, under eaves and other crannies on houses, farm buildings or rock cliffs. Lays 2–3 broods of 4–6 white eggs speckled with brown and grey; hatch after two weeks; fledged at three weeks. Aerial hunter, catching flying insects and ballooning spiders; flies close to ground around grazing animals to catch disturbed insects. Flies many hundreds of kilometres south to overwinter in subtropical savannahs.

Human/household impact: Celebrated as welcome herald of spring in its summer haunts, arriving from end of March to mid-May; mourned as it departs south again during late July to October. Some minor messing beneath nests or sometimes slight damage to decoratively painted cottages, but generally tolerated and admired.

SWIFT *Apus apus*

Size: Length 15–17cm, wingspan 38–40cm, weight 35–50g.

Description: Sleak, slim, streamlined master aeronaut. Uniformly dark sooty-brown except for small, pale grey chin-patch. Wings long and scimitar shaped, held motionless when soaring; short, forked tail.

Life history: Almost exclusively aerial; short legs (*apus* is Latin for 'no feet') used only for hanging on to vertical walls and cliff-faces – never lands on ground. Long-distance migrant; arrives in north in late April and May to breed. Nests in tree-holes, rock crannies and recesses in house roofs, thatch or under eaves. Lays 2–4 white eggs in May/June; hatch in three weeks; fledge in 6–7 weeks. Wheels and floats high in the air to catch airborne insects and ballooning spiders, but also races along streets and between houses, screaming, in gangs of 5–20. Leaves to fly south from July to August, travelling to subequatorial Africa and the Cape.

Human/household impact: Welcomed as magnificent announcer of spring, and admired for aerobatic prowess. Minor nesting mess usually tolerated.

HOUSE MARTIN *Delichon urbicum*

Size: Length 12–13cm, wingspan 25–30cm, 17–20g.

Description: Fast, sleek, slight aerobatic bird, dark blue-black above, white beneath, with distinctive and striking large white patch on rump. Wings long, slim and pointed; tail forked (less so than swallow's).

Life history: Long-distant migrant, arriving in north in May to build cup-shaped nests of daubed mud pellets under eaves of houses, and against stonework and exposed rafter beams. Two (sometimes three) broods of 3–6 white eggs; hatch in two weeks; fledge in three weeks. Catches flying insects on the wing. Gregarious, with clustered nest cups often touching. Flies south in July to October, from Europe to Sub Saharan and South Africa; from Asia to South-east Asia.

Human/household impact: Of the swifts/ swallows the most attached to houses, and perhaps the least appreciated. Large numbers of crammed nests may be seen as unsightly on pretty cottages. Messing under nests sometimes considered a problem.

BARN OWL *Tyto alba*

Size: Length 35–50cm, wingspan 75–110cm, weight 200–800g.

Description: Elegant, ghostly, long-winged and long-legged pale owl. Orange-buff upperparts, speckled with white and grey; underside pale to white, sometimes vaguely stippled with grey. Broad, heart-shaped face white, with large black eyes.

Life history: Nests in open, old or broken farm buildings, ruins, church towers and hollow trees, but also in house gables. Lays 4–10 round white eggs in April or May; hatch in five weeks; fledge at 12 weeks. Usually a second brood later, even into December. Nocturnal, usually seen as pale, ghostly shape gliding or in wavering flight, quartering low over the ground. Hunts small rodents, also birds and insects; prey is swallowed whole, and bone/fur pellets are regurgitated after digestion. Broad wings and soft wing-tip feathers (pinions) give silent flight. Does not hoot, but hisses a loud shriek.

Human/household impact: Long associated with farm buildings and welcomed (or at least tolerated) for its vermin control. Can be tamed and taught for falconry displays, but was never considered a proper bird for aristocratic hunting.

REPTILES

GECKOS order Gekkota

Size: Mostly small, up to 15–20cm long.

Description: Small, relatively plump, soft-bodied lizards, with short tails, prominent bulging eyes and broad, splayed toes. Some cryptically camouflaged, but others strikingly and brightly coloured.

Life history: Denizens of tropical, subtropical and other warm-habitat zones. Mostly nocturnal, but some species active during the day. Their broad toes, covered all over with branched, frond-like hairs, allow them to crawl up vertical surfaces, even glass, and across flat ceilings. Hunt insects by stealth and strike. Unlike other lizards (which are silent), geckos make sounds to communicate with each other, usually in the form of squeaks, trills, chirps and clicks.

Human/household impact: Tolerated in and around houses because they are seen as unthreatening (unlike other reptiles like snakes) and because they eat insects, including potential pests like house flies and mosquitoes. Because of their pretty colours and friendly chirrups, they are also seen as 'cute'. Many are kept in vivariums as domestic pets. Numerous species worldwide.

INSECTS

COLEOPTERA

BISCUIT BEETLE (or BREAD BEETLE, DRUGSTORE BEETLE) *Stegobium paniceum*

Size: Length 2–4mm.

Description: Small, short, nearly cylindrical beetle; pale yellowish-brown, covered with pale greyish hairs; legs and antennae slender. Larvae are small (1–4mm), grey-white grubs.

Life history: Larvae and adults infest wide variety of flour-based products, including biscuits, bread, flour, pasta, noodles and breakfast cereal. Adults fly readily, and infestations can attack food cupboards, cafes, restaurants, shops, warehouses, cargo ships, lorries and small areas of spilled crumbs behind a cooker. Once established will eat almost any human food product, chewing through paper, plastic and foil covers.

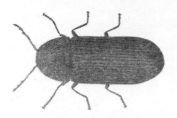

Human/household impact: Has been transported around the globe by human trade in food and products. Large infestations can cause serious damage, but even a small number will offend the sensibilities of the squeamish, though accidentally eating a few beetles is harmless. In the days when pharmacists dispensed flour- and sugar-based pills from unsealed storage containers, infestations would render them unsaleable.

CIGARETTE BEETLE *Lasioderma serricorne*

Size: Length 2–4mm.

Description: Small, short beetle, very similar to biscuit beetle, but distinguished under a microscope by its saw-toothed antennae.

Life history: Larvae and adults most famous for boring into cigars and cigarettes, and infesting tobacco leaves in stores and warehouses. Also attacks other plant-based stored products like dried beans, seeds, spices, ginger, liquorice and animal feeds such as oilcake and cottonseed cake. Once a major pest of cocoa beans in Nigeria.

Human/household impact: Although long known as a pest of many stored food products, it is the infestation of cigarettes for which it is chiefly noted, more or less concurrent with the swift rise of modern cigarette smoking (rather than cigars) in

the 1940s and '50s. This probably had more to do with perceived aesthetic damage to a high-value and high-status item, rather than a predilection by the beetle. Maybe, given the current health-led social distaste for cigarettes, there's a place for the beetle in anti-smoking campaigns.

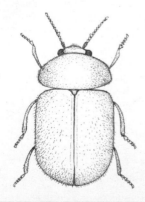

WOODWORM (or FURNITURE BEETLE)
Anobium punctatum (formerly *A. domesticum*)

Size: Length 2.5–4.5mm.

Description: Narrow, almost cylindrical beetle, with humped thorax and hidden head. Pitchy-brown, relatively long legs and narrow antennae dull red. Larvae typical grey-white, curled, nearly 'C'-shaped grubs.

Life history: Feeds inside almost all types of heartwood timber and wooden structures, softwoods and many hardwoods alike, boring twisting holes about 1mm in diameter that if left untreated can eventually completely riddle the wood. Adults fly readily.

Human/household impact: The most widespread and cosmopolitan of domestic wood-boring beetles. Outdoors lives in fallen branches, logs and stumps. Easily transported from building to building in infested furniture. Readily attacks any exposed wooden surface, but deterred by thick paint and varnish coats, and by injected or absorbed chemical treatments. When undetected can remain hidden for many years, reducing strength of structural timbers, and appearance and value of wooden furniture and household objects.

DEATH-WATCH BEETLE *Xestobium rufovillosum*

Size: Length 5–7mm.

Description: Stout, semi-cylindrical domed beetle, with hunched thorax and obscured, tucked-under head. Pitchy-black to dark reddish-brown, but dusted with pattern of small, dirty-yellowish scales, giving mottled appearance. Short legs and antennae dark brown to black.

Life history: Bores burrows 2–3mm diameter in heartwood of broadleaved hardwood trees, notably oaks and willows, where they are infected with fungal rot, and often in and around internal voids in the wood. Communicates to find mates by banging head against the timber substrate inside the voids, creating distinctly audible tapping. Can fly, but does so very rarely; many books claim that it does not fly.

Human/household impact: Inadvertently brought into large buildings with timber beams and joists during construction; not transferred in furniture. Slow growth and generation times result in it remaining undetected for decades or centuries, until large-scale internal damage is revealed by crumbling timber or catastrophic collapse. Ominous ticking of adult beetles in dead of night like a secret clock tapping out a cryptic message from some other world; most unnerving.

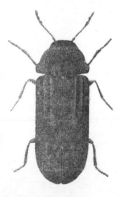

COFFEE WEEVIL (or NUTMEG WEEVIL)
Araecerus fasciculatus

Size: Length 3–5mm.

Description: Oval, robust and convex-bodied beetle; legs relatively long; antennae slender with slight, three-segmented club at apex. Brown or greyish, but covered all over with variegated pattern of short pale hairs, giving speckled or mottled appearance.

Life history: Larvae feed in plant seeds. Life cycle 30–45 days, with 8–10 generations per year. Tropical species originally from Indian subcontinent, which although transported around the world cannot survive cold winters.

Human/household impact: Widespread, but not quite cosmopolitan. Tropical pest of stored nuts and seeds, especially coffee and cocoa beans, broad beans and pigeon peas; also dried fruits, spices, cassava and other roots, papaya, cola nuts and nutmeg. May infest coffee beans on bushes, but heaviest infestations are only in long-term storage. Has been transported around the world in infested cargoes, but does not become fully established in colder temperate regions.

CAPUCHIN BEETLE *Bostrychus capucinus*

Size: Length 9–14mm.

Description: Almost cylindrical black beetle, with bright red or chestnut-brown wing-cases. Thorax with pronounced, hunched shoulders; head hidden underneath it, as if beneath a cowl, hence its name, after Capuchin friary monks, who always wore large hooded cloaks.

Life history: Adults and larvae bore tunnels 2–4mm in diameter into dead sapwood of hardwood trees, predominantly oaks.

Human/household impact: Not really a woodworm as such, but sometimes emerges indoors from poor-quality oak building timbers in which it was feeding, or firewood or rustic decorative objects. Only very minor pest, but often noticeable because of its bright colours.

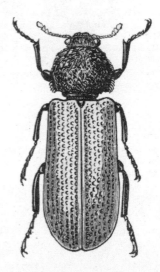

BAMBOO BORER (or GHOON) *Dinoderus minutus*

Size: Length 2.5–3.5mm.

Description: Small, short, cylindrical beetle. Dark brown to black; wing-cases sometimes reddish. Head tucked under knobbly thorax. Pale legs and short antennae.

Life history: Small, curled grey grubs feed in solid hardwood and bamboo stems. Life cycle complete in about five weeks under optimum conditions. Chews its way into stem where rind has been cut, for example where branches have been trimmed off.

Human/household impact: Feeds on bamboo, but also attacks other woods and has been found eating maize. In its pantropical homelands will destroy stored bamboo canes to dust. Many generations share the same stem, pushing through the accumulated droppings looking for remaining woody morsels. Often transported to temperate regions, where it emerges from imported bamboo objects, including ornaments, utensils and furniture, leaving unsightly holes. One instance of 30cm (1ft) length, 3cm (1in) diameter, having 800 exit holes.

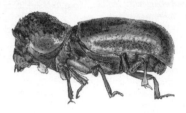

SWEETGUM SHOT BORER (or CAMPHOR SHOT BORER) *Cnestus mutilatus*

Size: Length 2.6–3.9mm.

Description: Short, squat, domed, cylindrical black beetle with head tucked under thorax; wing-cases very short and abruptly flattened and downturned at apex. Legs and antennae short, reddish.

Life history: Females chew borehole into various hardwoods – sweetgum, camphor, maples – in which to lay eggs. Larvae burrow up and out through wood. Native of Asia, where it is widespread. Introduced into southern USA since 1999.

Human/household impact: Normally outdoor species, a pest of nurseries, gardens and forestry, but there is a bizarre record of many females burrowing into plastic petrol jerry cans in a domestic garage.

LEAD CABLE BORER (or SHORT-CIRCUIT BEETLE) *Scobicia declivis*

Size: Length 4–6mm.

Description: Blunt-ended, cylindrical, shining black or dark brown beetle, sometimes with reddish patches at rear corners of thorax. Head hidden beneath squared-off thorax, which is sculptured with small, rounded, projecting tubercles. Legs dark reddish-brown.

Life history: Bores burrows 2–5mm into timber, but will also damage soft metal (lead) casings, probably because of textural confusion rather than nutritional need, hence its common name. Larvae spend many months, or a year, chewing in wood before adults emerge.

Human/household impact: Bizarre habit of chewing into lead cables leads it to cause a unique type of damage. Has a penchant for lead sheaths of aerial telephone cables, close to where they attach to a building. Bores are made next to cable-support rings, which are thought to give the beetle

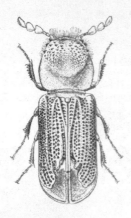

enough leverage to chew into the metal. In California damage is only revealed on the first serious rains after adult beetle has emerged, when water entering the borehole causes short-circuits. Due to changes in cabling and communications technology, this damage probably hardly ever occurs today.

LESSER GRAIN BORER *Rhyzopertha dominica*

Size: Length 2.5–3mm.

Description: Narrow, delicate, cylindrical shining beetle, dimpled all over with puncture marks, especially obvious and forming parallel lines on wing-cases; chestnut-red to dark brown. Head hidden under hunched thorax. Legs short; antennae short with last three segments broadened and triangular, forming loose club.

Life history: Adults and 'C'-shaped white grub larvae feed inside grain, seeds and kernels. Generation time can be 30 days, but average is 60 days.

Human/household impact: Widespread in warmer parts of the world. Attacks wide variety of stored seeds, including wheat, maize and rice, reducing them to empty husks. Also feeds on tobacco, nuts, beans, birdseed, dried fruits, dried meat and fish.

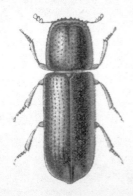

APPENDIX

BEAN WEEVILS (family Bruchidae), many similar species worldwide, including *Acanthoscelides obtectus*, *Callosobruchus chinensis*, *C. maculatus* and *Zabrotes subfuscus*.

Size: Length 2–6mm.

Description: Short, squat, rather dumpy, but convex beetles, with thorax strongly narrowed to small head. Black or very dark brown, but variously marked with indistinct patterns of pale hairs or minute scales, giving mottled or flecked appearance. Wing-cases do not completely cover abdomen so 'tail' is visible. Legs black or orange, hind pair thickened, but not for jumping. Antennae slim, but sometimes with triangular segments giving comb or saw appearance.

Life history: Feed inside wide variety of plant seeds. 'C'-shaped pale grub feeds inside pith of seed, avoiding poisons often found in hard seed shell.

Human/household impact: Major pest of stored seeds, especially legumes – beans, chickpeas, cowpeas, adzuki beans, lentils, gram and groundnuts, but also palm seeds and coconuts. Some other species (genera *Bruchus* and *Bruchidius*) attack field crops, laying eggs in young seed pods to emerge in stores, but do not reinfest other harvested dry seeds; they are minor pests because of perceived spoilage or contamination.

GOLDEN JEWEL BEETLE *Buprestis aurulenta*

Size: Length 18–22mm.

Description: Very handsome, long-oval, hemi-cylindrical, shining beetle, rounded at head, pointed at tail end. Metallic green, blue or bronze, with hints of gold or reddish-copper down back and around edges. Wing-cases marked with distinct longitudinal ridges.

Life history: Larvae feed in heartwood of various north-west American conifer trees, including Douglas fir, Ponderosa pine, western red cedar and spruce. Larval development may take many years, up to 51 recorded. Temperature has an effect, but so do genetics, and each egg batch has fast- and slow-developing larvae, perhaps an insurance against future environmental uncertainty.

Human/household impact: Eggs laid only on living trees (with some bark cover) or recently felled timber undergoing seasoning, but due to very long larval stage adults can emerge many years later from structural timber used in building, or from furniture. By this means beetle has been transported all around the world, but has not become established outside its home range.

HOUSE LONGHORN BEETLE (or OLD HOUSE BORER) *Hylotrupes bajulus*

Size: Length 8–25mm.

Description: Long, narrow beetle, with parallel-sided wing-cases, thorax rounded at sides, two prominent, shining, bulbous tubercles above; antennae and legs long. Greyish-brown to black; covered with short, pale greyish hairs giving a dusted appearance and producing four whitish marks on centres of wing-cases, of which front pair are usually most obvious.

Life history: Larvae burrow into sapwood and heartwood of various conifer trees like pines and firs, but also hazel, alder and poplar.

Human/household impact: Causes damage to structural timbers in houses, affecting joists, rafters and floorboards, especially in roofs. Can be originally introduced into a building during construction when, unbeknownst to the builders, the larvae are already chewing through the timbers. Larval development may take many months, and by the time adults emerge construction is complete. The beetle then reinfests other timbers. A predilection for loft spaces has sometimes been blamed on change from cooling thatch to warming slate and tile over the last century or more, but it may simply be that loft spaces are not regularly inspected and infestations go unnoticed.

BLUE CLERID BEETLE *Korynetes* (sometimes miss-spelled *Corynetes*) *caeruleus*

Size: Length 3.5–6mm.

Description: Long-oval beetle, with parallel-sided wing-cases and rounded thorax. Shiny metallic blue (sometimes slight bronzy-red thorax), but covered all over with sparse black hairs. Legs and antennae black, or slightly reddish.

Life history: Specialist predator of wood-boring beetles, particularly woodworm and death-watch beetles. Active narrow larvae explore woodworm tunnels and attack woodworm grubs.

Human/household impact: Occurs where there are particularly heavy infestations of woodworm or death-watch beetles, but never seemingly numerous enough to fully control outbreaks. Sometimes suggested as potential biocontrol agent, especially for death-watch beetle, where host larvae may live deep in massive timbers unreachable by chemical treatments. Most usually regarded as an indicator of a difficult woodworm situation.

MOULD BEETLES (family Lathridiidae), many very similar species worldwide, including *Aridius nodifer*, *Corticarina gibbosa*, *Enicmus minutus*, *Adistemia watsoni* and *Cartodere filum* (shown here).

Size: Length 1–3mm.

Description: Small to minute, narrow and usually slightly flattened beetles; wing-cases generally long-oval or narrow and parallel-sided; thorax small and rounded. Head, thorax and wing-cases all have separate outlines, giving distinctive appearance.

Life history: Mould feeders, eating spores and also fruiting bodies of various minute fungi. Away from human habitation occur in compost heaps and dead leaves, under bark of rotten logs, and in ants' and termites' nests.

Human/household impact: Sometimes considered pests in stored food products, but usually a sign that poor storage conditions have become damp, allowing mould and fungal decay to set in. As well as occurring in conventional food stores in houses, shops and warehouses, found on mouldy walls and ceilings, in museum herbaria (pressed plant collections), mouldy wine vats, old cheese and, according to one report, a pair of old boots in a cellar and an old hat.

GRAIN WEEVIL *Sitophilus granarius*

Size: Length 3–5mm.

Description: Long-oval, nearly parallel-sided beetle, with long snout on head. Shining black or dark brown, sometimes chestnut; may be marked with two or four vague pale marks on wing-cases; body strongly pocked with minute puncture-like dimples. Very similar to rice weevil, but punctures on thorax are oval rather than round, and lines of punctures along wing-cases are closer together.

Life history: Feeds on cereal seeds; pale grub hollows out grain from inside. Adult's snout has chewing mouthparts at end, with which it chews a deep drill hole into centre of grain. It then turns around and uses a telescopic egg-laying tube to lay an egg inside.

Human/household impact: One of the most important, longest known and most reviled pests of stored wheat and barley. Can quickly destroy grain stores by its chewings, and uric acid in its excreta renders any partly eaten husks unpalatable. Temperate and subtropical species. Known from prehistoric archaeological remains. Became more or less cosmopolitan right at the beginning of agricultural period 7,000–10,000 years ago. Flightless, so transported by humans during trade, exploration, colonisation and conquest.

RICE WEEVIL *Sitophilus oryzae*

Size: Length 3–5mm.

Description: Long-oval, shining black or dark chestnut-brown weevil, sometimes with vaguely paler patches; very similar to grain weevil, but dimpled punctures on thorax are round rather than oval, and lines of punctures along wing-cases are spaced slightly further apart.

Life history: Feeds on cereal seeds, but especially a major pest of milled rice. Like grain weevil, grub hollows out interior of rice grain, leaving a dusty husk.

Human/household impact: One of the most important pests of rice, and known in subtropical eastern rice-eating areas of the world for as long as grain weevil has been known in the West. Very similar species

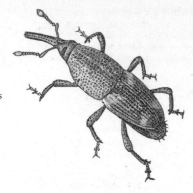

(once thought to be only a local variety), *S. zeamais*, is major pest of sweetcorn/ maize. It has adapted to the maize kernels, which are slightly larger than those of rice.

WOODWORM WEEVIL *Euophryum confine*

Size: Length 3–3.5mm.

Description: Narrow, parallel-sided subcylindrical beetle, with long snout on its head. Dark chestnut-brown to black, covered all over with dimpled punctures. Legs and antennae short, deep red or brown.

Life history: Riddles convoluted tunnels into rotten wood of almost all types of tree. A sluggish walker.

Human/household impact: Native of New Zealand, where it is a minor part of the natural fauna of decomposing logs. Accidentally introduced into UK in 1930s, it has become one of the most common domestic woodworm beetles in England and Wales, and is making headway into Scotland. Appears to only attack interior timber that has become damp and is suffering fungoid rot. Its congener *E. rufum*, another New Zealand species, was also introduced at the same time, but remains rare and poorly known. A very similar beetle, *Pentarthrum huttoni*, possibly a native of southern Europe (some say the Pacific Rim), is more widespread internationally, but is not common. It is also found in rotten timber, sometimes indoors; more often attacks on old casks are reported, suggesting that this is how it has been transported around the globe.

BLIND BARK BEETLE *Aglenus brunneus*

Size: Length 1.6–2.2mm.

Description: Minute, subcylindrical, rather parallel-sided beetle. Shining, pale to dark brown. Head lacks eyes.

Life history: In mouldy hay, manure heaps, stables and hotbeds, feeding on decaying organic matter.

Human/household impact: No longer really a synanthropic insect, but until the Middle Ages was a regular occupant of houses, living in straw, reeds or rushes strewn on trodden earth floors of hovels and rustic cottages. Regular find in archaeological digs from Ancient Egypt, Greece and Roman era until about AD 1600.

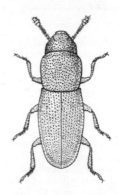

FUR BEETLE *Attagenus fasciatus*

Size: Length 3–5mm.

Description: Broad-oval, slightly flattened beetle. Black or dark brown, with areas of reddish. Thorax and undulating band across wing-cases thickly covered with pale hairs. Legs and antennae short and slim.

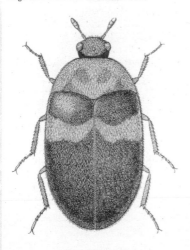

Life history: Narrow, elongate, bristly larvae attack animal products such as wool, feathers, sinew, silk and dead insects. Similar species regularly found in mammal and birds' nests, also feeding on dead bees at bottoms of their nests. Several generations a year, depending on temperatures and food quality.

Human/household impact: Pantropical species found in houses and warehouses, feeding on wool and silk carpets, furniture and clothes, skins, leather, furs, feathers, stuffed animals and museum insect collections. At a time when animal fur was a more important fashion and clothing commodity than it is today, it was considered a potential threat to the industry, hence its common name. Several other similarly cosmopolitan species have similar life histories, including *A. pellio*, which is black with a small round white spot on each wing-case, *A. piceus*, which is all black, and *A. smirnovi*, which is dark brown.

HIDE BEETLE *Megatoma undata*

Size: Length 4–6mm.

Description: Broad-oval, slightly flattened beetle. Black with scattered pale or white hairs that especially form two undulating white bars across wing-cases, and a patch at each rear corner of thorax. Legs and antennae slim and black. Male with last three segments of antennae enlarged to form long, broad club, much larger than female's.

Life history: Narrow, bristly larvae feed on various animal products, and in the wild it has been found under loose bark of old trees, feeding on dead insect remains.

Human/household impact: Only very minor nuisance (if any), and said to have been found occasionally indoors feeding on animal skins and furs.

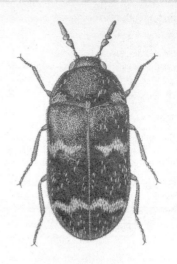

KHAPRA BEETLE *Trogoderma granarium*

Size: Length 2–3mm.

Description: Very small, broad-oval beetle. Brown to almost black, body surface shining, but obscured by dense covering of fine brown, yellowish or white hairs, forming a vague pattern of 2–3 indistinct bars across wing-cases. Legs and antennae short and slim.

Life history: Small, narrow, banded, bristly larvae feed on seeds and grains, and are renowned for being able to survive long-term starvation (eight years recorded) until food becomes available again. Adults do not feed.

Human/household impact: Major pest of stored grains. Tropical and subtropical, but has now spread around the world and is established in heated buildings, warehouses and maltings the world over. Two other very similar species, *T. inclusum* and *T. variabile*, are also grain-store pests.

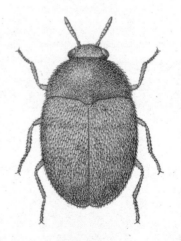

LARDER BEETLE (or BACON BEETLE)
Dermestes lardarius

Size: Length 7–9mm.

Description: Long-oval, smoothly rounded beetle. Black, front half of wing-cases pinkish-grey, caused by many small golden hairs over dull reddish body surface, with series of black spots arranged in vague zigzag bar across it. Thorax decorated with clumps of golden-grey scales forming irregular patches. Legs and antennae black, short and slim.

Life history: Long, banded, bristly larvae eat almost any human food product, but especially stored meat such as bacon, hence species' common name.

Human/household impact: Cosmopolitan and nearly ubiquitous – one of the most common household pests, often occurring in kitchens, and surviving on spilled food scraps behind a cooker or under cupboards. In earlier times major pest of factories making fishmeal and bonemeal, leatherworks, furriers and so on. Also recorded feeding on dried fish, bath sponges (natural, not latex foam), cheese and manure made from ground crabs.

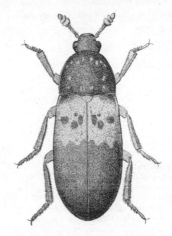

BROWN LARDER BEETLE *Dermestes ater*

Size: Length 7–9mm.

Description: Long-oval, smoothly rounded beetle. Black to dark brown, body surface shining, but obscured by fine, downy coat of brown hairs. Legs and antennae short and slim, brown or reddish.

Life history: Like larder beetle larvae, banded, bristly larvae of this species eat just about anything. Adults fly readily.

Human/household impact: Cosmopolitan; very common household pest, often found feeding in houses under kitchen cupboards, and in warehouses, store rooms and so on. Recorded feeding on copra, dried mushrooms, grain, cocoa and custard powder. Infestations of grain and other plant materials may be as a result of it feeding on dead remains of other insect pests. Several other very similar all-brown species also common, including *D. haemorrhoidalis* and *D. peruvianus*.

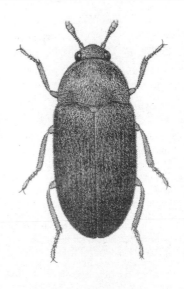

SPOTTED LARDER BEETLE *Dermestes maculatus*

Size: Length 5–10mm.

Description: Long-oval, smoothly rounded beetle. Black to chestnut-brown, body surface shining, but covered with a layer of greyish-brown hairs sometimes forming a vaguely tessellated pattern, or at least with the sides of the thorax densely dusted.

Life history: Like larder beetle larvae, banded, bristly larvae of this species eat stored and spilled food, especially meat and animal products.

Human/household impact: Cosmopolitan; very common household and warehouse pest. Apart from usual foods, also recorded from bizarre selection of habitats, including cork, fibre-board, stored tobacco, salt, sal ammoniac (smelling salts) and 'flexible asbestos'. Can chew through lead casing to get in or out of food containers. Often used to clean bird and animal skeletons for museum exhibits. Several similar species, including *D. carnivorus*, *D. dimidiatus* and *D. frischi*, which are distinguished by patterns of hairs, especially on underside of body.

VARIED CARPET BEETLE *Anthrenus verbasci*

Size: Length 2–4mm.

Description: Very small, convex, domed, almost spherical beetle. Black or dark brown, but covered all over with dense layer of scales coloured black, brown, yellow, orange and white, which form various patterns of bands, blotches and chequers. Legs black or brown.

Life history: Tiny, tufted, bristly larvae eat all types of animal fibre, including wool, silk and feathers.

Human/household impact: Cosmopolitan, ubiquitous and one of the most common domestic pests. Particularly damaging to wool carpets, silk rugs and furniture made of wool, but stuffed with horsehair. Attacks woollen clothes, horn (used for combs and cutlery handles), furs and leather (including book bindings). Away from domestic homes, is the greatest destroyer of museum collections of stuffed animals and drawers of insect specimens. Many a drawer of scientifically important specimens has been reduced to dust by years of unseen chewing. Numerous other very similar species, also highly destructive in this same way, notably *A. museorum* and *A. flavipes*.

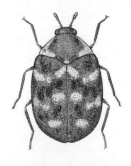

POWDER-POST BEETLES, *Lyctus* species

Size: Length 3–5mm.

Description: Long, narrow, parallel-sided, almost cylindrical beetles. Colour brown to almost black. Legs short and slim, and similarly coloured.

Life history: Tiny pale, hook-shaped grubs burrow into deep heartwood of a large number of tree types. Female beetle chews surface of timber to reveal xylem vessels, long, hollow tubes that transported water and dissolved nutrients up through the sapwood when the tree was alive. She then uses her extendible, telescopic, needle-thin ovipositor to lay an egg deep in the timber.

Human/household impact: Minor woodworm pest usually of furniture, and household and decorative objects, rather than of structural timber. Infestations usually small, but because beetles have a habit of continuously reinfecting the same wood, many generations of larvae can continue chewing away for years until the interior of the wood is reduced to a powder-filled void under a thin outer veneer – hence their common name. Large number of virtually identical-looking species that confuse even the experts.

DRIED FRUIT BEETLE *Carpophilus hemipterus*

Size: Length 2–4mm.

Description: Small, long-oval, rather flattened beetle with broad head, and with last two abdominal tail segments sticking out from behind short wing-cases. Reddish chestnut-brown to nearly black; wing-cases marked with two or four reddish-yellow patches. Legs short and stout, and antennae short with small compact club.

Life history: Tiny, worm-like maggots eat almost any type of fruit.

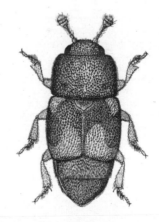

Human/household impact: Cosmopolitan and found in endless fruit-based situations, including grape skins around wine presses, dried figs, apricots, raisins, prunes and bananas. Also occurs in maize grain, cloves, fruit rind, cooked rice, fermented honey, copra, nuts and beans. Will feed outdoors on fallen and drying fruit in an orchard, so large numbers are present to invade storage warehouses, processing plants and canneries. Has been blamed for infecting stored fruits with yeast spores, causing them to ferment and souring the products. Can be conveniently reared in laboratory using commercially bought plum pudding.

WHARF BORER *Nacerdes melanura*

Size: Length 7–14mm.

Description: Long, narrow, parallel-sided beetle. Reddish or yellowish-brown, with black eyes, underbody and tips of wing-cases. Legs and antennae long and slender, reddish to black.

Life history: Skinny white maggot, 12–30mm long, bores into wood, but usually only at or near high-tide mark. Does not tunnel through sound wood, but chews rough voids in areas of damp where fungal decay has already started. Flies readily.

Human/household impact: A mainly maritime species. Attacks wharf timbers, piles, harbour walls, docksides and sometimes driftwood. In the days of wooden ships would bore into timber above water line. Also occurs away from estuaries

and the sea, and sometimes found along canals and rivers. Has additionally been reported from bases of wooden telephone poles where dogs have urinated, and in floorboards around bases of toilet pans.

6-SPOT SPIDER BEETLE *Ptinus sexpunctatus*

Size: Length 3–4mm.

Description: Small, subparallel beetle, with bulbous thorax and hidden head, giving appearance of having only two body segments (like a spider), rather than three (like an insect). Legs and antennae long and slender, adding to this effect. Black or dark brown, but with bright white hairs clustered into distinct spots: two at side of front third of wing-cases, two others (sometimes doubled, hence its scientific name) about one third from ends of wing-cases, and on head.

Life history: Bristly, 'C'-shaped grubs feed on a variety of dry organic materials. They roll into a ball if disturbed. Adults active and relatively fast moving, but will also feign death if molested.

Human/household impact: Feeds on almost any dried stored food product, including flour, cocoa powder, spices, dried fruits, nuts, corn and fish food. Several other similar species occur in these and other situations, notably Australian spider beetle *P. tectus*, which is uniformly dull brown, and *P. fur*, in which male is narrow and brown, female rounded and decorated with four white patches of hair.

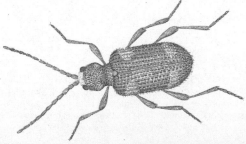

AMERICAN SPIDER BEETLE *Mezium americanum*

Size: Length 1.5–3.5mm.

Description: Minute, shining, globular beetle. Wing-cases fused into nearly spherical shield covering almost all of insect; thorax very small, head even smaller and hidden, tucked under. Wing-cases glossy chestnut-brown to black. Head and thorax pale, covered with yellowish hairs. Legs and antennae appear overly long and stout for so small a creature, pale dirty yellow or beige.

Life history: Minute, bristly 'C'-shaped larvae eat almost any dried material of animal origin. Adult beetles have two wing-cases fused together, are wingless and cannot fly.

Human/household impact: Small size and secretive habits make beetle easy to overlook, and in life it closely resembles a tiny seed. Occurs throughout the world, in stored products such as grain, nuts, animal skins, paper, dried fruits and cocoa powder, and in museum insect collections. Several similar species, including *M. affine*, which occurs mainly in Europe and the Mediterranean, and *Gibbium psylloides* and *G. aequinoctiale*, which are both shining brown.

HOUSE SPIDER BEETLE *Trigonogenius globulus*

Size: Length 2–4mm.

Description: Small, rather bulbous beetle, with rounded wing-cases, globular thorax and small head. Dull golden-brown due to dense covering of scales. Flecked with small patches of darker brown scales and with long outstanding hairs. Legs and antennae short, brown to whitish.

Life history: Breeds in wide variety of stored foods, usually of plant origin.

Human/household impact: Minor pest, but widespread around the world in both temperate and subtropical zones. Has been found in cornmills and granaries, but is especially noted for infesting chocolate factories. Also found in old buildings feeding on mouldy walls, perhaps

eating old flour-based pastes used for wallpapering. Several similar species, including golden spider beetle *Niptus hololeucus*, which is found with cereals, seeds, linen, cotton and leather.

SAW-TOOTHED GRAIN BEETLE
Oryzaephilus surinamensis

Size: Length 2–3.5mm.

Description: Tiny, narrow, slightly flattened beetle. Wing-cases smoothly parallel-sided, and edge of thorax armed with series of sharp teeth. Dull reddish-chestnut to dark brown. Legs and antennae short and brown.

Life history: Breeds in cereal grains and many other products, but may feed on mixture of stored food, and droppings of other grain-infesting insects; also partly predatory on other insect larvae. Cosmopolitan, but unlikely to have originated in Surinam, as its scientific name implies.

Human/household impact: One of the longest known and most vilified of stored food pests, recorded in warehouses and stores of grain, dried fruits, oil seed and nuts. Despite its reputation as a grain pest, seemingly unable to penetrate grain shells, and is rather a secondary pest, attacking after initial damage has been done by some other creature. Once considered the worst pest of flour-based baby and 'invalid' food factories.

RUST-RED GRAIN BEETLE *Laemophloeus ferrugincus*

Size: Length 1.2–1.8mm.

Description: Minute, parallel-sided, flattened reddish-brown beetle, with very long antennae.

Life history: Eggs laid in cracks in wheat grains, and adults feed in germ and endosperm. Also found in the wild, under rotten tree bark.

Human/household impact: In grain stores and flour mills. Usually a secondary pest, attacking grains after they have been damaged by other, more robust feeders. Several similar species.

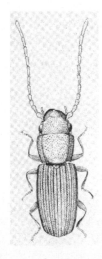

MEALWORM BEETLE *Tenebrio molitor*

Size: Length 12–16mm.

Description: Large, long, stout, parallel-sided subcylindrical beetle. Moderately shining, dark brown to almost black. Legs and antennae short, and black or brown. Larvae (meal 'worms') long, narrow, tubular, slightly shining and dirty yellow, sometimes banded darker orange-yellow or brown; head capsule orange-brown. Two very short antennae, and six very short legs close to head end.

Life history: Larvae feed on grain, bran, flour or similar foods. Larvae are long lived, with maybe an annual cycle, of which adults live three months. Adult beetles fly readily.

Human/household impact: Not a major storage pest because both adults and larvae are large, and relatively easily spotted and removed, but even small infestations are not tolerated. Usually recorded in 'old flour', in other words in abandoned sweepings in corners of disused warehouses and barns. Cosmopolitan. *T. obscurus* is similar, but adult body surface is duller, not shining, and larvae are darker. Commercially bred for production of larvae as food for pet lizards and garden birds.

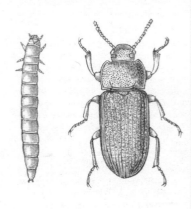

CELLAR BEETLE (or CHURCHYARD BEETLE) *Blaps mucronata*

Size: Length 18–23mm.

Description: Large, long-oval, convex, long-legged beetle. Entirely black and slightly shining. Antennae short and slim, and legs long. Wing-cases taper to short, drawn-out point at tail-tip. Cannot fly, and walks with clumsy clockwork gait.

Life history: Scavenger on whatever it can find. Life cycle may take 2–3 years; adult beetle very long lived, with up to 12 years recorded.

Human/household impact: Occasionally found in large numbers in grain dregs in stores and warehouses that have not been used for some years. Mostly a secretive and passive household visitor, living in old cellars or under floors, where it ekes out a living feeding on scraps that have fallen through gaps in floorboards above.

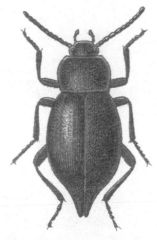

Nocturnal. Once much more widespread and common, but now considered rare. Several similar species.

RUST-RED FLOUR BEETLE *Tribolium castaneum*

Size: Length 2.5–4.5mm.

Description: Small, narrow, parallel-sided, convex beetle. Moderately shining, rust-red, to chestnut, to very dark brown. Legs and antennae short and brown.

Life history: Breeds in cereals, especially flour, although appears to do less well in 'short patent flours', the highest grade and whitest flours, made from the protein-rich endosperm part of the wheat grain; this type of flour is seemingly low in important B-group vitamins. Not very cold tolerant, so apparently unable to survive the winter in many temperate countries. Recurrent infestations constantly reinforced by newly arrived individuals in fresh imports of infected flour.

Human/household impact: Cosmopolitan, and one of the most common pests of stored flour and flour-based products. Also

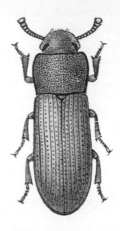

attacks oil seeds, bran, rice, maize and cocoa. At one time the most commonly found beetle in cargoes imported into UK. Several similar species, including *T. confusum* and *T. destructor*.

CADELLE *Tenebroides mauritanicus*

Size: Length 7–11mm.

Description: Small, almost parallel-sided, slightly flattened beetle. Both thorax and wing-cases are narrowed to give appearance of slight waist; sides of both flattened at edges, upturned and flange-like. Dark brown to almost black. Legs and antennae short and brown.

Life history: Mainly a predator of other insects infesting grain stores, but will also eat the grain.

Human/household impact: Pantropical, but only a minor pest. Despite being a predator of other insects, it is still seen as a contaminant of grain stores. Renowned for being long lived, and for passing many days without food (150 for larva, 50 for adult often quoted). Causes most damage by chewing through bolting silk, the fine and delicate silk mesh used in mills as a sieve to sort and grade flour grains. Also damages surrounding woodwork by burrowing into it.

APPENDIX

HOUSE GROUND BEETLE *Sphodrus leucophthalmus*

Size: Length 19–25mm.

Description: Large, long-oval to narrow, long-legged ground beetle. Typical ground beetle shape, with clearly distinct head (with narrow neck, large eyes and prominent jaws), rounded or heart-shaped thorax, and long abdomen covered with smooth wing-cases. Slightly shining, and black or with vague brownish tinge. Legs long and dark brown; antennae long; first four segments black, the rest dark reddish-brown.

Life history: Predator of other insects, especially larvae of cellar beetles, with which it is often found.

Human/household impact: Found with the cellar beetle in cellars, under floors and in cellar beetle-infested grain stores. Although never common it was once widespread; it has now declined considerably. In Britain, for example, in the 1890s it was regularly found in London cellars, but by 1950 it was regarded as very rare; it has not been recorded in Britain for 30 years. A similarly shaped and coloured but slightly smaller species is *Laemostenus complanatus*.

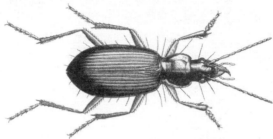

HARLEQUIN LADYBIRD (or ASIAN LADYBIRD, LADYBUG) *Harmonia axyridis*

Size: Length 7–8mm.

Description: One of the largest ladybirds, but still a relatively small beetle; round, convex and shining. Typical colour: head and thorax black and white, wing-cases bright reddish orange with about 20 small black spots, but highly variable; spots sometimes reduced in size or number, or large, to give harlequin chequer pattern. Other colour forms have black wing-cases with two or four red marks.

Life history: Adults and bristly black-and-red larvae are aphid predators; also eat other small insects. Form chrysalis on leaf or bark, have several generations a year and overwinter as congregated adults. Native to Far East.

Human/household impact: Deliberately transported around the world (especially North America and Europe) and released as biocontrol agent against problem aphids. Out-competes (and eats) native ladybirds and other aphid predators, leading to declines of local endemic species. Tendency to come indoors to hibernate in large clusters, causing consternation rather than damage.

235

7-SPOT LADYBIRD *Coccinella septempunctata*

Size: Length 6–7mm.

Description: Medium-sized ladybird; head and thorax black marked with white. Wing-cases bright reddish-orange with seven small, round black spots; central black spot just behind thorax bounded on each side by white mark. Legs and antennae short and black.

Life history: Adults and grey larvae are predators of aphids and other small insects. Orange and black chrysalids on leaf surfaces.

Human/household impact: Sometimes brought indoors on pot plants. Adults overwinter in tight huddles of 10–50 individuals. They return to the same crevice shelters year on year by detecting safety pheromone scents released there by the previous generation. Once indoors they become aroused by heating and are apt to wander off across walls and ceilings. However, since this immediately recognisable insect is generally regarded as a delight and as 'helpful' in gardens, it is tolerated and celebrated.

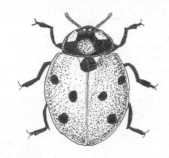

WASP NEST BEETLE *Metoecus paradoxus*

Size: Length 10–12mm.

Description: Sleek, parallel-sided, gently tapered beetle, with long legs and feathery antennae (especially in male). Black with yellow marks on thorax (female) or largely yellow/orange with black tail (male).

Life history: Lays eggs on rotten tree trunks and stumps; active larvae (triungulins) grasp any insect that comes near. Only those attaching to social wasps survive, getting taken back to the wasp's nest where they feed on the brood. Adults usually emerge after host wasps' nest has been abandoned at the end of the season.

Human/household impact: Can emerge indoors from social wasps' nests in a loft space or inside cavity walls. Harmless, but active and flighty, causing concern in those who dislike insects anyway.

HYMENOPTERA

HORNTAIL (or WOODWASP) *Urocerus gigas*

Size: Length to 50mm, wingspan 65mm.

Description: Large and striking, black-and-yellow, wasp-like insect. Four yellowish wings, with hind pair smaller and difficult to see at rest. Yellow, but with head (except eyes), thorax and broad bar across the abdomen deep black. Long legs and antennae. Female has a long, imposing, needle-like tail.

Life history: Needle tail is a saw-toothed egg-laying tube (not a sting), used to cut a drill into the conifer wood where the eggs are laid. Stout pale maggots feed in timber for 2–3 years before adults chew their way out to emerge.

Human/household impact: Frequently found in buildings where adults have emerged from larvae that have been boring through timber used in construction. Large size, wasp colours and dangerous-looking tail cause unnecessary consternation. Several other (usually smaller) species, including *Sirex juvencus*, which has a deep metallic blue-black body and yellow-red legs.

SOCIAL WASPS (or YELLOWJACKETS), *Vespula* and *Dolichovespula* species

Size: Length to 20mm, wingspan 40mm.

Description: Long, narrow, winged insects, with notably slender 'waist' between thorax and abdomen. Black, strikingly marked with yellow bars on abdomen; also yellow spots and side-stripes on thorax. Yellow legs and face.

Life history: Complex social colony with sterile females ('workers') building and foraging for food while queen lays eggs. Grubs fed caught insects (mainly flies), but adults visit flowers for nectar and fallen fruit. Large, chewed-wood paper nests of 10,000 workers at height, but all die off in winter; males mate but then die; mated queens hibernate and found nests anew in following year.

Human/household impact: Often nest in lofts, under eaves or inside floor spaces. Cause fear because they can inflict painful sting. Normally secretive and overlooked, but 'lost' individuals fly indoors. Generally 'helpful' as insect predators of garden pests. More dangerous when accidentally introduced into New Zealand, where mild winters allow colonies to persist all year, growing to several metres across with 100,000 occupants. Several similar species.

PAPER WASPS, *Polistes* species

Size: Length 20mm, wingspan 40mm.

Description: Slim, elegant winged insects with pronounced narrow waist between thorax and abdomen. Black, marked with bars and spots of yellow. Yellow legs and antennae.

Life history: Small, chewed wood paper nests made in the open, with brood combs arranged in hanging, domed umbrella formation from a narrow stalk above, not covered by a protective paper carton. Complex social colony of a few scores of workers (sterile females) and one or more queens (reproductive females). Grubs fed caught insects like flies, aphids and caterpillars.

Human/household impact: Can deliver painful sting. Apt to nest in 'awkward' situations like under porches, against window frames and in nooks in walls, so more likely to be accidentally disturbed than social wasps (*Vespula* species) and therefore seen as more aggressive. Several very similar species. Some regularly hibernate in houses, others attack household paper and books for nest material.

MASON WASPS, *Ancistrocerus, Odynerus* and others

Size: Length 8–12mm, wingspan 20–25mm.

Description: Small, slim wasps, with pronounced narrow waist. Black, marked with narrow yellow bars.

Life history: Make small, mud-lined nest in burrow in soil, hollow plant stem, old beetle burrow in wood or any small hole in a wall. Stock nest with insect prey on which eggs are laid. Nest entrance then sealed and grubs feed on provisioned insect food stores. New adults emerge next year.

Human/household impact: Occasionally make nests in mortar crevices, gaps around window frames or other domestic situations, like the hole in a cotton reel or in a keyhole. Many very similar species.

WESTERN HONEYBEE *Apis mellifera*

Size: Length 12–15mm, wingspan 25–30mm.

Description: Long-oval, but rather stout flying insect. Brown or black, marked with bands of lighter chestnut, red or orange-yellow across abdomen. Light covering of short hairs, often in bands. Not to be confused with fat, fluffy, brightly marked bumblebees.

Life history: Complex colony structure; many thousands of sterile females (workers) and one egg-laying queen. Visits flowers after nectar and pollen. Makes hanging wax combs for brood grubs and food storage in form of honey. Colony division by swarming, when queen and some workers fly off to make a new nest.

Human/household impact: Almost fully domesticated. Kept in artificial hives for harvest of honey and wax. Escaped swarms form feral colonies in hollow trees, and also in building voids, lofts and cavity walls. Can sting painfully, and alarm scents (pheromones) can trigger dangerous multiple attacks. Hybrid with disease-resistant but very aggressive African subspecies accidentally released in Brazil in 1957; now spread to USA, where it more regularly forms feral nests, so destruction is usually urged.

TREE BUMBLEBEE *Bombus hypnorum*

Size: Length 15–20mm, wingspan 25–35mm.

Description: Fat furry bumblebee, black but with thorax a striking tawny orange, brown or reddish, and tail tip bright white.

Life history: New nest started in spring by lone mated queen, which has hibernated over winter. At first she visits flowers for nectar and pollen to feed the first cohort of grubs. When they hatch, they are workers (sterile females) which assist with foraging and nest building. Further workers are reared. Nest in hollow tree, old woodpecker nest, or other cavity, jumbled mess of rough waxy cells. In summer grubs become males and fertile females (queens) which mate. All die off except sperm-storing queens.

Human/household impact: Unlike most bumblebees, which nest low down, in hedge bottoms, old mouse nests, grass tussocks or

small soil cavities, this species has tendency to nest high up in tree trunks, nest boxes and in loft spaces. It also has larger colonies than most other species, with up to 400 workers; energetic comings and goings may cause concern, but bumblebees are renowned for being docile and not aggressively defending their nests.

VIOLET CARPENTER BEE *Xylocopa violacea*

Size: Length 35mm, wingspan 65mm.

Description: Massive, shining blue-black bee. Large, heavy and stout. Body all-shining, inky blue-black. Large wings iridescent blue-black. Legs black and stout.

Life history: Female burrows into dead wood to make a cylindrical nest in which to lay her eggs. Tubular burrow is divided into cells, each stocked with a nectar/pollen cake on each of which a single eggs is laid. Grubs feed on the stored food, pupate, then emerge as adults usually the following year.

Human/household impact: Large size, heavy, buzzing flight and dramatic dark colours cause widespread fear. Burrows often in porch or window-frame woodwork, so sometimes apt to come indoors accidentally. Capable of stinging, but usually only if cavalierly picked up between finger and thumb.

MASON BEES, *Osmia* species

Size: Length to 12mm, wingspan to 20mm.

Description: Stout, moderately hairy bees. Black, but variously tufted with bands of reddish-brown hairs; abdomen or thorax often wholly lighter colours. Wings clear, legs short.

Life history: Make small nests in hollow plant stems, and also in vacated beetle burrows in dead wood. Tunnel is divided into cells by daubs of wet mud, hence the bees' common name. Each cell is stocked with nectar/pollen cake collected on flower visits, and a single egg is laid in each cell. Grubs feed on stored food, pupate and emerge the following year; males from outer cells appear first, females from interior cells a day or so later.

Human/household impact: Often nest in window and door frames, and also in loose mortar in old brickwork. Bees, especially those newly emerging from their cells, sometimes get lost and fly around indoors. Sting only if picked up in fingers.

FEATHER-FOOTED BEE *Anthophora plumipes*

Size: Length 9–12mm, wingspan 20–26mm.

Description: Small but plump, furry bee. Male has a brown thorax and black abdomen; middle legs tufted and feathery. Female all black except for red-haired legs.

Life history: Early spring flier; female, working alone, collects pollen/nectar to stock cells made in small tunnel nest in soil or a convenient narrow crevice, in which eggs are laid.

Human/household impact: Often nests in crumbling loose mortar of old walls, including inside disused chimney stacks. Sometimes takes a wrong turn and ends up indoors. Resembles a small, all-black bumblebee, and although it is not aggressive some people worry about stings.

LEAFCUTTER BEES, *Megachile* species

Size: Length to 20mm, wingspan to 35mm.

Description: Stout, broad-bodied bees. Black or very dark brown, but mostly covered in short hairs giving them a dull brown or fawn appearance. Underside of abdomen sometimes brightly orange, yellow, gold or silver because of thick hairs.

Life history: Cuts precise semicircles of leaf to line tubular nest tunnel made in the soil, a hollow stem, holes in woodwork or any suitable cavity. Nest is divided into cells, each stocked with nectar/pollen cake and each with single egg.

Human/household impact: Quite at home in domestic gardens and likely to nest in air-bricks, overflow pipes, loose mortar in old walls, and window and door frames. Will sting, but only if picked up in fingers.

PHAROAH ANT *Monomorium pharaonis*

Size: Length 1.5–2mm.

Description: Minute pale yellowish-brown ant. Typical ant shape with square head, slim thorax, very narrow, two-segmented waist and small, bulbous abdomen. Legs long and thin; antennae elbowed near middle. Entirely pale yellowish-brown, but end of abdomen is slightly darker.

Life history: Makes a large nest of up to 350,000 sterile females (workers) that forage for food, tend grubs and clear nest debris, and many (800 estimated) fertile females (queens) that lay eggs. Males are reared to order.

Human/household impact: A 'tramp' species transported all around the world. Although originally tropical, it lives in large, heated buildings and is a particular problem in hospitals. Nests are inaccessible deep in cavity walls. Workers traipse over food, dressings, surfaces and wounds, with potential to carry diseases. Also a nuisance in offices, apartment blocks and other centrally heated structures.

ARGENTINE ANT *Linepithema humile*

Size: Length 2–3mm.

Description: Minute, pale brown ant. Typical ant shape with broad head, slim thorax, very narrow waist and small, bulbous abdomen. Legs long and thin; antennae elbowed near middle. Entirely pale yellowish-brown, but abdomen is darker.

Life history: Forms large colonies of many thousands of sterile females (workers) and hundreds of fertile egg-laying queens.

Nests anywhere, in soil, leaf litter, under stones and in cracks in buidings. Native to South America, but genetic studies in North America and Europe show that entire invasive populations are supercolonies, with countless billions of genetically identical siblings, covering thousands of square kilometres.

Human/household impact: Invades buildings to nest and forage for food, especially in kitchens and stores. Foragers leave chemical trails for others to follow, thus marking a path to target food stocks.

BLACK ANT *Lasius niger*

Size: Length 3–4mm.

Description: Tiny black ant. Typical ant shape with broad, heart-shaped head, slim thorax, one-segmented waist and small, bulbous abdomen. Legs long and thin; antennae elbowed near middle. Entirely very dark brown to black.

Life history: Large nest in soil, under stones and logs, with many thousands of sterile females (workers) to forage, build and defend nest, and care for young, and one large egg-laying female (queen). Large mating flights of winged males and queens on warm, humid summer evenings. In the 'wild' ants tend aphid colonies, protecting them from ladybirds and other predators, and drinking their sugar-rich liquid excrement (honeydew).

Human/household impact: Ubiquitous species; very ready to invade kitchens and food cupboards. Foragers leave chemical trails to recruit other workers on their house-invading food trips. Many similar species worldwide.

RASPBERRY CRAZY ANT (or TAWNY CRAZY ANT) *Nylanderia fulva*

Size: Length 3–3.5mm.

Description: Tiny brown ant. Typical ant shape, mid to pale brown, more hairy than many other similar species.

Life history: Makes large colonies of many thousands of workers (sterile females), and multiple fertile egg-laying females (queens). Tends aphids, drinking honeydew, the sugar-rich aphid excrement. 'Crazy' because of its apparent madly erratic, circling, zigzag gait. Native of South America, but accidentally introduced into Texas, Louisiana, Mississippi, Georgia and Florida in USA. Named after Tom Raspberry, a pest-control agent who first noticed it.

Human/household impact: Seemingly attracted to magnetic fields (or warm wires) of electrical equipment and invades household appliances, including computers and monitors. On the plus side, away from the house it appears to displace another alien ant invader, the similarly South American fire ant *Solenopsis invicta*.

SIPHONAPTERA

HUMAN FLEA *Pulex irritans*

Size: Length 2–3.5mm.

Description: Minute dark brown, wingless, jumping insect. Tiny oval body flattened laterally; no easily obvious division into head, thorax and abdomen. Legs stout and short, with back pair longest and used for jumping. Under a microscope body is revealed as being decorated with rows of backwards-pointing spines. Entire body very dark brown, almost black.

Life history: Sucks blood using short but stout piercing stylet mouthparts. Faeces, which are more or less dried blood, are dropped into 'nest', where tiny pale, worm-like flea larvae eat them. Also found on cats, dogs, pigs, badgers and foxes.

Human/household impact: Long regarded with derision and as a sign of poor hygiene.

Now much less common than previously, at least in developed countries; reduced by advent of vacuum cleaners. Spreads diseases, notably bubonic plague. Humans are the only apes to have fleas. All other species in genus *Pulex* originate in Central and South America, previously a human-free continent; original host probably a peccary or guinea pig.

CAT FLEA *Ctenocephalides felis*

Size: Length 2–3mm.

Description: Minute dark brown, wingless, jumping insect. Tiny long-oval body flattened laterally; no easily obvious division into head, thorax and abdomen. Legs stout and spiny, with back pair longest and used for jumping. Under a microscope body is revealed as being decorated with rows of backwards-pointing spines. Prominent combs of heavy spikes along lower margin of head and behind neck. Entire body very dark brown, almost black.

Life history: Sucks blood. Faeces, which are more or less dried blood, are dropped into 'nest', where tiny pale, worm-like flea larvae eat it. They pupate, but adult flea remains dormant inside cocoon until heat or vibration signals return of host; fleas then quickly 'hatch' and jump aboard.

Human/household impact: Readily picked up by domestic pets from habit of sleeping outdoors in regular coverts frequented by other animals. Dormant cocoon phase allows synchronised emergence on return of humans from holiday to find seeming major infestation. Freshly emerged fleas jump on human legs to bite. Minor nip, but associations of dirt and disease quickly cause revulsion. Dog flea *C. canis* is very similar.

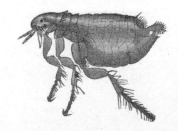

DIPTERA

WINDOW FLY *Scenopinus fenestralis*

Size: Length 4–6mm.

Description: Small, dark, narrow fly. Black, legs reddish. Walks with hunched appearance; relatively short wings held tight flat against abdomen. Flies in short, hopping skips.

Life history: Grubs are predators of other insects, notably larvae of carpet and larder beetles, and house-moth caterpillars; also flea larvae and fly maggots.

Human/household impact: Secretive and most often found singly, crawling around

insides of windows. Having newly emerged as an adult the first instinct is to fly to the light, towards the nearest window. Harmless, or helpful in that it destroys real domestic pest insects. Much less common than once was the case, probably as a result of vacuum cleaner control of its carpet beetle prey.

BOW-WING FLY *Palloptera* (formerly *Toxoneura*) *muliebris*

Size: Length 5mm, wingspan 10mm.

Description: Tiny, pale-bodied fly; thorax grey, abdomen yellowish-pink. Wings have prominent narrow, sinuous loop markings of alternating black and yellow.

Life history: Little known, but larvae thought to be predatory on other small fly maggots, usually in rotten logs and tree stumps, and leaf debris and soil. Holds wings out at near right angles and waves them independently, like semaphore flags; purpose of behaviour unknown, but may be connected to courtship or territoriality.

Human/household impact: Not really considered a domestic insect, but found indoors (on ceilings usually) surprisingly often by entomologists. May be feeding on carpet beetle larvae.

SCUTTLE FLIES, *Phoridae*

Size: Length 0.5–6.5mm, wingspan 1.2–12mm.

Description: Tiny to minute, variously dark dirty yellow to black, humpbacked flies, with short, rounded wings. Run and jump well in preference to flying.

Life history: Hugely diverse life histories, from earthworm parasites and insect egg predators to leaf miners, dung feeders and general scavengers.

Human/household impact: Really rather insignificant, but known to breed in bizarre list of odd places, including in boot polish (animal-fat based), pickled food, human cadavers and a tin of blue paint.

ANOPHELINE MOSQUITOES, *Anopheles* and other species

Size: Length to 10mm, wingspan to 15mm.

Description: Small, narrow-bodied, narrow-winged, long-legged flies. Body and wings sometimes decorated with patches of minute scales, causing blotches and mottles. Mouthparts long. At rest on wall or ceiling, or when biting, head is held down and tail up at a nearly 45-degree angle.

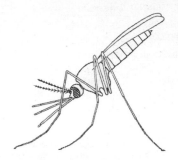

Life history: Eggs laid in still water – ditches, ponds, puddles, flooded tin cans and other rubbish. Wriggling larvae feed on microscopic decay particles in the water. Adults visit flowers, but females take blood from vertebrates, and need this nutritional top-up in order to mature eggs.

Human/household impact: Annoying and painful bloodsucking leaves red spots and swollen welts on victim. Can spread malaria, a microscopic protozoan blood parasite causing illness and death. Arguably the most dangerous animals in the world and responsible for more human suffering and death than any other creatures. Spreads several other debilitating diseases including elephantiasis. Disease spread mainly in, but not limited to, tropical zones.

AGUE MOSQUITO *Anopheles atroparvus*

Size: Length to 10mm, wingspan to 15mm.

Description: Small, narrow-bodied, narrow-winged, long-legged fly. Body and wings spotted and speckled with distinct dark patches of minute scales. Mouthparts long. At rest, or when biting, body is held tail-up, head-down.

Life history: Eggs laid in still water – mostly brackish ditches, or lowland ponds on coastal marshes. Wriggling larvae feed on microscopic decay particles in the water. Adults visit flowers, but females take blood from vertebrates, and need this nutritional top-up in order to mature eggs.

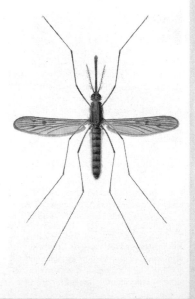

Human/household impact: Annoying and painful bloodsucking leaves red spots and swollen welts on victim. More likely to come indoors than other closely related species. Previously (to end of 19th century) spread malaria (ague) in Britain. Very many similar species worldwide, some of which still spread the disease in tropical zones (*A. gambiae* is the major African vector).

HOUSE GNAT *Culex molestus*

Size: Length to 10mm, wingspan to 15mm.

Description: Small, narrow-bodied, narrow-winged, long-legged fly. Body and wings more uniformly covered with minute scales than in *Anopheles*. Mouthparts long. At rest, or when biting, body is held parallel to surface.

Life history: Eggs laid in still water – ditches, ponds, puddles, flooded tin cans and other rubbish. Wriggling larvae feed on microscopic decay particles in the water. Adults visit flowers, but females take blood from vertebrates, and need this nutritional top-up in order to mature eggs.

Human/household impact: Annoying and painful bloodsucking leaves red spots and swollen welts on victim. More used to venturing inside houses than other species in genus, but there are many very similar species worldwide, some of which can spread viruses like yellow fever and dengue.

ASIAN TIGER MOSQUITO *Aedes albopictus*

Size: Length to 10mm, wingspan to 15mm.

Description: Small, narrow-bodied, narrow-winged, long-legged fly. Dark brown to black; head and thorax with strong white median stripe and side flecks; abdomen brightly ringed with white; legs with white joints. Wings more or less uniformly clear.

Mouthparts long. At rest, or when biting, body is held parallel to surface.

Life history: Eggs laid in water, especially in small pots, discarded rubbish and rain slops in old tyres. Wriggling larvae feed on microscopic decay particles in the water. Adult females suck blood.

Human/household impact: Urban specialist, day flier and aggressive biter. Native of Far East, but transported to southern Europe, North and South America, and nearly to Australia, in secondhand car tyres shipped across the world. Very many similar but less strikingly marked species on all continents; this one and some others capable of transmitting yellow fever, dengue, West Nile fever and other viruses. Perhaps the most sinisterly threatening new pest species to arrive in developed Europe, North America and Australia.

FRUIT FLIES, *Drosophila* species

Size: Length 2–3mm, wingspan 4–6mm.

Description: Small, dark, slow-flying flies; different species variously marked with streaks or spots in dull browns, reddish-orange or yellow.

Life history: Tiny pale grey larvae feed in over-ripe, rotting, usually semi-liquid fruit or decaying vegetable matter such as garden compost and kitchen waste.

Human/household impact: Usually outdoor species, but will come indoors to infest fruit bowls, vegetable racks and stores. Attracted to wine left in glasses, vinegar and yeasty bread. Mildly irritating, but not generally considered a health hazard. Very many almost identical species. *D. melanogaster* has been used for the last 100 years as the subject of intense genetic studies in classrooms and biology laboratories around the world. Mutations caused by random genetic changes in the DNA have created lineages with white (as opposed to red) eyes, longer or shorter wings, extra wings, shorter or longer legs, and legs where antennae should grow.

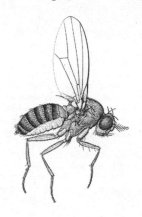

HORNET HOVERFLY *Volucella zonaria*

Size: Length to 20mm, wingspan to 40mm.

Description: Very large, broad, boldly marked and striking hornet-mimic hoverfly. Body black, marked with broad, pale orange bands across abdomen and brown marks on thorax. Large wings clouded with dark shadow near tips, and infused with yellow-orange near bases.

Life history: Larvae feed in wasps' nests, scavenging on fallen food (dead insect prey brought back to nest by foraging wasps), and also on wasp brood.

Human/household impact: Indoor wasps' nests, under floors or in ceiling spaces, may be home to this fly. Large, fat grey maggots often found crawling about on floors; in the wild they would migrate away from host wasps' nest to pupate. Likewise, emerging flies may appear indoors the following year, long after wasps' nest has finished. Slow, heavy, loud flight, combined with wasp-like markings, may cause alarm, but species is harmless. *V. inanis* is slightly smaller, with more yellow markings.

CHEESE SKIPPER *Piophila casei*

Size: Length 5–6mm, wingspan 7–8mm (adult); length to 10mm (maggot).

Description: Adult fly shining black, with red eyes and yellowish legs. Pale, legless maggot. White, pointed at head end, blunt, and armed with two short, pointed horns at tail end.

Life history: Larvae feed in cheese; also in bacon, stored fish and other dried animal protein, but not in starchy foods. Life cycle can be as little as 12 days. Larvae are the skippers, and get their name from the habit of biting their own tails, tensing the muscles, then suddenly letting go, flinging themselves into the air a short distance.

Human/household impact: Apart from causing revulsion when seen in cheese or meat products, larvae are often implicated in myiasis, the infestation of the human body with maggots. If eaten in cheese maggots are resistant to stomach acid; they may damage the intestines and be voided alive. They are also an important forensic tool for estimating time of death, when found in putrescent corpses.

YELLOW SWARMING FLY
Thaumatomyia notata

Size: Length 3mm, wingspan 6mm.

Description: Minute, yellow and black, shining, convex, short-legged fly. Body mostly yellow; thorax has three broad black stripes and abdomen usually has broad black bar on each segment.

Life history: Lives outdoors, mostly in grasslands; larvae predatory on aphids feeding at grass roots.

Human/household impact: Long known to accumulate in large numbers in houses, especially in lofts and roof spaces, where they are blown from fields, and trapped by eddies under eaves on sheltered sides of buildings. Harmless, but slightly annoying.

HOUSE FLY *Musca domestica*

Size: Length 6–7mm, wingspan 13–15mm.

Description: Wings clear; body grey, with four dark streaks down thorax; abdomen grey with sides pale translucent yellow. Legs dark grey to black.

Life history: Pale grey maggots breed in manure, sewage and other semi-liquid decaying organic matter. Adult flies feed on this same breeding material, but are also attracted indoors where they crawl on ceilings, walls and surfaces, including food plates. They eject digestive juices onto food, along with contaminants from their last meal. They also traipse over food.

Human/household impact: Implicated in spread of very many diseases and micro-organisms, and blamed for countless millions of human deaths. In developed countries less often found in domestic homes than a generation ago; more usually occur near farms, where manure heaps are available. Similar bush fly *Musca vetustissima* in Australia.

LESSER HOUSE FLY *Fannia canicularis*

Size: Length 3–4mm, wingspan 8–9mm.

Description: Grey, with thorax obscurely dark streaked; each side of abdomen with 2–3 small yellow/orange spots contrasting with dark dorsal line. Legs dark grey to black. Wings clear.

Life history: Brownish-grey, bristly larvae live in leaf litter or soil layer, where they are scavengers on decaying organic matter. Adults (usually males) come indoors and fly ceaselessly in erratic, vaguely triangular zigzags beneath hanging ceiling lights.

Human/household impact: Mild nuisance – perhaps visually disturbing. Not generally attracted to human food, and not implicated in disease spread. Very many similar species occur naturally out of doors.

CLUSTER FLY *Pollenia rudis* and other species

Size: Length 9–11mm, wingspan 18–20mm.

Description: Medium-sized grey fly, dusted with short, golden-grey hairs that produce a shifting pattern of blotches and bars. Dull red eyes and black legs.

Life history: Parasitoids of earthworms and perhaps other soil-dwelling invertebrates. Adult flies active in sun, and visit flowers.

Human/household impact: Named for habit of congregating in large numbers, sometimes thousands, in lofts and porches, and under eaves, in winter, and appearance of sluggish individuals in spring. Clustering is a result of resting on roof or wall surfaces, and climbing until a suitable dry nook or cranny is found. Dead flies and slow-flying spring emergers may be annoying, but are not implicated in disease spread. Several similar species.

STABLE FLY *Stomoxys calcitrans*

Size: Length 6–7mm, wingspan 13–15mm.

Description: Medium to small grey fly. Similar in appearance to house fly, but thorax not as clearly streaked and abdomen all-over mottled grey, without yellow markings. Head has long, narrow proboscis sticking out in front, clearly visible in resting individuals.

Life history: Pale white/grey maggots breed in manure, compost, grass cuttings and other decaying organic matter. Adults suck vertebrate blood. Particularly prevalent around farms.

Human/household impact: Usually outdoor species, but will bite humans in farm buildings. Both sexes bite, and large numbers can be distressing to humans and stock animals alike. Not implicated in spreading blood-borne diseases.

BLOW FLY *Calliphora vomitoria*

Size: Length 8–14mm, wingspan 15–25mm.

Description: Large, bristly, agile fly; black with glints of metallic blue, green or grey. Dull red eyes and black legs. Thorax and abdomen dusted with microscopic hairs, giving appearance of shifting pattern of blotches and bars.

Life history: Eggs laid in carrion, rotten meat and wounds. Maggots feed on flesh that has started to become liquefied by bacteria, or by enzymes secreted from larvae themselves. Fully grown maggot wriggles up to 30m away from food source to find pupation sites. Complete life cycle in about three weeks.

Human/household impact: Meat spoiled by eggs (called fly blown) and resulting maggots. Lazy buzzing indoors can be annoying. Sometimes useful in forensic murder investigations; can be used to determine time of death when found on a corpse.

TUMBU FLY *Cordylobia anthropophaga*

Size: Length to 9mm, wingspan to 20mm.

Description: Medium-sized, rather squat, brown and orange fly. Dull brownish-orange; thorax marked with vague greyish stripes; abdomen darkened at tip.

Life history: Lays eggs in the soil where a host animal is likely to rest, and hatching maggots burrow into the skin, feeding on blood and pus until mature. It then pops out to change to a pupa. Found in Africa.

Human/household impact: Original hosts were likely to have been aardvarks *Orycteropus afer* and wild pigs *Sus scrofa*, but now mainly occurs in dogs, chickens and humans. Single maggot (grows up to 15mm long) forms boil-like swelling with a small breathing hole through which excrement and discharge are passed. Multiple burrows cause skin thickening or gangrene. Gross. Congo floor maggot *Auchmeromyia lutcola* has a similar form and life history.

MOTH FLIES (or DRAIN FLIES), family *Psychodidae*

Size: Length less than 5mm.

Description: Tiny, broad-winged, fluffy-looking insects. Two broad-oval wings held flat or tent-like over hunched body, and dense covering of hairs or scales makes them resemble tiny moths. Pale to dark grey, often mottled.

Life history: Tiny, bristly larvae live in decaying organic matter, leaf litter, compost and manure; some are semi-aquatic in the liquid putrescence.

Human/household impact: Often found in compost bins, but also breeds in kitchen sink waste pipes, washbasin overflows and drains, and emerges to flutter around sinks and kitchen work surfaces. Not implicated in disease spread. Harmless.

CRANEFLIES (or DADDY-LONG-LEGS), family *Tipulidae*

Size: Length to 35mm, wingspan to 75mm.

Description: Very large, long, narrow-bodied, narrow-winged, very long-legged flies. Usually grey-bodied, but can be marked with black or yellow patterns. Wings sometimes streaked or patterned with dark marks. Legs extremely long.

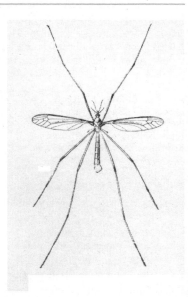

Life history: Narrow, tubular larvae (sometimes called leatherjackets) feed in soil, rotten wood, mud or water, eating grass roots or general decaying organic matter. Many species quite seasonal, appearing at fixed times every year.

Human/household impact: Some of the lawn-dwelling species, derided as minor garden pests, are attracted to lights and regularly visit lighted porches or enter through open windows to fly around indoors with heavy bobbing flight. Harmless. Very many similar species.

LEPIDOPTERA

ANGOUMOIS GRAIN MOTH *Sitotroga cerealella*

Size: Length 8–10mm, wingspan 15–18mm.

Description: Small, pale, narrow-winged moth. Forewings pale golden coloured, hind wings pale grey, fringed with long hairs.

Life history: Short, dumpy caterpillars feed in grain, usually on the plant, during ripening and before harvesting.

Human/household impact: First noticed as potential grain pest in French region of

Angoumois during 1840s. Cannot survive outdoors in cold temperate central and northern Europe or North America, although it sometimes appears in transported cargoes. If it emerges in a store, having been brought in with the crop 'from the field', it will crawl upwards through heaped bulk and lay eggs on the surface grains, to reinfest, but it will not burrow back down into the lower part of the silo. However, it is a major pest of sorgum in Africa, and will crawl down through much more of a crop if it is stored on the ear, with its larger air spaces.

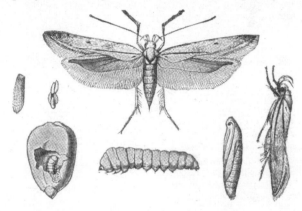

WHITE-SHOULDERED HOUSE MOTH *Endrosis sarcitrella*

Size: Length 8–10mm, wingspan 12–22mm.

Description: Small, pale silvery and white moth. Forewings coarsely speckled with greyish-brown; each has three small dark spots arranged subequally. Fresh specimens very distinct, with head and thorax, and extreme wing bases, brilliant white.

Life history: Long, narrow, cylindrical pale caterpillar lives in a silken gallery in a variety of habitats, including stored cereals, rotten wood and birds' nest detritus, and is a general feeder and scavenger. Several generations a year.

Human/household impact: Very common and widespread inhabitant of barns, farm buildings, warehouses, granaries and houses, wherever grain or flour products are stored, and where undisturbed corners accumulate crumbs and dust.

BROWN HOUSE MOTH *Hofmannophila pseudospretella*

Size: Length 9–13mm, wingspan 15–22mm.

Description: Small bronze-brown moth; wings flecked with darker spots. Generally mid-brown, but wings speckled with darker scales. Two dark spots or dashes at one-third along wing, larger circular spot at two-thirds, and series of small spots or dashes along edge of wing-tip.

Life history: Long, narrow, cylindrical caterpillar, pale grey with brown head capsule, feeds on wide variety of foodstuffs, and makes a slight silk web. Adult moth flies out of doors and is attracted to lighted windows, porches and so on. At least two generations a year.

Human/household impact: Omnivorous scavenger in any warehouse or store where corners acquire heaps of crumbs or dust. If left untreated attacks bagged flour, beans, peas and other stored foods. In houses also attacks clothes, carpets, soft furnishings, furs and leather.

COMMON CLOTHES MOTH (or WEBBING CLOTHES MOTH) *Tineola bisselliella*

Size: Length 6–8mm, wingspan 12–17mm.

Description: Tiny, subcylindrical, silvery-brown moth. Under a lens wings are pale golden, sometimes darker near base, and shining. Wings furled and curled around body. Runs actively, and flies rather ineffectually.

Life history: Small pale caterpillars make a light silken tube from which to feed, and often several feed together under a silk webbing. Eats animal material such as wool, feathers, fur and hair. Continuously brooded, with several generations per year.

Human/household impact: Larvae chew holes in wool and silk clothes, carpets, soft furnishings, curtains, duvets, eiderdown quilts and fur coats. One of the most common household insects, found in most houses at some time or other. Usually occurs in low numbers, but can cause considerable damage if clothes are put into storage in lofts or cupboards, and are not examined for several years, by which time an outbreak of many generations can build up large numbers of larvae.

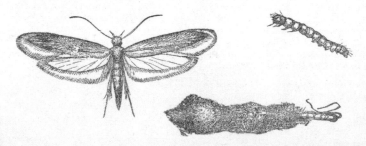

CASE-BEARING CLOTHES MOTH *Tinea pellionella*

Size: Length 5–9mm, wingspan 12–17mm.

Description: Tiny, subcylindrical, dusty brown moth. Under a lens wings are pale silvery grey-brown with two or three darker brown spots, the largest two-thirds along wing. Wings are held close, tent-like, against body.

Life history: Tiny pale caterpillar with dark head capsule makes a tubular silk case 6.3–9.5mm long, and carries it about as it moves. Case is whitish, but incorporates fibres from the food fabrics so can be bizarrely coloured. Caterpillar dies if case is removed. Two or three generations a year.

Human/household impact: Feeds on wool, silk, hair and feathers, and attacks clothes, carpets, soft furnishings, curtains, quilts, furs and occasionally food products. Most damage is done to stored clothes that are not examined for some time.

TAPESTRY MOTH *Trichophaga tapetzella*

Size: Length 5–9mm, wingspan 13–22mm.

Description: Small, slim, grey and white moth. Generally mottled white or very pale grey, but basal third of wings dark brownish-grey, sometimes purplish; tip of wings sometimes with vague grey fleck. Wings tight furled along body at rest. Good bird-dropping mimic.

Life history: Tiny pale caterpillar feeds inside a dirty silken tube case about 10mm long, which it carries about with it as it moves. Feeds in bird and animal nests, on moulted fur, feathers, wool; also in owl pellets and disused wasp nests. One generation in temperate zones, adults fly May–August.

Human/household impact: Will feed on horse-hair furniture stuffing, feathers in pillows, rough woollen fabrics (including tapestries). Much less common nowadays (at least in the UK, where it is currently considered very rare), and although can be found in unheated outbuildings and stables, more likely to be found in natural reservoir habitats.

CORN MOTH *Nemapogon granella*

Size: Length 6–9mm, wingspan 10–14mm.

Description: Tiny mottled moth. Forewings cream or beige, mottled with patches of light and dark brown. Hind wings grey. Head with tuft of white or pale yellow hairs.

Life history: Larvae feed in stored grain, but also outdoors in large, tough bracket fungi on rotten trunks and logs.

Human/household impact: Minor pest in Europe and North America, but has spread around the world. In Europe most prominent in Baltic region, where it seems particularly associated with stored rye, perhaps because of the high moisture content at which it is stored. Very minor pest of wheat, but apparently hardly ever occurs in oats or barley.

RICE MOTH *Corcyra cephalonica*

Size: Length 12–15mm, wingspan 14–24mm.

Description: Small, buff-brown or greyish moth. Forewings uniformly drab grey/brown, hind wings pale.

Life history: Short pale grey to white cylindrical caterpillars feed in various grains, especially rice.

Human/household impact: Although first found in Greece, infesting rice, it is now cosmopolitan. In North America regarded as serious pest of cocoa and confectionery. In the tropics a major pest of flour mills.

INDIAN MEAL MOTH *Plodia interpunctella*

Size: Length 8–11mm, wingspan 15–22mm.

Description: Small grey and white moth. Forewings brown, with strong, broad, pale grey, almost white, band covering most of basal half of wings, edged with blue-grey cross-line.

Life history: Pale pinkish-white caterpillars feed on a variety of grains, usually in a silken web.

Human/household impact: Attacks cereal grain, rice, flour, nuts and dried fruits in warehouses, mills and shops, including pet shops. Household infestations often arise from birdseed and dry pet food.

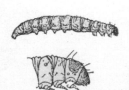

MEDITERRANEAN FLOUR MOTH *Ephestia kuehniella*

Size: Length 9–14mm, wingspan 17mm.

Description: Small grey moth. Forewings brownish-grey with two vague irregular, dark-edged cross-lines at one-quarter and three-quarters; two small black dots between them.

Life history: Slim pale caterpillars feed on all types of grain, making silk galleries as they go, sometimes clumping together into a webbing. Breeds continuously.

Human/household impact: Long known as pest of flour mills, but also recorded feeding on chocolate, tobacco, oats, rice, nuts, pet-food biscuits and dried fruits. High infestations spoil more flour than is destroyed, and silk threads block and clog delicate machinery. Similar dried-fruit moth *Vitula serratilinella* is occasional pest in dried prunes.

SMALL TORTOISESHELL *Aglais urticae*

Size: Wingspan 45–62mm.

Description: Medium to large butterfly; upperside dusky red marked with dark brown and cream, and series of scalloped blue marks round wing edges. Underside very dark brown mottled with lighter shades.

Life history: Spiny black caterpillars feed on stinging nettles in woods, parks and gardens. One or two generations a year. Overwinters as adult butterfly.

Human/household impact: Often attracted into buildings to hibernate, folding wings together and remaining unmoving for several months. Unnoticed in sheds and garages, but sometimes disturbed in spare room by central heating. Harmless.

MOTHS attracted to lights, very many species

Size: Wingspan 10–150mm.

Description: Vast diversity of forms, mostly mottled browns and greys, camouflaged to look like dead leaves or tree bark, but some very brightly coloured reds, oranges and whites.

Life history: Caterpillars (huge variety of shapes and sizes) feed on plants, with different species on leaves, buds, flowers, seeds, stalks, roots and/or bark of one or more different plant species.

Human/household impact: Many moths are attracted to lights, whether single candles or powerful floods. No one is really quite sure why. They also fly in through open lighted windows to rest on walls and ceilings, or get trapped in light fittings. Their appearance at night is often seen as

sinister, but it is a good predator-avoidance tactic. Despite media misconceptions vast majority of moths are harmless plant feeders.

HEMIPTERA

KNOBHEAD BUG *Metopoplax ditomoides*

Size: Length 3.5–4mm.

Description: Long-oval and parallel-sided, tiny black-and-white ground bug. Head and thorax black, and wing-cases pale beige with darkened veins. Head with distinct bulbous projection between eyes.

Life history: Feeds on mayweed, chamomile and related plants, usually in warm, dry waste places like verges and field edges.

Human/household impact: Sometimes recorded in large numbers overwintering in houses, including in lofts. Harmless.

ASSASSIN BUG (or FLY BUG, MASKED HUNTER) *Reduvius personatus*

Size: Length 17–22mm.

Description: Dark brown to black, with shining wings folded tight onto body. Nymph (immature) covers itself in dust and debris to disguise itself.

Life history: Stout and powerful beak mouthparts are for stabbing and eating small invertebrates, including bed bugs.

Human/household impact: Most usually found in old houses, where it feeds on other insects. Will bite if picked up, but not really a bloodsucker. Several related species worldwide do suck human blood. In South and Central America *Rhodnius prolixus* and others are vectors of Chagas disease, caused by parasitic protozoan *Trypanosoma cruzi*.

BED BUG *Cimex lectularius*

Size: Length up to 5mm.

Description: Broad, oval, flat bug, pale yellowish-brown to dark reddish in colour. Wingless, with body segments visible.

Life history: Sucks human blood. Hatchling bugs, 1mm long, start feeding immediately. Complete life cycle in about 30 days; adult bugs long lived, with 18 months recorded.

Human/household impact: Hides in cracks in bedframes, under loose wallpaper, under peeling paint, in cracks in plaster, around light switches and electrical sockets, and behind skirting boards. Emerges at night to suck blood from sleeping victims. Leaves tell-tale speck blotches of faeces around sheltering places. Emits distinct smell, detectable to the familiarised noses of expert bug hunters. Once widespread, but declined during late 20th century; recent outbreaks in plush hotels have made media headlines.

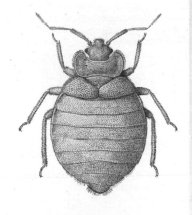

WESTERN CONIFER BUG *Leptoglossus occidentalis*

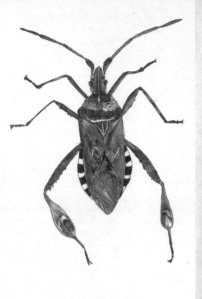

Size: Length 16–22mm.

Description: Long-oval, long-legged brown bug with narrow head and parallel-sided body. Brown, marked with pale flecks along sides of abdomen, and with distinctive white 'W' mark on each shiny front wing-case. Back legs noticeably long and spatulate (broadened).

Life history: Feeds by puncturing seeds in cones of various conifer trees.

Human/household impact: Native of California, Oregon and Nevada; somehow crossed the Rockies in the 1950s and spread right across USA, reaching New York in 1990. Arrived in Europe in 1999 and is spreading widely. Often attracted indoors to hibernate. Although harmless to humans its strange (new) appearance and relatively large size can be disconcerting, and it gives off a powerful, but not unpleasant, scent.

BOXELDER BUG *Boisea trivittata*

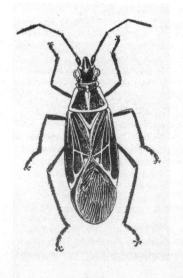

Size: Length to 13mm.

Description: Long-oval bug, dark brown or black in colour, streaked along thorax and wing edges with bright orange-red. Wingless nymph has bright red abdomen.

Life history: North American species. Feeds on seeds of maple trees, and also those of ash and box elder.

Human/household impact: Harmless to humans and causes no damage, but has a tendency to enter houses to hibernate. Usually clusters under loose tiles, behind metal and wooden sidings, but will come indoors through loose windows and doors. Forms tight knots in corners, giving off distinct acrid smell.

PHTHIRAPTERA

HEAD LOUSE *Pediculus capitis*

Size: Length 0.5–3.5mm.

Description: Minute pale, cadaverous ashy-white, narrow, soft-bodied, short-legged, wingless insect.

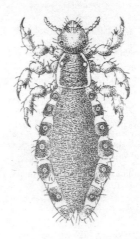

Life history: Lives entire life on human heads. Eggs ('nits') glued to bases of hairs hatch after a week into tiny lice ready to start sucking blood immediately. Large claws on legs grip hairs. Full life cycle in about one month.

Human/household impact: Does not spread disease, but stigma of infestation causes embarrassment and stress. Despite popular myth, does not spread by chair backs, pillows, hats, scarves, combs or brushes, but only by head-to-head physical contact. Most often appears in children 3–10 years old and their cuddling mothers. Very similar-looking body louse *Pediculus corporis*, better called the clothing louse, is not a household pest; it only occurs in morbidly poor and dirty homeless refugees and famine victims, whose only possessions are the clothes they stand up in (and lie down in).

CRAB LOUSE (or PUBIC LOUSE)
Pthirus pubis

Size: Length 0.5–2mm.

Description: Minute, squat, round, dark grey, wingless, stout-legged insect.

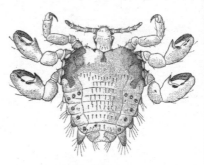

Life history: Lives entire life on human body, especially in groin and perianal area. Eggs glued to hairs hatch after a few days, and tiny lice start to suck blood immediately. Huge claws (especially on middle and back legs) grip hairs. Full life cycle in about one month.

Human/household impact: Does not spread disease, but infestations cause extreme embarrassment. Despite sometimes being called pubic louse, this is really the louse of human body hair (but not generally on the head), and occurs on men's hairy chests and backs, beards and moustaches, as well as armpits, eyebrows and eyelashes. Despite claims of catching the lice from dirty bed linen, they are most usually caught by intimate sexual contact; sometimes found in infants' eyelashes, caught from cuddling parents.

PSOCOPTERA

BOOK LOUSE *Lepinotus reticulatus*

Size: Length 0.5–1.5mm.

Description: Tiny pale, dirty-yellowish insect. Head subtriangular, wings reduced to small, round stubs.

Life history: Sticky eggs get covered in dusty debris. Saw-like egg burster on top of embryo membrane cuts through eggshell as head pulsates beneath. Grazes on wide variety of materials.

Human/household impact: Feeds on moulds and fungal hyphae (often invisible) in stored (and spilled) foods, on debris where other domestic pests have been feeding/defecating, and on flour-based glues under wallpaper and in books, hence the common name. Very many similar species.

FLOUR LOUSE *Liposcelis bostrychophila*

Size: Length 0.5–1.5mm.

Description: Tiny dirty-yellowish-grey insect. Head triangular, wingless, back legs with first segment swollen and with tooth-like bump on outer edges.

Life history: Sticky eggs get covered in dusty debris. Grazes on spilled food and mould hyphae. Has tendency to run in short, curved sprints of 10–20mm. Looks like animated dust.

Human/household impact: Common in houses, where it feeds in backs of

cupboards and drawers. Does no real harm, but resemblance to head lice causes confusion and upset. Very many similar species.

THYSANOPTERA

THRIPS, THUNDERFLIES or **THUNDERBUGS**

Size: Length 1-5 mm

Description: Minute, narrow, short-legged insects, mostly black, but some red or orange. Most species with four narrow feathery wings.

Life history: Nymphs like miniature wingless adults; all stages feed on plants, sucking juices, either leaves, flowers, stems; or on fungi in leaf litter or under rotten bark; some are predatory. A few are international pests of cereal crops, large

numbers can migrate, often on weather fronts, hence thunder association.

Human/household impact: Incidental in homes, but sometimes brought inside on washing hung out to dry, but taken in when that thunder storm approaches. Has well-publicised tendency to insinuate themselves, terminally, under the glass of picture frames. Very many similar species.

DICTYOPTERA

TERMITES, *Reticulitermes, Nasutitermes,*
and many other similar species

Size: Length 1–15mm.

Description: Tiny to small, pale, often white insects; head relatively large and round on soft, narrow body. Sometimes called white ants for superficial resemblance to ants, but they are unrelated.

Life history: Burrows in soil and wood, and makes complex nests, some species forming huge 'concrete' mounds in grassland and savannah. Complex community of sexual male and female, and various infertile worker castes, often many thousands, to forage, build and tend young; larger specimens are soldiers that defend nests.

Human/household impact: Majority of about 4,000 world species harmlessly recycle fallen trees, stumps and logs, but about 350 species are known to attack

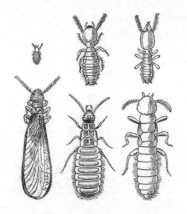

building timber, especially in tropical and subtropical zones. They burrow deep into wooden piles, beams, rafters, walls and flooring, and the honeycomb-like damage may go unnoticed until critical collapse.

GERMAN COCKROACH *Blattella germanica*

Size: Length 10–15mm.

Description: Slim, flattened, buff-brown insect. Legs long, and antennae very long. Pale yellowish wings completely cover body. Thorax has two dark streaks.

Life history: Eggs laid in purse-like container (ootheca), and carried by female in her genital opening until just before they hatch. Nymphs wingless. They scavenge almost any organic matter, and mature in 5–6 weeks. Breeds all year round. Mostly nocturnal, hiding during the day.

Human/household impact: Cosmopolitan, despite its name. Prefers warm, moist environment. Common domestic pest in houses, bakeries, restaurants and other buildings. Feeds in filth but also attracted to human food. Blamed for traipsing disease germs over any food left out. Can reach pest proportions.

COMMON COCKROACH (or BLACK BEETLE) *Blatta orientalis*

Size: Length 20–24mm.

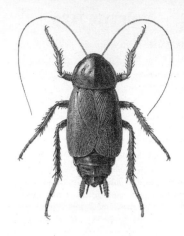

Description: Large, dark reddish-brown to black, flattened insect. Legs long, and antennae very long. Male has shining wing-cases that cover two-thirds of abdomen; female wing-cases reduced to short stubs.

Life history: Egg case (ootheca) carried by female until just before the eggs hatch. Nymphs of both sexes wingless. They scavenge all decaying organic matter. Generation time about one year. Nocturnal.

Human/household impact: Tolerant of cooler conditions, and usually found on ground floor and lower levels; often occurs in cellars and basements. Feeds on filth, and blamed for traipsing disease germs over any food left out. Surinam cockroach *Pycnoscelus surinamensis* is similar but broader, with longer wings covering all of abdomen; parthenogenetic in Europe and North America, and only females known away from South-east Asia, where it originated.

AMERICAN COCKROACH *Periplaneta americana*

Size: Length 28–44mm.

Description: Large, shining, deep reddish-brown to almost black, long-oval, flattened insect. Thorax with edges broadly marked with yellow; legs also yellowish.

Life history: About 16 eggs carried by female in purse-like bag (ootheca) until near hatching. Wingless nymphs pass through 10–11 moults before reaching adulthood. Life expectancy up to three years, during which time 90 oothecae may be produced.

Human/household impact: Prefers warm, moist environments. Mainly pest in tropical and subtropical zones the world over, despite its name. As well as living in buildings, frequents sewers, drains and latrines. Traipses disease germs over any food left out. Very fast runner, 1.5m/s (3.4mph). Similar *P. japonica* is a cold-adapted species from the Far East that has recently been recorded outdoors in New York City.

AUSTRALIAN COCKROACH *Periplaneta australasiae*

Size: Length 30–35mm.

Description: Large, shining, deep reddish-brown to nearly black, long-oval, flattened insect. Thorax edged with yellow; streak at base of leathery forewings also yellow.

Life history: About 24 eggs carried by female in pouch (ootheca) until hatching. Wingless nymphs moult 10–11 times before adulthood. Generation time about one year. Adult life expectancy 4–6 months.

Human/household impact: Scavenger in any organic rubbish, spilled or stored food. Despite its name it is circumtropical, occurring in and out of doors.

DERMAPTERA

EARWIG *Forficula auricularia*

Size: Length 15–25mm.

Description: Unmistakable narrow, dark brown insect with dark reddish-brown forceps at tail end. Legs, thorax and ends of wing-cases pale yellowish-buff.

Life history: Eggs laid under logs and stones tended by female until hatching. Wingless nymphs resemble small adults. Scavenge on decaying plant material, but will also eat small insects.

Human/household impact: Little more than intruders from the garden, apt to enter through windows surrounded by creepers and climbing plants. Forceps are harmless, though waved threateningly if picked up. Can fly, but very rarely does so. Lesser earwig *Labia minor* is smaller and narrower; it was once more widespread, especially in cities, when transport was horse drawn. Breeds in manure heaps, flies readily and is attracted to and through lighted windows.

ORTHOPTERA

HOUSE CRICKET *Acheta domestica*

Size: Length 18–25mm.

Description: Yellowish-buff to brown grasshopper-like insect. Stout, cylindrical body, blunt head, long legs (especially back pair), very long antennae.

Life history: Eggs laid in soil, or cracks in rock, brick or plaster. Nymphs are miniature wingless versions of adult. Nymphs moult 9–11 times; generation time about two months. Omnivorous, eating small insects or scavenging almost any plant or foodstuff.

Human/household impact: More or less harmless, but infestation seen as unhygienic and high numbers can be unnerving. Also breeds in rubbish dumps, so there is potential for traipsing disease spread. High-pitched, purring song made by adult males rubbing hardened wings together. Pegs arranged on underside of right wing like a comb are strummed by plectrum on upperside of left wing, and amplified by smooth area called the 'harp'. Loud calling can disturb sleepers. In the Far East pet crickets of various species were traditionally kept in cages, for appreciation of their songs.

ZYGENTOMA (THYSANURA)

SILVERFISH *Lepisma saccharina*

Size: Length 9–12mm.

Description: Slim, sleek, sinuous, cylindrical, silver, wingless insect, with long antennae and three long tail bristles. Covered all over with shining scales, giving it a metallic appearance and its 'fish' name.

Life history: Tiny eggs laid in cracks in woodwork and plaster hatch in three weeks into tiny miniature versions of adults. Scavenges animal and plant protein. Is able to digest cellulose. Continues to moult even after reaching adulthood, and may live for several years.

Human/household impact: In houses throughout the world, often occurs in kitchens and bathrooms. More or less harmless, scavenging spilled food or nibbling detritus, but large numbers can cause damage to wallpaper and other materials by nibbling to get at starch-based glues.

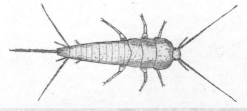

FIREBRAT *Thermobia domestica*

Size: Length 10–15mm.

Description: Brisk, cylindrical, mottled brown, wingless insect, with long antennae and three long tail bristles. Similar to silverfish but larger, stouter and bristlier.

Life history: Similar to that of silverfish, but requires higher temperatures to develop. Scavenges after animal and vegetable protein.

Human/household impact: Most often found in heated places like bakeries and heating ducts, and originally around open cooking fires, hence its name. More or less harmless, but large numbers can cause minor damage to food and household items.

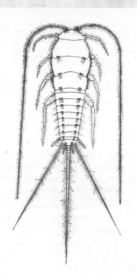

MITES

DUST MITES, *Dermatophagoides* species

Size: Length 0.2–0.4mm.

Description: Microscopic, domed, cushion-shaped, pale grey-white, eight-legged mite. Legs short and slim; tiny, down-facing, pointed head.

Life history: Feeds on sloughed human skin particles. One egg laid per day over period of 30–45 days; adult lifespan about 75 days. First nymph has six legs, but at first moult fourth pair appears.

Human/household impact: Generally unseen, but large numbers can build up in furnishings, especially bed mattresses, where humidity from regular occupants is an important requirement for their survival. 100–500 animals per gram of dust are quoted. Mites themselves are harmless, but dry airborne particles of their faeces cause asthma in susceptible individuals.

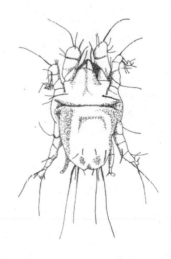

FLOUR MITE *Acarus siro*

Size: Length 0.3–0.6mm.

Description: Microscopic, domed, pale pearly-white, eight-legged mite. Legs short and slender; tiny, down-pointed head.

Life history: Eggs scattered over moist flour, and hatch in 3–4 days. Life cycle complete in 3–4 weeks. Adult life about six weeks.

Human/household impact: Despite tiny size can cause great losses to stored flour and grain. Infestations occur where relative humidity is high (RH 80–85 per cent quoted), and mites die out below RH 60 per cent. Heavy infestations taint flour with droppings and moulted skins, producing a strong odour called 'mintiness' by bakers, and colouring flour grey, making it unsuitable for consumption.

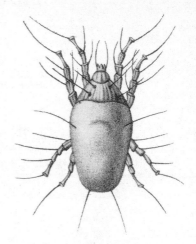

CHEESE MITE *Tyrolichus casei*

Size: Length 0.45–0.47mm.

Description: Microscopic, pale yellowish or orange, eight-legged, oval mite.

Life history: Eggs hatch into miniature adults that start feeding immediately. Life cycle takes about three weeks.

Human/household impact: Feeds on cheese, and also in damp or mouldy flour. Generally considered a nuisance if found on maturing cheeses, but deliberately inoculated into brands produced by various central German dairies, notably Altenburg and Milbenkäse, where its presence in the rind is said to produce the distinctive flavour. Cheese is sold with live mites still feeding on it, and they are eaten along with the cheese.

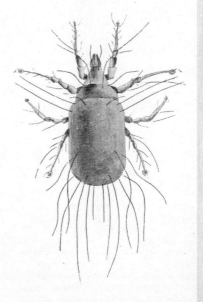

SPIDERS

BLACK WIDOW *Latrodectus mactans*

Size: Body length 4–7mm, leg span 25–40mm.

Description: Black, long-legged, round-bodied spider. Body round, abdomen almost spherical. Legs long and slim. Shining black all over, but with distinctive red hourglass shape on underside of abdomen.

Life history: Makes untidy web of loose strands and draped silk, usually under logs, stones or in hollows, and sits to wait for prey to walk over it, then pounces.

Human/household impact: Mostly outdoor species, but will enter outbuildings, garages, privies and houses. Well known for venomous bite, which feels like a very painful wasp sting, sometimes followed by aching, sweating and nausea. Reputation much over-stated; bites only very rarely fatal to healthy humans. Only bites if picked up, or partly crushed in clothing or bedding.

FALSE WIDOWS *Steatoda nobilis*, *S. grossa* and other species

Size: Body length 6–8mm, leg span 12–15mm.

Description: Female black or dark brown, body shining, abdomen round and bulbous, marked with red or cream crescent on front edge, and other slight patterns on top. Male slimmer and brown, with abdomen also patterned with pale marks.

Life history: Makes irregular untidy web of sticky silk in corners of cupboards, sheds, garages and outbuildings.

Human/household impact: Although small, has relatively long fangs and can pierce human skin if picked up between finger and thumb; bite said to be like wasp sting. Related to infamous black widows, so can cause unnecessary anxiety, especially whipped up in tabloid media.

BROWN RECLUSE SPIDER *Loxosceles reclusa*

Size: Body length 7–18mm, leg span 45–65mm.

Description: Medium-sized, long-legged spider. Mid- to dark brown, sometimes marked with black violin-shaped mark near head. Six eyes, rather than usual spider complement of eight eyes.

Life history: Spins messy web of loose strands in log pile, under rocks or inside hollow log. Pounces on prey that walks over web. Eggs laid in batches during spring hatch in about one month; adulthood in one year, life expectancy up to two years.

Human/household impact: Often enters cellars, outbuildings, sheds, porches and houses, particularly infrequently disturbed storage spaces. Danger much exaggerated by reputation. Bite feels like jabbing wasp sting, causing redness, swelling and possibly ulceration. Most bites occur through partial crushing when stored item sheltering spider is picked up.

SYDNEY FUNNEL-WEB SPIDER *Atrax robustus*

Size: Body length 10–35mm.

Description: Large, stout, dark, glossy, short-legged spider. Deeply coloured blue-black, plum or brown. Abdomen and cephalothorax sometimes differently coloured.

Life history: Makes untidy tunnel web under log or stone, with trip-wire spokes radiating out; in response to vibrations in silk pounces on prey walking over it. Occurs in eastern and southern Australia.

Human/household impact: Usually secretive, but sometimes found near houses and reputed to often fall into swimming pools. Males known to wander in search of mates. Highly venomous so bites are painful, causing various symptoms from breathlessness and nausea to death. Antivenom has been available since 1981 and no deaths have been reported since its availability. Several similar species.

HOUSE SPIDER *Tegenaria domestica* and other species

Size: Body length to 20mm, leg span to 100mm.

Description: Mottled grey-brown, usually with alternating light/dark chevron marks down sides of abdomen; legs appear chequered because of repeated small dark blotches down their lengths.

Life history: Secretive, making untidy matted web in form of rough undulating white sheet, twisted into dark tunnel retreat inside crevice or corner. Sits and waits for prey to cross web and pounces in response to victim's vibrations. Males especially tend to wander at night in search of mates, and if they fall into an empty bath are unable to climb the smooth, steep sides.

Human/household impact: Generally harmless, but very largest individuals might just be big enough to bite (slight pinprick nip) if picked up between finger and thumb. Helpful in that they eat potential household pests like cockroaches and flies. May cause anxiety or fear in some individuals, but true arachnophobia (irrational and paralysing phobia) is very rare.

DADDY-LONG-LEGS SPIDER *Pholcus phalangioides*

Size: Body length to 10mm, leg span to 110mm, but legs usually angled.

Description: Dull grey, sometimes whitish, knees darker; tiny body compared with very long and very thin legs.

Life history: Hangs upside down in feeble and untidy web on cornices and ceilings. Remains motionless, apparently unmoving for months, but will vibrate web wildly, so as to appear as a blur, if disturbed. Rapidly wraps any fly or other insect that blunders into its flimsy silk strands. Also eats other spiders.

Human/household impact: Harmless, helpful even, as it eats house flies, mosquitoes and other pests. Webs unlikely to be tolerated by the overly houseproud.

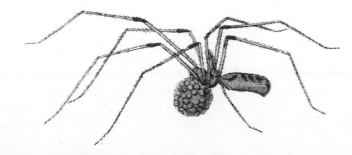

WOODLOUSE SPIDER *Dysdera crocata*

Size: Body length to 18mm, leg span to 40mm.

Description: Abdomen pale pinkish-cream, head and thorax red, legs bright pinkish-orange, long, articulated fangs red.

Life history: Secretive, usually living under stones and logs in garden, but nocturnal and comes out to hunt woodlice at night. Long, sharp fangs allow it to puncture hard woodlouse shell from above and below.

Human/household impact: Will sometimes wander indoors if woodlice are regular visitors too, but usually restricts itself to porches and cellars. Fangs are long and sharp enough to puncture human skin and will give painful bite, like a wasp sting, if it is picked up between finger and thumb.

OTHER INVERTEBRATES

SCORPIONS, various species

Size: Body length 10–100mm.

Description: Unmistakeable form; flattened long-oval body of head carapace and seven segments, long, slim tail of five segments and sting, eight legs and two pincered claws. Mostly dull yellow-buff, brown or black.

Life history: Eggs hatch into minute versions of adult. Hunt food by stealth, gripping with claws, stinging, or both. Usually nocturnal.

Human/household impact: Mostly outdoor species, but some have tendency to enter outbuildings, garages, privies, sheds and cellars. Mostly occur in dry tropical and subtropical zones. Hide in crevices and cracks during day to crawl about ceilings and walls to hunt by night. Despite being helpful in killing mosquitoes, house flies and other pests, fear of their stings makes them unpopular house guests. Most species are harmless, or sting like a wasp.

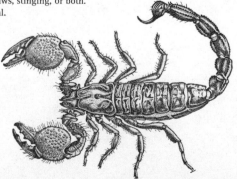

WOODLOUSE *Oniscus asellus* and other species

Size: Length 3–18mm.

Description: Broad, oval, flattened, multi-segmented, 14-legged land crustaceans. Mostly mottled grey, but sometimes with yellow, white or pink marks.

Life history: Eggs carried in brood pouch (marsupium) between legs; white hatchlings (mancas) released after one day. Scavenge on decaying organic (mostly vegetable) matter, including rotten wood. Nocturnal, sheltering under moist logs and stones. Body flanged at edge so animal clamps down onto substrate, pulling in legs to protect itself. Other, more cylindrical species run away fast; highly domed species roll into ball.

Human/household impact: May live in damp cellars and sheds, but ventures indoors are little more than exploratory visits. Although they need to keep moist and avoid drying out, they sometimes enter houses to avoid drowning in very wet weather.

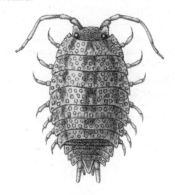

HOUSE CENTIPEDE *Scutigera coleoptrata*

Size: Length 25–50mm.

Description: Yellowish-brown body slightly flattened, with three darker brown stripes running along it. Up to 15 pairs of very long, thin legs, and one pair of long antennae.

Life history: Catches and eats small insects using speed and stealth. Venomous fangs are modified from limbs.

Human/household impact: Harmless, perhaps even beneficial as it runs around on walls and ceilings killing mosquitoes and other pests. Fangs nowhere near powerful enough to puncture human skin, but species does run very fast, which can startle some nervous people. *S. forceps* is a very similar North American species.

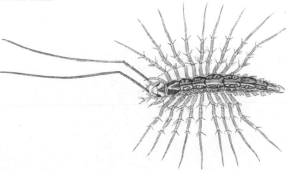

SNAILS, various species

Size: Diameter 5–50mm.

Description: Unmistakeable whorl-shelled molluscs, with soft, slimy bodies. Head with two short feeler tentacles and two longer telescopic-eyed tentacles. Body generally whitish-grey/brown. Shells variously mottled or streaked.

Life history: Graze on various plant materials. Body secretes mucus as lubricant. Retreat into shell if disturbed or to avoid desiccation.

Human/household impact: Occasionally venture indoors by accident, but mostly brought in on cut flowers, vegetables and so on. Move outwards and up walls, a natural escape response, and afterwards are found clinging to a ceiling or top of a wall, hidden in the shell after secreting a tough moisture-retaining layer.

SLUGS, various species

Size: Length 25–300mm.

Description: Unmistakeable long, thin, slimy molluscs. Head with four tentacles, longer upper two eyed. Variously coloured grey, black and brown, but also red and bright orange.

Life history: Graze on decaying organic matter, including dead plants; also carrion, dung and fungus. Mucus coating thicker than that of a snail. Push down into moist soil to avoid desiccation.

Human/household impact: Occasionally enter cellars, basements and very damp ground-floor dwellings. Harmless but unpleasant, leaving silvery slime trails on floors, walls and ceilings.

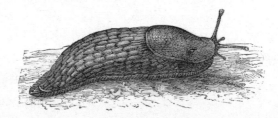

MILLIPEDES, various species

Size: 25–100mm.

Description: Long, thin, cylindrical, segmented arthropods, with very many short legs, blunt head and short antennae. Dark-coloured orange-brown to black, and sometimes vaguely striped along sides or back.

Life history: Push through soil and leaf litter grazing on (usually dead) plant material. Coil into tight spiral if disturbed or picked up.

Human/household impact: Most incursions into buildings are accidental visits into damp basements or cellars. Will not tolerate warm, dry conditions.

BRISTLY MILLIPEDE *Polyxenus lagurus*

Size: 2–3mm.

Description: Minute, short, stubby millipede. Pale to dark grey-brown, covered all over with rows of short, stout bristles, especially visible in splayed, frond-like tufts down sides. Two longer, horizontal, more parallel tufts at tail.

Life history: Lives gregariously, grazing on lichen, mould or algae from substrate surface, often with litter of cast skins. Usually on tree trunks, under loose bark, and on bare stones in walls, quarries and marine cliffs. Mostly nocturnal.

Human/household impact: Has been found, though not often, grazing on mould on ceilings.

BEER MAT NEMATODE *Panagrellus redivivus*

Size: Up to 1mm long.

Description: Microscopic worm.

Life history: Feeds in moist or wet substrate where starch-like food is available.

Human/household impact: Named after its discovery in German beer mats, but now known to be widespread in many wet and moist foodstuffs. Reared as microfood for fish fry by aquarium keepers. Harmless.

References

Alfieri, A. 1931. Les insects de la tombe de Toutankhamon [Insects in the tomb of Tutankhamun]. *Bulletin de la Société Royale Entomologique d'Egypte* 15: 188–189. (In French.)

Anon. 1918–1921. *Reports of the Grain Pests (War) Committee.* London: Harrison & Sons.

Anon. 1948. *Economic Report. Salient Features of the World Economic Situation, 1945–47.* New York: United Nations Department of Economic Affairs.

Anon. 1965. Thomas H. Morgan biographical. In: *Nobel lectures, Physiology or Medicine 1922–1941.* Amsterdam: Elsevier Publishing Co.

Axelsson, E., Ratnakumar, A., Arendt, M.-L., Maqbool, K., Webster, M. T., Perloski, M., Liberg, O., Arnemo, J. M., Hedhammer, A. & Lindblad-Toh, K. 2013. The genomic signature of dog domestication reveals adaptation to a starch-rich diet. *Nature* 495: 360–364.

Barrows, W. B. 1889. *The English Sparrow (Passer domesticus) in North America, Especially in its Relation to Agriculture.* US Department of Agriculture Division of Economic Ornithology and Mammalology Bulletin 1. Washington: Government Printing Office.

Beavis, I. C. 1988. *Insects and Other Invertebrates in Classical Antiquity.* Exeter: Exeter University Press.

Bedel, L. 1872. Note sur la manière de vivre du *Ptinus sexpunctatus* [Note on the lifestyle of *Ptinus sexpunctatus*]. *Bulletin de la Société Entomologique de France* 1872: li. (In French.)

Bell, W. J., Roth, L. M. & Nalepa, C. A. 2007. *Cockroaches: Ecology, Behaviour and Natural History.* Baltimore: Johns Hopkins University Press.

Berry, R. J. 1970. The natural history of the house mouse. *Field Studies* 3: 219–262.

Blair, K. G. 1935. Some ancient beetles from Egypt and Mesopotamia. *Proceedings of the Royal Entomological Society of London* 10: 19.

Bonnefoy, X., Kampen, H. & Sweeney, K. 2008. *Public Health Significance of Urban Pests.* Copenhagen: World Health Organization.

Boyce, R. W. 1910. *Mosquito or Man? The Conquest of the Tropical World.* 3rd edn. London: John Murray.

Brown, P., Sutikna, T., Morwood, M. J., Soejono, R. P., Jatmiko, Wayhu Saptomo, E. & Rokus Awe Due. 2004. A new small-bodied hominin from the late Pleistocene of Flores, Indonesia. *Nature* 431: 1055–1061.

Brown, S. W. 1973. Genetics – the long story. In: Smith, R. F., Mittler, T. E. & Smith, C. N. (eds) *History of Entomology.* Palo Alto: Annual Reviews Inc.

Buckland, P. C. 1981. The early dispersal of insect pests of stored products as indicated by archaeological records. *Journal of Stored Product Research* 17: 1–12.

Buckland, P. C. 1990. Granaries stores and insects. The archaeology of insect synanthropy. In: Fournier, D. & Sigaut, F. (eds) *La préparation alimetaire des cereals. Rapports présenté à la table ronde, Ravello au Centre Universaire pour les Biens culturels, avril 1988.* Rixensart: Pact.

Buckland, P. C. & Panagiotakopulu, E. 2001. Ramses II and the tobacco beetle. *Antiquity* 75: 549–556.

Buckland, P. C. & Sadler, J. P. 1989. A biogeography of the human flea, *Pulex irritans* L. (Siphonaptera: Pulicidae). *Journal of Biogeography* 16: 115–120.

Budgen, L. M. [Acheta Domestica] 1850. *Episodes of Insect Life*. London: Reeve & Benham.

Burgess, N. R. H. & Cowan, G. O. 1993. *A Colour Atlas of Medical Entomology*. London: Chapman & Hall Medical.

Burr, M. 1939. *The Insect Legion. The Significance of the Insignificant*. London: J. Nisbet & Co.

Busvine, J. R. 1976. *Insects, Hygiene and History*. London: Athlone Press.

Butler, E. A. 1896. *Our Household Insects. An Account of the Insect-pests Found in Dwelling-houses*. London: Longmans, Green & Co.

Byrne, K. & Nichols, R. A. 1999. *Culex pipiens* in London Underground tunnels: differentiation between surface and subterranean populations. *Heredity* 82: 7–15.

Carlton, C. & Bayless, V. 2011. A case of *Cnestus mutilatus* (Blandford) (Curculionidae: Scolytinae: Xyleborini) females damaging plastic fuel storage containers in Louisiana, USA. *The Coleopterists Bulletin* 65: 290–291.

Cloudsley-Thompson, J. L. 1976. *Insects and History*. London: Weidenfield & Nicolson.

Cobb, N. A. 1914. North American free-living and freshwater nematodes. *Transactions of the American Microscopical Society* 33: 69–164.

Constantine, B. 1994. A new ecological niche for *Gibbium aequinoctiale* Boieldieu (Ptinidae) in Britain, and a reconsideration of literature references to *Gibbium* spp. *The Coleopterist* 3: 25–28.

Cornwell, P. B. 1968 & 1976. *The Cockroach*. London: Hutchinson, The Rentokill Library, 2 vols.

Cucchi, T., Vigne, J.-D. & Auffray, J.-C. 2005. First occurrence of the house mouse (*Mus musculus domesticus* Schwarz & Schwarz, 1943) in the western Mediterranean: A zooarchaeological revision of subfossil occurrences. *Biological Journal of the Linnean Society* 84: 429–445.

de Lumley, H. & Boone, Y. 1976. Les structures d'habitat au Paléolithique inférieur [Habitat structures of the Lower Palaeolithic]. In: de Lumley, H. (ed.) *La préhistoire française*, vol. 1. Paris: CNRS. (In French.)

Disney, R. H. L. 1994. *Scuttle Flies: the Phoridae*. London: Chapman & Hall.

Donaldson, H. H. 1915. *The Rat, Reference Tables and Data for the Albino Rat (*Mus norvegicus albinus*) and the Norway Rat (*Mus norvegicus*)*. Memoirs of the Wistar Institute of Anatomy and Biology No. 6. Philadelphia: Wistar Institute.

Driscoll, C. A., Menotti-Raymond, M., Roca, A. L., Hupe, K., Johnson, W. E., Geffen, E., Harley, E. H., Delibes, M., Pontier, D., Kitchener, A. C., Yamaguchi, N., O'Brien, S. J. & Macdonald, D. W. 2007. The Near Eastern origin of cat domestication. *Science* 317: 519–523.

Ealand, C. A. 1916. *Insect Enemies: Enumerating the Life histories and Destructive Habits of a Number of Important British Injurious Insects, Together with Descriptions Enabling Them to be Recognised, and Methods by Means of Which They May be Held in Check*. London: Grant Richards.

Eaton, R. A. & Hale, M. D. C. 1993. *Wood: Decay, Pests and Protection*. London: Chapman & Hall.

Edwards, F. W., Oldroyd, H. & Smart, J. 1939. *British Bloodsucking Flies*. London: British Museum.

Edwards, R. 1980. *Social Wasps: Their Biology and Control*. East Grinstead: Rentokil Limited.

Felemban, H. M. 1997. Morphological differences among populations of house sparrows from different altitudes in Saudi Arabia. *Wilson Bulletin* 109: 539–544.

Ferris, H. 2009. The beer mat nematode, *Panagrellus redivivus*: a study of the connectedness of scientific discovery. *Journal of Nematode Morphology and Systematics* 12: 19–25.

Fletcher, R. 1993. Mammoth bone huts. In: Burenhult, G. (ed.) *The First Humans: Human Origins and History to 10,000 BC.* pp. 134–135. New York: HarperCollins.

Garret-Jones, C. 1951. The Congo floor maggot, *Auchmeromyia luteola* (F.), in a laboratory culture. *Bulletin of Entomological Research* 41: 679–708.

Goddard, J. 2009. Bed bugs (*Cimex lectularius*) and clinical consequences of their bites. *Journal of the American Medical Association* 301: 1358–1366.

Gotzek, D., Brady, S. G., Kallal, R. J. & LaPolla, J. S. 2012. The importance of using multiple approaches for identifying emerging invasive species: the case of the Rasberry crazy ant in the United States. PLoS ONE 7(9): e45314. doi:10.1371/journal.pone.0045314.

Gratuze, B. 1999. Application to prehistoric trade in the Mediterranean and the Near East: sources and distribution of obsidian within the Aegean and Anatolia. *Journal of Archaeological Science* 26: 869–881.

Green, M. & Pitman, A. J. 2002. The role of olfaction in substrate location by *Euophryum confine* (Broun) (Coleoptera: Curculionidae). In: Jones, S. C., Zhai, J. & Robinson, W. H. (eds) *Proceedings of the Fourth International Conference on Urban Pest*s. Blacksburg: Pocahontas Press.

Hall, E. R. & Russell, W. C. 1933. Dermestid beetles as an aid in cleaning bones. *Journal of Mammalology* 14: 372–374.

Halmschlager, E., Ladner, C., Zabransky, P. & Schopf, A. 2007. First record of the wood boring weevil, *Pentarthrum huttoni*, in Austria (Coleoptera: Curculionidae). *Journal of Pest Science* 80: 59–61.

Harcourt-Smith, W. E. H. 2007. The origins of bipedal locomotion. In: Henke, W. & Tattershall, I. (eds) *Handbook of Paeoanthropology*. Vol. 3. New York: Springer.

Harpaz, I. 1973. Early entomology in the Middle East. In: Smith, R. F., Mittler, T. E. & Smith, C. N. (eds). *History of Entomology*. Palo Alto: Annual Reviews Inc.

Harris, D.H. (ed.) 1996. *The Origins and Spread of Agriculture and Pastoralism in Eurasia*. London: Routledge.

Hawley, W. A., Reiter, P. Copeland, R. S., Pumpuni, C. B. & Craig, G. B. Jr 1987. *Aedes albopictus* in North America: probable introduction in used tires from northern Asia. *Science* 236: 1114–1116.

Henry, D. O. 1989. *From Foraging to Agriculture: the Levant at the End of the Ice Age*. Philadelphia: University of Pennsylvania Press.

Hewitt, C. G. 1914. *The House Fly,* Musca domestica, *Linnaeus. A Study of Its Structure, Development, Bionomics and Economy.* Manchester: University of Manchester Press.

Hickin, N. E. 1947. The status of *Hylotrupes bajulus* L. (Col. Cerambycidae) in Surrey. *Entomologist's Monthly Magazine* 83: 132.

Hickin, N. E. 1963. *The Woodworm Problem.* London: Hutchinson.

Hickin, N. E. 1975. *The Insect Factor in Wood Decay. An Account of Wood-boring Insects with Particular Reference to Timber Indoors.* 3rd edn. London: Associated Business Programmes.

Hinton, H. E. 1943. Natural reservoirs of some beetles of the family Dermestidae known to infest stored products, with notes on those found in spider webs. *Proceedings of the Royal Entomological Society of London* (A) 18: 33–42.

Hinton, H. E. 1945. *A Monograph of the Beetles Associated with Stored Products.* Vol. 1. London: British Museum.

REFERENCES

Hole, F. 1992. Origins of agriculture. In: Jones, S., Martin, R. & Pilbeam, D. (eds) *The Cambridge Encyclopedia of Human Evolution*. Cambridge: Cambridge University Press. pp. 373–379.

Holt, V. M. 1885. *Why Not Eat Insects?* Reprinted 1967, Farringdon: Classey, and 1992, Whitstable: Pryor Publications.

Hopberg, E. P., Alkire, N. L., Queiroz, A. D. & Jones, A. 2001. Out of Africa: origins of the *Taenia* tapeworms in humans. *Proceedings of the Royal Society* B 268: 781–787.

Hope, F. W. 1836. Notice of several species of insects found in the heads of Egyptian mummies. *Transactions of the Entomological Society of London* 1: xi–xii.

Howard, L. O. 1931. *The Insect Menace*. New York: The Century Company.

Howe, R. W. 1965. *Sitophilus granarius* (L.) (Coleoptera, Curculionidae) breeding in acorns. *Journal of Stored Product Research* 1: 99–100.

Jones, R. 2001. [Live head louse exhibited at indoor meeting of British Entomological and Natural History Society, 11 September 2001] *British Journal of Entomology and Natural History* 14: 239.

Jones, R. A. 2011. Understanding the honeybee. In: *The Beekeeper's Bible*. London: HarperCollins.

Jones, R. A. 2012. *Mosquito*. London: Reaktion Books.

Jones, R. A. & Crow, J. 2012. *The Little Book of Nits*. London: Bloomsbury.

Kenward, H. K. 1975. The biological and archaeological implications of the beetle *Aglenus brunneus* Gyllenhal in ancient faunas. *Journal of Archaeological Science* 2: 63–69.

King, G. A. 2009. *The Alien Presence: Palaeoentomological Approaches to Trade and Migration*. PhD thesis. University of York.

King, G. A. 2013. Establishing a foothold or six: insect tales of trade and migration. In: Preston, P. R. & Schörle, K. (eds) *Mobility, Transition and Change in Prehistory and Classical Antiquity. Proceedings of the Graduate Archaeology Organisation conference on the fourth and fifth of April 2008 at Hertford College, Oxford, UK*. Oxford: Archaeopress.

Kirby, W. & Spence, W. 1815. *An Introduction to Entomology: or Elements of the Natural History of Insects*. London: Longman, Hurst, Rees, Orme & Brown.

Kittler, R., Kayser, M. & Stoneking, M. 2003. Molecular evolution of *Pediculus humanus* and the origin of clothing. *Current Biology* 13: 1414–1417.

Krinke, G. J. (ed.) 2000. *The Laboratory Rat*. London: Academic Press.

Kroukamp, G. & Londt, J. G. H. 2006. Ear-invading arthropods: a South African survey. *South African Medical Journal* 96: 290–292.

Landsberger, B. 1934. Die Fauna des alten Mesopotamien nach der 14 Tafel der Serie Har-ra = Hubullu [The fauna of ancient Mesopotamia as described in the 14 tablets of the Har-ra (Hubulla) series]. *Abhandlungen des Sächsischen Akademie der Wissenschaften zu Leipzig Philologische-historische Klasse* 42: 1–144. (In German.)

Lattin, J. D. & Wetherill, K. 2002. *Metopoplax ditomoides* (Costa), a species of Oxycantharidae new to North America (Lygaeoidea: Hemiptera: Heteroptera). *Pan-Pacific Entomologist* 78: 63–65.

Lehane, B. 1969. *The Compleat Flea*. London: John Murray.

Lehane, M. 2005. *The Biology of Blood-sucking in Insects*. 2nd edn. Cambridge: Cambridge University Press.

Levinson, H. & Levinson, A. 1994. Origin of grain storage and insect species consuming desiccated food. *Anzeiger für Schädlingskunde, Pflanzenschutz, Umweltschutz* 67: 47–59.

Linsley, E. G. 1942. Insect food caches as reservoirs and original sources of some stored products pests. *Journal of Economic Entomology* 35: 434–439.

Little, L. K. (ed.) 2007. *The Plague and the End of Antiquity. The Pandemic of 541–750.* Cambridge: Cambridge University Press.

Marshall, J. T. & Sage, R. D. 1981. Taxonomy of the house mouse. In: Berry, J. (ed.) *Biology of the House Mouse. The Proceedings of a Symposium held at the Zoological Society of London on 22 and 23 November 1979.* Symposia of the Zoological Society of London No. 47, pp. 15–25.

Marshall, S. A. 2012. *Flies: the Natural History and Diversity of Diptera.* New York: Firefly Books.

Martin, P. S. & Klein, R. G. (eds) 1984. *Quaternary Extinctions: a Prehistoric Revolution.* Tucson: University of Arizona Press.

Maunder, J. W. 1983. The appreciation of lice. *Proceedings of the Royal Institution of Great Britain* 55: 1–33.

McGovern, P. E. 2010. *Uncorking the Past. The Quest for Wine, Beer and Other Alcoholic Beverages.* Berkeley: University of California Press.

Merdic, E. & Vuljicic-Karlo, S. 2005. Two types of hibernation of *Culex pipiens* complex (Diptera: Culicidae) in Croatia. *Entomologia Croatica* 9: 71–76.

Messenger, M. T., Su, N.-Y. & Scheffrahn, R. H. 2002. Current distribution of the Formosan subterranean termite and other termite species (Isoptera: Rhinotermitidae, Kalotermitidae) in Louisiana. *Florida Entomologist* 85: 580–587.

Millais, J. G. 1911. Catapult shooting. In: The Earl of Suffolk and Berkshire (ed.) *The Encyclopedia of Sport and Games.* London: William Heinemann. Vol. 1, pp. 402–403.

Moufet, T. 1634. *Insectorum sive minimorum animalium theatrum.* London: Thomas Cotes.

Munro, J. W. 1966. *Pests of Stored Products.* London: Hutchinson.

Noble-Nesbitt, J. 1969. Water balance in the firebrat, *Thermobia domestica* (Packard). Exchanges of water with the atmosphere. *Journal of Experimental Biology* 50: 745–769.

Panagiotakopulu, E. 2001. New records for ancient pests: archaeoentomology in Egypt. *Journal of Archaeological Science* 28: 1235–1246.

Panagiotakopulu, E. & Buckland, P. 2009. Environment, insects and the archaeology of Egypt. In: Ikram, S. & Dodson, A. (eds) *Beyond the Horizon: Studies in Egyptian Art, Archaeology and History, in Honour of Barry J. Kemp.* Cairo: American University in Cairo Press.

Pettigrew, T. J. 1834. *A History of Egyptian Mummies and an Account of the Worship and Embalming of the Sacred Animals by the Egyptians with Remarks on the Funeral Ceremonies of Different Nations and Observations of the Canary Islands, of the Ancient Peruvians, etc.* London: Longman, Rees, Orme, Browne, Green & Longman.

Phelps, G. 1976. *Squire Waterton.* Wakefield: EP Publishing.

Pickering, G., Lin, J., Riesen, R., Reynolds, A., Brindle, I. & Soleas, G. 2004. Influence of *Harmonia axyridis* on the sensory properties of white and red wine. *American Journal of Enology and Viticulture* 55: 153–159.

Plarre, R. 2010. An attempt to reconstruct the natural and cultural history of the granary weevil, *Sitophilus granarius* (Coleoptera: Curculionidae). *European Journal of Entomology* 107: 1–11.

Preston, C. 2006. *Bee*. London: Reaktion Books.

Rackham, D. J. 1979. *Rattus rattus*: the introduction of the black rat into Britain. *Antiquity* 53: 112–120.

Ritchie, S. A., Moore, P., Carruthers, M., Williams, C., Montgomery, B., Foley, P., Ahboo, S., Van Den Hurk, A. F., Lindsay, M. D., Cooper, B., Beebe, N. & Russell, R. C. 2006. Discovery of a widespread infestation of *Aedes albopictus* in the Torres Strait, Australia. *Journal of the American Mosquito Control Association* 22: 358–365.

Robinson, W. H. 1996. *Urban Entomology. Insect and Mite Pests in the Human Environment*. London: Chapman and Hall.

Roy, H. E., Brown, P. M. J., Frost, R. & Poland, R. L. 2011. *The Ladybirds (Coccinellidae) of Britain and Ireland*. Wallingford: Biological Records Centre.

Rydell, J. & Speakman, J. R. 1995. Evolution of nocturnality in bats: potential competitors and predators during their early history. *Biological Journal of the Linnean Society* 54: 183–191.

Scheffrahn, R. H., Cabrera, B. J., Kern, W. H. Jr & Su, N.-Y. 2002. *Nasutitermes costalis* (Isoptera: Termitidae) in Florida: first record of a non-endemic establishment by a higher termite. *Florida Entomologist* 85: 273–275.

Shute, P. G. 1951. *Culex molestus*. *Transactions of the Royal Entomological Society of London* 102: 380–382.

Smith, D. & Kenward, H. 2011. Roman grain pests in Britain: implications for grain supply and agricultural production. *Britannia* 42: 243–262.

Smith, D. N. 1962. Prolonged larval development in *Buprestis aurulenta* L. (Coleoptera: Buprestidae). A review with new cases. *Canadian Entomologist* 94: 586–593.

Smith, K. G. V. (ed.) 1973. *Insects and Other Arthropods of Medical Importance*. London: British Museum (Natural History).

Smith, R. L. & Olson, C. A. 1982. Confused flour beetle and other Coleoptera in stored marijuana. *Pan-Pacific Entomologist* 58: 79–80.

Southall, J. 1730. *A Treatise of Buggs; Shewing When and How They Were First Brought into England, How They are Brought into and Infect Houses, Their Nature, Several Foods, Times and Manner of Spawning and Propagating in this Climate...etc*. London: J. Roberts.

Stebbing, E. P. 1909. *Insect Intruders in Indian homes*. Calcutta: Spink & Co.

Tattershall, I. 2012. *Masters of the Planet: the Search for Our Human Origins*. New York: Palgrave Macmillan.

Thompson, H. V. 1953. The edible dormouse (*Glis glis* L.) in England, 1902–1951. *Proceedings of the Zoological Society, London* 122: 1017–1024.

Trewin, B. J., Kay, B. H., Darbro, J. M. & Hurst, T. P. 2013. Increased container-breeding mosquito risk owing to drought-induced changes in water harvesting and storage in Brisbane, Australia. *International Health*, first published online November 13, 2013 doi:10.1093/inthealth/iht023

Trpis, M. & Hausermann, W. 1978. Genetics of house-entering behaviour in East African populations of *Aedes aegypti* (L.) (Diptera: Culicidae) and its relevance to speciation. *Bulletin of Entomological Research* 68: 521–532.

Tudge, C. 1998. *Neanderthals, Bandits and Farmers: How Agriculture Really Began*. London: Weidenfield & Nicolson.

Van Andel, T. H. 1994. *New Views on an Old Planet*. Cambridge: Cambridge University Press.

Verkerk, R. H. J. & Bravery, A. F. 2004. A case study from the UK of possible successful eradication of *Reticulitermes grassei*. Report of a presentation at Environmental Optimisation of Wood Protection, Lisbon, Portugal, 22–23 March 2004.

Vigne, J.-D., Guillaine, J., Debue, K., Haye, L. & Gérard, P. 2004. Early taming of the cat in Cyprus. *Science* 304: 259.

Waring, C. 2011. Bees and beekeeping history. In: *The Beekeeper's Bible*. London: HarperCollins.

Waslkov, G. A. 1987. Shellfish gathering and shell midden archaeology. *Advances in Archaeological Method and Theory* 10: 93–210.

Wetterer, J. K. 2010. Worldwide spread of the pharaoh ant, *Monomorium pharaonis* (Hymenoptera: Formicidae). *Myrmecological News* 13: 115–129.

Williams, F. X. 1928. The natural history of a Philippine nipa house with descriptions of new wasps. *Philippine Journal of Science* 35: 53–118.

Winston, M. 1992. *Killer Bees: the Africanized Honey Bee in the Americas.* Cambridge, MA: Harvard University Press.

Winston, M. L. 1997. *Nature Wars. People vs Pests.* Cambridge, Massachusetts: Harvard University Press.

Withers, P. 1989. Moth flies. Diptera: Psychodidae. *Dipterists Digest* 4: 1–83.

Woodroffe, G. E. 1953. An ecological study of the insects and mites in the nests of certain birds in Britain. *Bulletin of Entomological Research* 44: 739–772.

Zinsser, H. 1935. *Rats, Lice and History.* Boston: Little Brown & Co.

Acknowledgements

First, some apologies. Most human domestic pests have become cosmopolitan, spread throughout the world by trade and exploration, but each region also has its own peculiar specialities. I've tried to include examples of all typical household visitors here, but I realize that this offering is decidedly skewed towards insects. As an entomologist, I'm biased, obviously, but also insects are the dominant creatures when it comes to invading our houses. Actually, they're the dominant creatures all over the Earth, but that's another discussion, in another book. Insects are, however, very important because there are so many of them, and they are so diverse. And by virtue of their unfamiliarity to most people, insects offer some of the most unusual and interesting associations with humans down the years that we've been building shelters to keep them out.

I live in England, and this book is also decidedly Anglocentric. This is mainly because I've tried to lace the text with some of my own personal experiences of the household pests and guests that have come my way. I hope, though, that the biological lessons are international, and that householders all over the world will be able to put aside some of the revulsion they feel at the unwarranted intrusions they suffer, so that they, too, can marvel at the wondrous adaptations of their myriad trespassers.

I've been helped on my way through this book by many hands. As ever, my late father, Alfred Jones, was always happy to lend me many of his old books and came up with anecdotes from his own domestic pest-ridden past. I've also roped in my daughters: Lillian Ure-Jones, who proof-read the text, and Verity Ure-Jones who took time out from GCSE studies to paint some pen-and-ink portraits of several of the animals mentioned in the book. Many helpful correspondents have answered obscure questions and contributed their own ideas, facts and figures, including: Christie Bahlai, Viktor Baranov, Max Barclay, Roger Booth, David Clements, John Dittes, Scotty Dodd, Michael Geiser, Stefan Harrison, Tony Irwin, Dafydd Lewis, Keith Lugg, Crystal Maier, Joseph Parker, Matt Smith and Claudia Watts. My grateful thanks go to all of them.

Index

aardvark 174
Acanthoscelides obtectus 114, 221
Acarus siro 268
Acheta domestica 179, 180, 266
acorns 117, 118
Adistemia watsoni 188, 223
Aedes 161
Aedes aegypti 163
Aedes albopictus 164, 247
Africanised honeybees 72, 73
Aglais urticae 65, 257
Aglenus brunneus 176, 177, 225
agriculture 32, 34, 53, 88, 107–109, 112, 180
agrobiocoenosis 36
ague 161
American cockroach 98, 99, 264
Ancistrocerus 238
Ancistrocerus domesticus 38
Angoumois grain moth 151, 253
animal skins 17
Anobium domesticum 132, 217
Anobium punctatum 132, 217
Anopheles 161, 246
Anopheles atroparvus 165, 246
Anopheles gambiae 246
Anopheles maculipennis 165
Anopheles messeae 165
Anoplophora glabripennis 137
ant hills 126
Anthophora plumipes 145, 241
Anthrenus flavipes 228
Anthrenus museorum 158, 228

Anthrenus verbasci 156, 228
anthropobiocoenosis 37
Apis mellifera 70, 71, 72, 239
Apodemus sylvaticus 84, 115
Apus apus 56, 57, 213
Araecerus fasciculatus 149, 218
Argentine ant 242
Aridius nodifer 223
Asian longhorn 137
Asian tiger mosquito 164, 247
assassin bugs 172, 259
Atrax 76, 270
Attagenus fasciatus 225
Attagenus pelio 225
Attagenus smirnovi 225
Auchmeromyia luteola 173, 251
Australian cockroach 98, 99, 264
Australopithecus 13, 17, 20

bacon beetles 48, 201, 227
badgers 181
bamboo borer 149, 219
barley 53, 83, 107, 109–111
bats 61, 62, 170, 171, 210
bean weevils 114, 115, 221
beans 53, 114
bed bug 166–171, 259
bee nests 122–124, 144
bee villages 145
beer 109
beer mat nematode 189, 275
bird nests 101, 104, 105, 120, 153
biscuit beetle 106, 107, 123, 148, 216
black ant 243
black rat 86, 87, 208
black widows 76, 269
Blaps mucronata 41, 42, 43, 44, 233

Blattella germanica 98, 99, 263
Blattella orientalis 95, 98, 264
bloodsucking 14, 16, 159–174
blow flies 251
blue clerid beetle 179, 222
Boisea trivittata 260
Bombus hypnorum 239
Bombyx mori 115
book louse 262
bookworms 147
Bostrychus capucinus 218
boxelder bugs 260
bread 30, 50, 106, 107
brown rat 88, 89, 209
brown recluse spiders 76, 270
Bruchidius 114, 221
Bruchus 114, 115, 221
Buprestis aurulenta 136, 221
bush fly 92

cabbages 53
cacao moth 149, 151
cadelle 234
Calliphora vomitoria 251
Callosobruchus chinensis 221
Callosobruchus maculatus 221
camphor shot borer 190, 219
Canis familiaris 29, 206
Canis lupus 29, 206
cannabis 148
capuchin beetle 218
carpenter bees 240
carpet beetles 156–159, 200, 228
Carpophilus hemipterus 229
Cartodere filum 223
cats 15, 85, 86, 206
cattle 18, 31, 53
caves 12, 17, 24, 25, 58, 75, 170